WHY IS IT?

… We are Afraid of Being Descendants of Monkeys but Not Incest?

HARRY MARGULIES

Under Licence to: Why is it Publishing AB

Copyright © 2021 Harry Magulies and Why is it Publishing

All rights reserved. This book, or any portion thereof, may not be reproduced or used in any manner by any means without the written permission of the publisher.

Cover: Darwin's Monkey

Why is it Publishing AB
Kronudden, 18532 Vaxholm. Sweden

🌐　　Web: www.whyisitpublishing.com

@　　Email: why@whyisitpublishing.com

Links to all video clips recommended in this book will be accessible through our website. Scan the QR code and it will take you straight there.

ISBN:
978-1-80227-082-2 (hardback)
978-1-80227-083-9 (paperback)
978-1-80227-084-6 (eBook)

It's easier to fool people than it is to convince them that they have been fooled.
~ Mark Twain

Contents

Foreword xi

Introduction 1

CHAPTER 1
    Why is it ... that the Bible is viewed as a book of utmost morality when your children should really not be allowed to read it? 8

CHAPTER 2
    Why is it ... that when scientists or religious figures try to show that science and religion are compatible, the result ends up being unscientific? 23

CHAPTER 3
    Why is it ... that Pope Francis' fine words about making the world a fairer place bring us no closer to closing the income and wealth gap? 44

CHAPTER 4
    Why is it ... that we are afraid of being descendants of monkeys but don't mind being descendants of incest? 67

CHAPTER 5
Why is it ... that so much violence in recent times has come from followers of Islam while followers of Christianity have decreased their levels of violence? 77

CHAPTER 6
Why is it ... that we accept so many errors in holy scripture that elsewhere would have made us stop reading? 103

CHAPTER 7
Why is it ... that we believe that we are in possession of the true religion when we don't really know what that is? 125

CHAPTER 8
Why is it ... that, in spite of best efforts, creationism does not make it into other than pseudo-science?................................155

CHAPTER 9
Why is it ... that so much anti-Semitism from Christianity and Islam has been directed against the Jews when, at least in Christianity, the Jews must be acknowledged to be God's chosen people? 176

CHAPTER 10
Why is it ... that we are eager to believe that we have free will in relation to God but don't know what free will is? 201

CHAPTER 11
Why is it ... that the pope of the Catholic Church is considered infallible when so many mistakes have been made by the church?.........216

CHAPTER 12
Why is it … that Christianity decided to be anti-sex in spite of having its roots in sexy Judaism? 239

Afterword 263

Postscript 269

Acknowledgements 275

Index 279

In this book big questions are being asked…and answered.

We are all faced with the problem of how to negotiate our way through the world, and over the millennia, billions of people have turned to God for answers. Now, Harry Margulies has turned the tables and poses 12 pressing questions, of us, and of God.

He tackles – fearlessly – the big subjects: divine omniscience; the sometimes-wilful obscurity of religious texts and the opaque meaning of God's word; the seeming carelessness, callousness and cruelty of God; violence enacted in the name of God; the problems of reconciling religious belief and scientific knowledge; a whole raft of issues surrounding the always vexed issue of religion and morality, with lengthy, forensic discussions of money, intolerance, hypocrisy, sex. As that list – one that only scratches the surface of the breadth and depth of the themes dealt with in the course of the book – suggests, this is not for the faint-hearted (or the simple-minded). It is a deeply serious, challenging piece of work, but it is also at all times lucid and accessible, and often funny.

It is never glib, but is in fact the result of decades of reading, research, questioning, deep thought.

It is a book unafraid to ask the difficult questions, in the same way that every faith, every religious person should be. We should all be willing if not eager to explore and question the foundations on which we choose to build our lives, the very rules and guidelines that underpin our quotidian existence. Harry confronts religious thinkers, religious leaders, religious texts head-on, without fear or prejudice, and sees how they look, how they shape up in the bright, unforgiving light of clear- thinking and in the face of tough, serious interrogation. Whether you are deeply religious, agnostic or atheist, you will be, by turns, intrigued, infuriated, perhaps enlightened by much of this, and, most of all, you will be challenged to think afresh on everypage.

Karl French
Editor

FOREWORD

Harry Margulies is one of the most clear-sighted people I have ever met. He has an unerring ability to convey his points of view in a lucid and thought-provoking way. What more could you want from a writer?

So, how can I convey all of this? It's actually quite simple. I have been privileged to follow Harry's life, both privately and professionally, for almost 50 years, so of course I feel I know him rather well by now. We first met back in the early 1970s. I was an ambitious, young reporter on what was then Sweden's biggest newspaper. Harry was working as a tax advisor and had just co-written a book about tax planning, a virtually unknown concept at the time.

I was immediately impressed by Harry's ability to look at problems in a fresh way, while at the same time always treating facts and rules with proper respect. He also had an impressive ability to get his message across.

What began as a purely professional relationship developed over time into a close personal friendship. As Harry's career developed, it took him into the world of international taxation. Sweden wasn't enough for him – he needed to widen his perspective, so he moved to Canada and from there to London, his current base.

For me, our long friendship has entailed participation in a number of incredibly interesting seminars, stimulating and eye-opening discussions on all manner of subjects, not least religion – and many memorable dinners. And so many funny stories.

Over the years, I have been able to follow the evolution of Harry's professional qualities, and this has indeed been impressive to behold. He soon became much sought-after as an advisor. He has worked for a number of notably demanding and distinguished clients, in many cases involving extraordinarily complicated tax problems. One particular quality of Harry's is that he doesn't just analyse the rules and the facts – he has that rare ability to think outside the box and see things that others have simply missed. He is also conscious, at all times, of how any information is experienced by the recipient, and he possesses an enviable ability to communicate. This is a gift that I, as a journalist and publicist, have noticed and valued.

What have religion and taxation got in common? Not a great deal, but then this is not important. What is important are Harry's analytical powers and his unstinting ambition to look behind first impressions.

Over the years, Harry and I have often discussed the different religions and their varying effect on people, and I have repeatedly been amazed at the ambition, effort and time that Harry has devoted to penetrating the different religious texts and mythical tales. He is exceptionally well-read.

Harry has, of course, been published before in his professional field, for instance in a number of articles in Swedish tax journals. He has also co-written a number of books on taxation, but this is the first time that he has tackled something other than taxation in book form. I am delighted to recommend this book, especially as it is written in such accessible language and with a light touch. The book is cumulatively compelling and there is a discernible narrative thread, but nevertheless every chapter can stand on its own.

I find this book eminently readable and accessible, whether you are a believer, an atheist or an agnostic. Either you will have your belief confirmed, or you will be furious to find that someone can have such different ideas, which can also be useful and even inspiring. Whatever your belief, I can promise you that you will be faced with observations and arguments that you have never encountered before. The worst that could happen is that you might end up an atheist... and would that be such a bad thing?

Jan Sterner
Journalist and publisher

INTRODUCTION

This is not a scientific work. There is already so much scientific writing on the subject matter of this book that the choice had to be made between exactness and a certain ease of reading and understanding. I opted for the latter, and you will therefore find neither footnotes nor a bibliography in this writing. One can only hope that it succeeds in being both understandable and entertaining.

I will be asking a few questions, and I hope that the process of trying to find answers to these questions will entertain you and make you think about your own answers. My questions, and my attempts to answer them, are of course based on my own experiences and observations.

The psychology of belief starts to affect you very early in life. If you, like me, were indoctrinated into certain beliefs in your childhood, you may find it very difficult, almost physically painful, to shed those beliefs. I have a feeling that many will not go through the agony of letting reason win over belief. Rather than actively taking charge of the process that leads from belief to reason, it is probably easier to live in doubt and semi-consciously ignore the fact that, deep down, you know what is true and what is not.

It is not only childhood indoctrination that can bring one to faith. We should not ignore the fact that some people find reason to believe, or rather find their faith, later in life. There are also adults who, in their own mind, find some rationale or inspiration that motivates them to convert to a different religion, believing that within this new faith, they have found the truth.

I note with interest that after a certain movie was released, a telegenic young Catholic priest was interviewed on American television and complained about the indoctrination into atheism the movie represented. Not a word was spoken about the indoctrination into belief which the church starts early on in the lives of its Catholic adherents.

I have been fascinated with religion for most of my adult life. The more I have studied it, the more I have come to the conclusion that you have to make a choice: you can either understand reality based on observation and science, or allow yourself just to believe.

The scientific approach dictates that you should believe in something only because of the evidence and, as new evidence arises, you are prepared to revise your understanding. Religious belief, on the other hand, requires that you believe in something with no evidence or perhaps even in spite of evidence to the contrary. The extent of this requirement is such that you are made to be proud of the fact that you claim to believe in something that you might well know, deep down, is scientifically impossible.

I will be concentrating on Judaism, Christianity and Islam. My questions may be about holy texts, religious figures or religious practices. I may sometimes come back to the same issue from a somewhat different angle. When I investigate these belief systems, I do so with an eye on the holy texts of these Abrahamic religions.

There are many who do not identify with any of the Abrahamic religions, and their belief systems and holy texts will not be subject to scrutiny in this book. There are quite a few who don't quite embrace any holy texts but may still find comfort in believing – or perhaps even knowing – that there is some form of supernatural being out there who may bring comfort, especially when circumstances become difficult. There are also quite a few who feel that they belong to one of the Abrahamic religions but are, at the same time, prepared to ignore what the holy texts of these three religions actually say. It may help some in this category to find comfort in the God who is created – in effect by themselves – as they embrace certain appealing passages of these holy texts while rejecting other, rather less agreeable passages.

INTRODUCTION

For the sake of this writing, God will be treated as masculine because that is how He is described in Judaism, Christianity and Islam. I am not a believer in God, but, for the sake of convenience here, I will use the term God or Lord to describe Him.

I am myself convinced that if Jesus even existed as a historical person, he was not the son of God, but, for the sake of argument, we will visit the Jesus of the holy writings.

We know that Muhammad existed and that he was a great warrior. I myself have difficulty believing that he was the last prophet who gave us the final and only truth forever. But when we visit Islamic holy texts, I will talk about both Muhammad and Allah from the Quran and the Hadiths.

In these times, it is important to ensure gender neutrality, so I use "he" and "she" other than in references to God or Jesus. Where appropriate, he and she are interchangeable, and each will include both genders. I am very happy to stipulate that any reader who belongs to a different gender outside of the binary "he" and "she" is also included. Rest assured that "he" or "she" includes all gender non-conforming persons.

Did God know what was or is going to happen with the universe, our planet and ourselves after creation and not care? Did the all-seeing and all-knowing God not understand how his holy texts were going to be given many different interpretations and often used to spite or even kill believers with a different interpretation of the same texts?

God is supposed (to the extent that it is not actually his own words) to at least have inspired the writing of the holy texts. Could He not, at the same time, have inspired better understanding in order for us not to have such trouble interpreting his will, indeed his meaning? We know that in the Old Testament, the 10 Commandments were, according to the Bible, written by His own hand on top of a mountain next to the burning bush, a bush that was not consumed by the fire. Knowing all the languages and all the translations that would come up, knowing how to communicate in a way that we would absolutely understand, could He not even get His own writing clear enough for us to understand absolutely?

In the Old Testament, God is described as having many positive traits, but He is also vengeful (for several generations) and jealous, He can get extremely angry (wrathful) and is so stubbornly, needlessly mysterious that humanity would forever struggle to understand Him. The inconvenience of all these traits will be made evident throughout this book.

These are some of the not-so-likeable traits one would find in human beings. Should we really have to find these negative human traits in our God?

I'm a big fan of Occam's razor. Occam (1285–1347) was an English philosopher, and Occam's razor is a problem-solving framework that basically lets us decide which answer to a question is normally the correct one. He says that the answer that requires the least number of assumptions is normally the correct one. In simple terms, the simplest answer is almost always right.

With all the human traits in our Lord, with all the spite and incomprehensible calls for murder, torture or genocide, with all the bad editing and lack of clarity in the holy books, one must wonder: is that really what the all-seeing, all-knowing God wants from us? We are supposed to believe and accept that God's ways are mysterious and that is why we do not understand them. We are, however, made to believe that when, for instance, God acts angrily or in revenge against us, He is really acting in our best interests and that the fault somehow is ours; we just do not know why. This, of course, leads us into the thorny issue of free will. Can we have free will if we do not know what is right or wrong and what outcome God really wants?

One has to ask the question that requires an Occam's razor answer. Which is more likely? Is it that God created humanity in his image, to have something to toy with as He pleases? Or is it that man invented God in his image to have something to worship?

Where does this leave us? As God is all-seeing, His plan must have been that in different regions there would be different ways of worshipping Him. He would be looking down on us while we continue to fight over who is in

INTRODUCTION

possession of the most correct, the most holy, and the most God-inspired interpretation of the holy texts.

The fighting between the various interpreters of the same texts should not be taken lightly. A lot of wars and killing have occurred in God's name. In Northern Ireland, not so long ago, Catholics and Protestants were at each other's throats for generations, even though both sides are Christian. In the Muslim world, Shia and Sunni have been similarly hostile to each other's way of believing in basically the same holy text.

My thanks go to God Himself and the holy texts, commands, commandments, and interpretations issued in His name, as well as to Moses, Jesus, Muhammad, the popes, the rabbis, the mullahs, and the ayatollahs. Otherwise, these questions could not have been asked. Of course, I also owe thanks to all the thinkers and writers who have had a much more scientific approach to examining the issues of belief. I finally want to thank some great comedians who, in a simple manner, have been able to cast a light on the difficulty of belief. Let me especially point you to George Carlin's God Loves You, which can be found on YouTube at https://youtu.be/QZ8hefESt7c and also Ricky Gervais's The Bible which can be found at https://www.dailymotion.com/video/x4toj3w.

My own journey started with reading James Michener's *The Source* in my teenage years. I found it fascinating that in the book, which is about an archaeological dig, he wrote a short story around every archaeological find, and I became curious whether the stories could be biblically accurate. So, I started reading the Bible, first the Old Testament and then the New Testament, and finally ventured into the Quran.

Further understanding came from *The Unauthorised Version: Truth and Fiction in the Bible* by Robin Lane Fox.

There are many more authors and debaters. I will mention a few, such as Christopher Hitchens, Sam Harris, Stephen Fry and, of course, Richard Dawkins. If you have not or will not be reading their books, I encourage you to at least look up these brilliant authors on YouTube and follow some of their debates. Hopefully, you will marvel, as I have, at the clarity and simplicity with which they convey their message, the clarion call for reason over belief.

If you are now reading this foreword, it means you have the book in your hand. What is required of you now is that you do not get upset, or angry, or worse. If you feel that you need to be violent in God's name, you are almost proving your own disbelief in that you believe God cannot handle His own defence. If you truly believe, it is required of you to understand that God can take care of Himself.

If you continue reading this book, do not forget that God is all-powerful, all-knowing, and all-seeing. In simple terms, having the power to do anything means there is nothing God cannot do. Being all-knowing means there is nothing He does not know, having knowledge far superior to our own humble beliefs and scientific knowledge. Lastly, being all-seeing, by definition, must mean that there is nothing that will happen in the future, potentially all different futures, that He cannot see or foresee. A reasonable conclusion is that if the God of anybody's belief would not want me to publish my writings, He could have ensured that they never came to be written. All-knowing and all-seeing, He must somehow have approved the publication of this writing.

When you read the questions and the short discussions around them, you must do so in the light of God's being all-powerful, all-knowing and all-seeing. Let us delve into the God of the three religions – Judaism, Christianity and Islam – all originally stemming from Abraham. We should not allow ourselves to forget that even within these three religions there are so many different branches with so many different interpretations.

Anyone who has decided to read on should realise how easy it is to find fault and errors in the beliefs of others who do not believe in the same way you do. You should then remember that a person with other beliefs may look at yours and be similarly happy to point out each and every fault and error as you may have done in regard to their belief system, without the filter of childhood indoctrination. Let us try hard, when we discuss all of these errors and faults, to

INTRODUCTION

at least understand them in the same way we are prepared to do in terms of the religious beliefs of persons with different faiths and beliefs.

What, then, is the difference between a religious person and a non-believer? Even a fervent believer must admit that she believes in her own God but not in the God or Gods of other religions or faiths. To borrow from Richard Dawkins, everybody is an atheist about other gods than the one of their own religion. In defining an atheist, he draws the conclusion that the atheist has only gone one step further and taken the last God out of the equation.

When I write "we", rest assured that I am not talking about the royal we but the reader and myself and anybody and everybody else that exists.

Where I perhaps write that we discuss something, it is while knowing, of course, that we are not actually engaged in discussion but I imagine a discussion between the reader and myself.

The chapters can best be seen as independent, subtly interconnected, and, I trust, thought-provoking essays.

CHAPTER 1

Why is it … that the Bible is viewed as a book of utmost morality when your children should really not be allowed to read it?

We need to start by remembering that both Jesus and his brother James were in favour of following the laws of Moses from the Old Testament. Christianity, or perhaps better stated, all the various Christian faiths, were very likely not anything either Jesus or James had anticipated. Jesus, after all, came to fulfil the law. Both Jesus and James were in favour of following the laws of Moses.

The evil in the Bible starts very early on. It begins, as long as we overlook, for the moment, the eating of the forbidden fruit, when Adam and Eve had two sons, Cain and Abel, and Cain killed his brother. Despite this egregious sin, Cain's only punishment was banishment from the Garden of Eden. Remarkably, the eternal God nonetheless provided Cain, at his request, with a mark on his forehead which offered him full protection against anyone outside of the Garden of Eden intent on killing him. We are left to wonder who these others could possibly be, since, according to the biblical story of Adam and Eve, their family were the first and thus far only ones to inhabit the earth. So, we get off to a confused start both in terms of ethics and narrative.

I believe we are almost all familiar with the story of Sodom and Gomorrah. Sodom has become synonymous with really bad behaviour. It is also the root of the verb sodomise, which implies homosexual activity, specifically anal penetration. Sodom and Gomorrah, in biblical terms, were really awful places. God did not like the amount of sinning occurring in these places and felt that He had to take action. The writer of the Sodom and Gomorrah story in the Bible clearly forgot that God must have known about all the evil that was to take place in Sodom and Gomorrah a long time before it happened. In fact, He already knew about this at the time of creation, if not before. But now, God decides it is time for severe action against the sinners in these particular locations.

The story reads that as angels are engaged in a discussion with Abraham, God reveals Himself to Abraham and expresses his outrage at the horrific, sinful behaviour of the inhabitants of Sodom and Gomorrah. Amazingly, Abraham starts negotiating with God and asks for mercy if just 50 God-fearing people can be identified in the sinful city. Do we believe that this negotiation actually occurred? In the story, God agrees and Abraham thinks that his hand has been strengthened and continues to negotiate. He asks God to consider 45 righteous men, moving down to 40, then 30, then 20 righteous men, and finally settling for 10 righteous men. God seems to be in a benevolent mood and agrees each time.

We must admire Abraham's gall and his incredible negotiating skills in his dealings with the Lord. We must also admit that we have reason to be disturbed by this negotiation with the God who has foreseen what will happen in Sodom and Gomorrah and knows what He will do about it, since way back in human time (or before). We must speak of "human time" as it is difficult to speak about time in relation to God. For the sake of good order, let us note that God knows where this negotiating is going before Abraham even initiates it.

The story continues with two angels being sent down to Sodom to visit with Lot, the nephew of Abraham. The angels are invited to stay in Lot's house and be served food. That night, a mob of men, both young and old, from everywhere in the city, ask Lot to produce the men that have come to visit him. The mob want them sent out so that the mob may "know them". To *know* them is, in fine biblical language, to have sex with them, which in this case obviously means that the mob wish to engage in group rape. How titillating when new flesh arrives, is it not?

Lot, being the righteous man he is, does his best to prevent the mob from violating the male angels. And, intent on protecting his angelic visitors, instead, lo and behold, he offers the mob his two virgin daughters "which have not known man". Lot assures the mob that they can do as they please with his daughters. The mob, of course, refuse his offer and complain that a foreigner such as Lot thinks he can judge them. It is only when the mob come close to breaking down the door that the angels finally rescue Lot and turn the mob blind.

The remainder of the story is well-known. The angels explain that they have come to destroy the city but would like to make Lot and his family leave first, thus saving their lives, but with one key condition: they must not look back while the city is being destroyed. Lot's wife is far too curious not to look back and is punished for her curiosity by being turned into a pillar of salt.

So here we are, very early on in the Bible, and already we find ourselves reading about the desire for homosexual gang-rape and the distracting counter-offer – an offer made by their father, lest we forget – of young virgin girls for gang-rape by the same mob.

I do not think anybody would disagree that had this not been a holy text, no responsible parent would want their children to read such a story. Yet children are sent to Jewish school and to Sunday school to learn about the goodness of the Lord and the morality of the holy book.

But the story does not end here. We now come to Lot's virgin daughters. Lot supposedly had four daughters, two of whom were likely either married or engaged to be married. Lot was left with his remaining two virgin daughters who had fled with him from Sodom. One could argue that perhaps God's intention was to protect Lot's virgin daughters; nevertheless, Lot remained unpunished for offering his daughters' virginity to a violent mob, in an act which would constitute the sin of pre-marital sex, at the very least.

Lot and his two daughters end up living in a cave. The daughters are afraid that they are the last people on earth and decide to procreate. While God is

CHAPTER 1

watching over them – as He watches over all of us – they decide to get their father drunk and take turns having sexual intercourse with him in order to become pregnant. Both of them do, indeed, get pregnant; the older one has a son called Moab, and the younger daughter gives birth to a son named Ammon. We watch in amazement at how incest is perceived to be the only way to keep the earth populated. God could have sent down angels to explain the situation to the daughters or could even have sent a few men outside of the family for the daughters to procreate with, but He did not, and we must assume that He chose not to do so. Let us not forget that incest starts early in the Bible. The original inhabitants of the Garden of Eden are one and the same family and have no other way of procreating than to engage in incestuous relationships with their immediate family members.

Had this story not been found in a holy book; would we have wanted our children to read the story about Sodom and Gomorrah?

Almost all of us must be aware of the story of Noah's ark. Noah was, of course, a direct descendant of Adam, nine generations down. Who else could he be a descendant of? In the story, God is very disappointed with humanity and decides to drown just about all living creatures in the entire world but picks Noah and his family to start the world over again so that the human race can carry on.

Noah is told to build an ark with very specific measurements. Noah and his family are to board the ark and also invite seven pairs of "clean" animals and only one pair of "unclean" animals, male and female, to shelter on the ark. The ark will float on the waters which are to flood the earth and drown all of humanity except Noah's family. All the animals will also be left to drown, except the ones safely on board the ark. It seems that God wanted to have a margin for procreation with seven pairs of clean animals boarding the ark. But why would He need that margin of safety? God has created everything from nothing, anyway. And, besides, God sees all futures.

The story about the ark has many parts that remain untold. We can imagine that this multitude of animals and Noah's family have ample drinking water from the heavy rain. But how do they get food? Clean animals must relate to the ones which eventually become, according to later-introduced dietary laws, clean to eat or kosher. God certainly knows that animals are going to be divided into clean and unclean or kosher and non-kosher. How did Noah know?

The explanation for how the animals and Noah's family on the ark were fed could be – although we are not told – that God just suspended the need to feed during the time on the ark. We do note that Noah and his family are supposedly vegetarian, at least until they leave the ark, and do not need kosher meat. Perhaps they could plant food to grow on the Ark, but what would the animals eat? What would the predator animals eat?

Both humanity and all the different kinds of animals would start over and populate the earth once it had dried up and Noah and his family, as well as all the animals, could disembark.

God knows what His creation is going to bring about. He has, of course, foreseen that the people are going to be wicked, and He has already, long ago, known what He is going to do with them. He could have just made them understand how to behave or, in modern terms, programmed or re-programmed them and let them live, but He decided not to. We remember that God, at the beginning of the Bible, was very happy with his creation and patted Himself on the back, stating that He saw that it was good. Should we perhaps draw the conclusion that it was not that good a creation after all? Should we perhaps draw the conclusion that the creation story is man-made?

Would you like your children to read or be instructed by any other book that contains the harshness of wiping out all of humanity in a deliberate drowning? But you would allow them to read the Bible. With most of humanity having drowned, we must realise that there was only one family left on earth. Since Noah and his wife came on board with their three sons, who also brought their wives, procreation was only possible between cousins one generation down. Is this biblical tale a good example of high morality for our children?

The animals, by the way, really had nothing to do with it. God could have chosen some other way than the total flooding of the earth and saved them instead, but He chose to drown them as well, which, of course, would affect all land animals. He could just have killed every family on earth apart from Noah's without having to drown the animals, but He did not. Animals supposedly do not have any free will, and man had been given dominion over them. Why were they drowned? What wrong did they do other than living their lives the way God created them? Is this an example of high morality for us and our children to be guided by?

God could have found a more humane way of killing the world's population than drowning. He could also have revealed Himself and let people understand how important it is to follow His wishes and commands. He could have just re-programmed His creation, but that would imply that He was not all-seeing and had not already foreseen human behaviour when He created them.

There are, even today, efforts being made to identify where the ark landed after the flood. The location that frequently comes up is Mount Ararat in modern Turkey. Do we not realise that the story is so unrealistic that the whole thing must be deemed impossible? There was never such a huge ark that could house all the massive creatures (leaving aside the thorny issue of dinosaurs which can't be made to fit into the problematically abbreviated Biblical timeline anyway) and all other animals down to the smallest. It would further have been virtually impossible to keep predators from attacking the prey. What would the predators eat? Would it be possible to prevent the predators from attacking all the other creatures? In short, do we have any reason to believe that Noah's ark ever existed?

You would not think that deception and theft would be allowed in the Bible. Let us therefore turn to the story of Jacob and his brother Esau to see if God does not, after all, mind either deception or stealing. In the 10 Commandments, God forbids bearing false witness and theft. We fully understand that the 10 Commandments came later, but we must understand that God already knew what was right.

Isaac, in the biblical story, is the father of two sons. The elder son is named Esau and the younger one is Jacob. In his old age, Isaac is turning blind. He requests that his elder son, Esau, goes to hunt for some game and prepare a delicious meal that he is craving. Isaac's intentions are to bless Esau, his firstborn, before his passing, in accordance with custom. This delicious meal is meant to be a celebration.

Rebecca, Isaac's wife, happens to hear what he says to Esau but wants the fatherly blessings for his younger and her favourite son, Jacob. Rebecca instructs Jacob to go out and from the flocks bring two fine young goats that she will use to prepare his father's favourite dish. Jacob is instructed to take the food prepared by his mother to his father. His father will eat it and at the end of the meal bless the wrong son, the younger one, Jacob.

Jacob, who is not stupid, complains to his mother that his older brother is a very hairy man and that his own skin is smooth. He is afraid that his father might touch him and find out that the wrong son is seated next to him. He is also afraid that when his father finds out that he is being tricked, he will end up cursing him instead of blessing him. Do we observe here that Jacob is not at all concerned about the deception itself but eager to ensure a positive outcome from the deception? Jacob's issue is with his father finding out that the wrong son is being blessed, not the fact that he is being blessed by deception and wrongfully, given the firstborn's natural rights.

Jacob's mother does not mind about any curse that could come from father Isaac. In fact, she both eggs her son on and gives him comfort by saying that should Isaac discover the ongoing deceit, "Let the curse fall on me, your mother." It is really rather amazing that two mortals can decide on the deceit to get a father's blessing. It is equally amazing that this mother and son feel that they possess the power to shift whatever curse may result from their actions from the son over to the mother. They must obviously believe that they can get away with it because Jacob goes along with the scheme as a willing participant. He wants the blessing for himself, knowing full-well that he was stealing the blessing from his older brother. And even believers must wonder what force, power and authority are contained within a curse issued by a mere mortal?

CHAPTER 1

The deception continues as Jacob goes out, gets the young goats and delivers them to his mother. Mother Rebecca prepares a delicious meal, knowing precisely how Isaac likes it. She takes the older brother Esau's best clothes and gives them to the younger son Jacob to wear. She takes the skin of the goats and puts them on Jacob's hand and neck so that he will feel very hairy and thus more closely resemble his brother, should his blind father, Isaac, want to touch him. Thus prepared, Jacob goes to his father with the meal and freshly-baked bread.

"My father," says Jacob to Isaac. Isaac answers by asking him if he is Esau or Jacob. Jacob, well-aware of what he is up to, lies and says that he is Esau, the firstborn son. He kindly explains to his father that he has done as instructed; he has arrived with wild game and asks his father to eat it and give him his blessing.

Isaac, still a bit suspicious, asks how his son managed to find the game so quickly, and Jacob has the perfect reply when he says that it was God who put the game in his path. Jacob has no hesitation in invoking God to make his trickery more plausible.

Still wanting to be sure that his blessing goes to the right son, Isaac says, "Come close so I can touch you and make sure that you really are Esau." Jacob moves over to his father, who touches him and says that the voice is Jacob's but the hands are Esau's. He has obviously felt that Jacob's hands are hairy, just like those of his elder brother. His father then asks Jacob to come over and kiss him, which allows Isaac to smell his clothes, and we know that he is wearing his brother's clothes.

The story is well told by the writer and there is no lack of suspense. Isaac does not go straight to blessing Jacob but wants to eat the meal, after which the blessing will come from his lips. Time passes while the suspicious Isaac continues to probe the identity of the son beside him. We are meant to be waiting in suspense to see whether Jacob's older brother will arrive at the scene in time to stop the trickery, which would supply a moral ending to this tale.

But Isaac is indeed convinced that it is the elder of the two brothers in front of him and so gives him his blessing, a blessing that includes the promise that many nations will become the servants of this son and will bow down to him, and further still that he will be the master of his brothers and that his mother's sons will bow down to him. Finally, Isaac blesses him, saying, "All who curse you will be cursed, and all who bless you will be blessed."

Still in suspense, we sit and wonder when the older brother is going to show up. At last he does, just as Isaac has finished blessing Jacob and the blessed son has left his father. Esau has himself prepared the meal from the wild game he has hunted and prepared for his father's blessing. The confused Isaac asks him who he is, and he replies that he is his firstborn son, Esau. Isaac is upset and asks who it was, then, who had just served him the wild game that he had finished eating and who it was, therefore, that received his blessing.

Fully understanding that he has been tricked and has blessed the wrong son, Isaac nevertheless concludes that the blessing must stand. Esau begs his father to bless him as well, but Isaac refuses. Esau understands that his younger brother has taken away the blessing meant for him. His father, in the end, explains that he has in his blessing given Jacob everything, including the promise that all his brothers will be his servants, and he has also granted him an abundance of grain and wine. Isaac concludes that there is nothing left for him to give to his son Esau, despite Esau's being the firstborn and therefore the one entitled to his father's blessings.

The conclusion of this story is tragic. Esau ends up hating his brother, and Rebecca is afraid that he will kill Jacob. She has him flee to her brother, Jacob's uncle, and stay with him until Esau cools down.

I believe we can all agree that deception should not be rewarded. And surely there would be no reason for Jacob to keep the benefits of the blessing since it was received by pure deception and trickery. But Isaac lets it stand, and what is even more notable is that God lets it stand. Jacob, on the run, has a dream where God appears to him and tells him that the land where he lies will be given to him and his offspring. God promises him that his offspring shall be as many as the dust of the earth and that they shall spread in all directions. God declares that He is with him and will keep him safe wherever he goes and will not leave him. It is abundantly clear from all this that God is not upset about the deception but takes it for granted that the trickery must and will be rewarded. One could perhaps, if somewhat facetiously, say that God's actions make Him an accessory after the fact. Not only does God let the deception stand but He even adds to it with the extra promises given to Jacob.

The story is so well told that one could easily forget that this is a tale of unalloyed deception, and a deception that stands and indeed prospers despite all the trickery. Is this a story that you would like your children to read and be taught? Do we find this to be a story of moral rectitude? Would we have accepted the story as moral in any other context than the Holy Bible?

We have so far merely gone over some of the lighter stuff. If we want to see who God really is and what He prescribes for humanity, there is substantially more to be reviewed.

In Psalm 137: 8–9, God tells people that they should be either blessed or happy, depending on how you want to translate it, when they take the babies of daughters of Babylon and in revenge dash them against the rock. Does this somehow constitute a moral high point, a fitting part of the Bible serving its vital role as a guide to morality? Perhaps we should remind ourselves that God is a vengeful being, one who continues to dole out his punishments even generations after the perpetrator of sin.

The famous prophet Isaiah puts forth very similar sentiments and speaks of the Lord promising a cruel day full of anger against the arrogant: "their infants will be dashed to pieces before their eyes; their houses will be looted and their wives violated." We do not want to leave this without understanding that, in this context, *violated* means raped. Is this another example of high morality?

Isaiah has more warnings and this time threatens that God will go after attractive women by exposing their nakedness. What the infinitely wise God says, according to Isaiah, is that because the daughters of Zion are arrogant and walk with stretched-forth necks and eyes full of desire, God will uncover their secret parts. There's a lot of sexual repression in this writing. Is this something in which we want our children to be educated and indoctrinated?

WHY IS IT?

Let us not forget that slavery was not a problem in either the Old or the New Testament. Slaves should be happy with their lot and mostly be rewarded in the next life. In fact, the Holy Bible has no prohibition against a man going so far as to sell his own daughter into slavery. We can just imagine in what kind of slavery she would end up in relation to her master. As opposed to male slaves, she is not to be freed the same way as male slaves, who are entitled to freedom after serving their master for six years. If this female slave, acquired from her father, does not please her new master, he should let her go. He has no right to sell her on to a foreign people as it is he who has broken faith with her. If he hands her over to become the property of his son, the master shall see her as if she were his daughter. Do we find this to be high morality? Would you like your own daughter to understand and accept this notion of selling a daughter into slavery to be treated even worse than male slaves?

Perhaps it would be a good start to understand what the biblical texts actually say. That would require us to remove the blinders of childhood indoctrination and to see through the patina of old language, which is somewhat hard to understand.

Women are not terribly important in most of the Bible. They do, however, come in handy for purposes of sacrifice. Jephthah is a general who is at war with the Ammonites. He is very keen on winning the war and he promises God that if He gives him victory against the Ammonites, he will sacrifice, as a burnt offering, whoever first emerges out of his house. When the general returns to his home in triumph, it is his daughter who is the first to come through the door. The general keeps his promise and does, indeed, burn his daughter, for which God rewards him with the prestigious position of judge, and Jephthah is, when he dies, buried with great honour.

Is there any way we can see this as a reasonable story with a valuable moral lesson for us? The promise to God is one thing, but He could have stopped the burning of the general's daughter in the same way that He stopped Abraham from sacrificing his son Isaac or intervened in some way as He did for Lot's two virgin daughters.

CHAPTER 1

Can we find anything moral in the story? Or are we simply disgusted with both the promise to God and the fulfilment of the promise by a general who was also a father and who burnt his daughter?

We must not forget King David, who is seen as one of the big heroes of the Old Testament. We have come to believe that, as a young shepherd boy, David manages to defeat Goliath with a sling, ultimately saving King Saul's soldiers. King Saul makes David the leader of his army but becomes anxious about David's immense popularity among the people. The king is afraid that David may take the kingdom from him. The king's son, Jonathan, loves David very much, and that becomes very helpful to David when Jonathan warns David about the king's plotting to kill him. Jonathan even confirms that he sees David as the future King. David hides in various territories outside of King Saul's control. Eventually, war ensues, and, after both King Saul and his son Jonathan are killed in battle, David becomes the anointed king over Judah while Saul's elder son, Ish-Bosheth, is king of Israel. War starts again and Ish-Bosheth is murdered, which leads to David' becoming king over all of Israel. Nathan the prophet prevents David from building the temple which he claims will be built by King David's son. Nathan also makes a prophecy about God's special relationship with the house of David in the words, "Your throne shall be established forever." God's inspirational powers must not be up to par since there is, in 2 Samuel, a second story about the killing of Goliath. In this story, Elhanan is the victorious killer of the giant Goliath. We're just noting.

The 10 Commandments were well-known at the time, and so let us see what acts David commits in spite of the law. He sees a married woman bathing and calls for her. He starts having sexual relations with her and she gets pregnant while her husband, Uriah, a Hittite, is in active battle for the king. King David, as it is written in the Bible, covets another man's wife and engages in sexual activity with her, although it is not clear from the biblical text whether the woman, Bathsheba, consents.

So, the sex with King David gets his married mistress pregnant, and the scheming King David calls Uriah back from the war zone to be with his wife in the hope that the child will be presumed to be Uriah's. Uriah, however, is a very good man and does not want to have the comforts of life while his troops are battling. Therefore, he does not lie with his wife. King David has to find a different way of solving his problem. The king obviously has no difficulty with bearing false witness. King David sends Uriah back to battle with a note to his commanding officer that he be put on the front line, obviously with the intention that he be killed. Uriah dies in battle and King David marries his widow, Bathsheba. King David is therefore effectively guilty of killing the husband of his mistress. The good man, Uriah, is sent to his death. The sinner, King David, does not suffer for now.

The prophet Nathan advises the king that his sin is forgiven but that his child will die. Eventually, David's son Absalom is indeed killed. We have here another completely immoral story in the Bible, and yet King David is seen as the ancestor of the future Messiah, and in fact both ancestral lines of Jesus in the New Testament go over King David so that Jesus can be described as descending from him. The intention in both ancestral lines described in the New Testament is to fulfil the Old Testament prophecy that the Messiah would come from the house of David. Although it must be noted that, when writing that lineage of ancestors, both the Gospel according to Matthew and the Gospel according to Luke seem to have completely forgotten that Joseph was only the stepfather of Jesus, with God being the true father and with Mary as mother. We should all know that the immaculate conception refers to Mary, Jesus' mother, who was without original sin all the way back to her conception. This belief was meant to set the stage for the Virgin Mary to become the father of Christ. This leaves us asking: did God really care? Why in the eyes of God is everybody else born with original sin?

Would you really want your children to read this extremely immoral story where the king breaks quite a few of the 10 Commandments and yet gets rewarded? Your children would come to understand that lusting for somebody else's wife, getting her pregnant, trying to trick her husband into sleeping with his wife and plotting to have her husband killed are all bad acts but obviously in

CHAPTER 1

King David's case, they are still forgivable by the Lord Himself. After all of this, David was still, according to both the Old and New Testaments, the ancestor of the coming Messiah.

In many instances, God orders genocide to make room for His people to occupy lands that already have occupants. In some instances, God orders torture. We can stop here, but we should be reminded that if we were to continue our investigation, there would be so many more tales to be found in the Bible of a nature that we should, or even must, consider completely immoral.

Are we still okay calling the Old and New Testaments books of high moral value? The New Testament has no problem with slavery – is that a book of high morality? The New Testament has Jesus saying that he has come to fulfil the law. We should not misunderstand what that means. It means incorporating the teachings and rules of the Old Testament into the teaching of Christ Himself. The New Testament is in no way an independent Bible. The New Testament is built on the foundations of the Old Testament. The Old Testament is part of Christian teaching as holy scripture.

Would we now be willing to concede that, had both the Old and New Testaments not been holy books, there is no way we would have wanted our children to either read these books or be instructed in accordance with the perceived wisdom in those books? Are we willing to look at the texts, without the blinders of childhood indoctrination, for what they actually teach and prescribe?

Stephen Fry has a lot on his plate. He is a Jewish nonbeliever; he is gay; he has admitted to certain mental health struggles. He has not allowed his two minority labels and mental health issues to impede him in his task of calmly and comically analyzing the world around us and describing it as is. He readily employs his wit to critique religious notions. Despite his personal issues, Mr. Fry has turned out to be both a very good comedian and a very good debater.

This is a fitting place to remind ourselves of Stephen Fry's interview in 2015 which can be found on YouTube and is a must-see (https://youtu.be/-suvkwNYSQo). The interviewer asks Stephen Fry what he would say to God if he were to meet Him up at the Pearly Gates. Stephen Fry brilliantly answers, "I'd say, bone cancer in children? What's that about?" Mr. Fry continues with, "How dare you? How dare you create a world in which there is such misery that is not our fault? It is not right, it is utterly, utterly evil. Why should I respect a capricious, mean-minded, stupid God who creates a world that is so full of injustice and pain? That's what I would say."

Many probably believe that it is only in conservative Muslim societies where blasphemy could become a police matter, but in Ireland, Stephen Fry's remarks about God prompted a police investigation. The idea to be investigated was that Mr. Fry was in breach of the Defamation Act.

We ought to be willing to look at the holy books and find that there are some good passages that could serve as moral guides but that there are evil passages aplenty that on balance should not allow us to come to the conclusion that the Holy Bible is a good moral guide. We should understand that, and we should not let our children be fooled by either rabbis, ministers or priests who expend a lot of effort trying not to explain but to explain away the fact that so much immorality and evil is prescribed in God's name.

One explanation that is often put forward is that when God orders it, or God Himself commits immoral acts, it is automatically good. It is good because God is, by definition, good, and we humans just do not understand it. It is a very circular argument. Bad acts by God are good because God is good. So why does a good God commit bad acts?

In areas that are not religious, such as the military, orders from a commanding officer are not supposed to be followed if they, for instance, go against the rules for warfare. An Occam's razor question could be: are we meant to lose all personal morality and just give in to God's commands, even if they are horrendous?

CHAPTER 2

Why is it ... that when scientists or religious figures try to show that science and religion are compatible, the result ends up being unscientific?

We, or at least most of us, now know and take for granted that the earth is round and not flat. We also now know that the earth is not the centre of the universe, with the sun and the moon circling our planet. We also know that our light comes from the sun and not because, according to the biblical creation story, darkness and light were separated before the sun was created. It is because of centuries of scientific progress in explaining the natural world that the vast majority of us no longer believe those things. We needn't dwell here on the very few who still cling to provably unscientific beliefs concerning the nature of things.

If you were to pick up a book built upon the premise that the earth is flat, most of you would probably stop reading right there. If, for some reason, you did continue reading, it would be with a smile on your face to see what other absurd untruths might have made their way into this book.

But here, we will be examining holy scripture. A great many probably know, or sort of know, the real truth about the nature of things but let it slide so as not to have to take a painful stand against the religion of their childhood indoctrination. Indeed, a great number of scientists and religious figures have made heroic efforts to show that religion, or religious beliefs, and scientific knowledge can and should coexist.

For this chapter, let us follow Dr. Francis Collins as he explains how a *Scientist Provides Evidence for Belief*. Let us together note that it is, in his own words, **evidence** he brings to the table. He does so in his book *The Language of God* with *A Scientist Provides Evidence for Belief* as the subtitle of his book. He does set the bar high himself, so we have the right to have great expectations of the evidence he brings forth. He is, after all, a renowned scientist and he fully understands what evidence is. We should understand that what Dr. Collins is providing evidence for is not just any belief. It does not take much science to provide evidence for belief. We know that many people can believe many stupid things. When we turn to Dr. Collins and his book *The Language of God*, we are made to understand that what he intends to demonstrate is that belief and science are compatible.

Why can we pick Dr. Collins as a representative of the scientists who are not only believers (or claim to be) but also claim the right to explain to the rest of us how things really work? Francis Collins is an American physician and geneticist. He managed to pair certain genes with particular diseases, which led to the Human Genome Project. He eventually became the director of the NIH, the National Institutes of Health, in the USA.

As we can see, Dr. Collins is a scientist with substantial scientific credentials, especially as the leader of the project to sequence the human genome, one of the greatest scientific accomplishments of our age. When working with DNA and genes, he is working in the field of evolution and must find himself at the crossroads between science and belief. It is therefore particularly interesting how he presents his evidence for belief.

Even more interesting is that for him, as he states in his book, faith was not an important part of his childhood. In other words, he did not start with childhood indoctrination into a certain set of beliefs. Rather, his religious beliefs grew while he was becoming an educated and accomplished scientist. Dr. Collins' journey towards faith came from nonbelief. He says that a few months into his college career he became convinced that while many religious faiths had inspired interesting traditions of art and culture, they held no foundational truth. And he further states that he gradually shifted from agnosticism to atheism. And yet, he found his way to belief. Very notably, he believes that he has found a way of demonstrating to the rest of us that there is no real conflict between science and religion, or, expressed somewhat differently, between reason and belief.

From the religious side, we will follow Pope Francis. The pope needs no introduction as he is the leader of the Catholic Church. That does not mean that science is unimportant to him. He has shown his interest in science in many statements and also in his *Encyclical on Climate Change & Inequality* published in 2015. He clearly demonstrates that he does not mind taking a scientific approach to issues of concern to humanity and the world around us.

Finally, we will delve into a book named *Encyclopedia of Bible Difficulties* authored by Dr. Gleason L. Archer and published in 1982. It is a promising title. As the title indicates, there are difficulties in the Bible that need or at least may need an explanation.

An objective analysis of each difficulty would be interesting, and the more difficulties found in the Bible, the more one should probably question the truthfulness of the Bible, or preferably Bibles, as Christianity holds that there is both an Old and a New Testament.

Let us now start with Francis Collins' book. In this book, he describes a moment when he felt that he, as a scientist, could not draw conclusions without considering the data. As he says, "Could there be a more important question in all of human existence than 'Is there a God?'." Thus began his journey to further study the major religions of the world, and his reading of the CliffsNotes left him with little reason to be drawn into one or other of the many possibilities. That was until he started to read C.S. Lewis's *Mere Christianity*, which he found intelligent and, in a way, made him see the light. The big question for him became how to understand "Moral Law".

I think we would all find it interesting how he answers the question *Why would a loving God allow suffering in the world?* He quotes C.S. Lewis again, who, in *The Problem of Pain* argues, "If God were good, he would wish to make his creatures perfectly happy, and if God were Almighty, he would be able to do what he wished. But the creatures are not happy. Therefore, God lacks either goodness or power or both."

Francis Collins' answer to this dilemma is that a large fraction of our sufferings and that of our fellow human beings is brought about by what we do to one another. Please observe with me that he mentions *a large fraction* of human suffering. There must, since humans are not responsible for all but only a large fraction of our sufferings, be quite a bit left that should, therefore, fall under God's responsibility. I believe it would be good to keep these thoughts in mind as we now venture into three specific points in this scientist's writing.

Firstly, Collins' journey to faith became serious when his daughter was raped. He wonders why God did not stop the perpetrator or interfere with the free will of the perpetrator. Collins comes down to the point that, for the most part, "the existence of free will and of order in the physical universe are inexorable facts." He concludes that "while we might wish for such miraculous deliverance to occur more frequently the consequence of interrupting these two sets of forces would be utter chaos." His scientific conclusion is that God cannot constantly interfere in the acts stemming from the free will of bad people or even in the occurrence of natural disasters or disease as that would create utter chaos. To be crystal clear, he posits that there is, indeed, an all-powerful God, but His constant intervention would wreak havoc on his creations. This does, in Collins' mind, even excuse God from having to interfere and prevent the evil act experienced by his daughter.

It may be difficult for us to follow this because where and when God intervenes, we, for the most part, would not even know that He had intervened. There could even be reason to question to what extent we do or do not really have free will in relation to God.

It is reasonable to ask why God could not have stopped the perpetrator before the rape. We have to ask ourselves how scientific Dr. Collins' methods are when he comes to the conclusion that if God intervened there would be utter chaos. On the contrary, it would seem reasonable to assume that if this all-powerful, all-knowing, benevolent God were to interfere, He would do it in such a way as to prevent chaos – He does have that power.

Outside of the Bible, rape is never forgivable. Let us anyhow, and only for the sake of our analysis of Dr. Collins' statement that God's intervention in the material world would wreak havoc on His creation, assume that God would actually have intervened. The intention here is not to make light of Dr. Collins' daughter's predicament, but, since Dr. Collins brought it up, we should be allowed to investigate the occurrence and whether God's intervention would have had such dire consequences as stated by Dr. Collins. Let's therefore assume that God would have intervened by rendering the rapist limp and tying him up on a chair with his trousers down while waiting for the police to arrive. It is hard to see that our universe would be subjected to any catastrophic effects because of this. Dr. Collins' family would surely suffer no catastrophic effects from God's hypothetical intervention. All that would have happened would've been that the benevolent God would have saved Dr. Collins' daughter. The earth, our solar system, the universe and life on earth would have continued, after God's hypothetical intervention to save Dr. Collins' daughter, as if nothing had happened.

Collins moves on, while putting on his scientific hat, to explain that, "Science reveals that the universe, our own planet, and life itself are engaged in an evolutionary process." His take is that God set all of His creation in motion, which led to the inevitability of other painful consequences. One would almost want to cry out and wonder how a scientist can come to the conclusion that the all-seeing God, the God who knows all the futures that may occur, could not have done a better job by assuring a peaceful development in the natural world. Is it really so, we wonder, that once God had turned his creation into an ongoing evolution, painful consequences were inevitable? The rape of Collins' daughter can be linked back to God's creation when He somewhat sloppily let evolution take over and run its course while He was watching. Was He enjoying the scene? Was He indifferent to what went on?

Furthermore, with Dr. Collins' religious hat on, he should understand that no matter what science reveals about the universe and our planet and ourselves – that is not what the Bible reveals. The Bible reveals that the earth was created by God, who created all the living creatures on it, as well as man and woman. The Bible also reveals that the sun and the moon and the stars were created around the earth, the earth being the centre of the universe.

Collins is being choosy. He believes some but not all. Once you start down this path, one can conclude that perhaps Collins has chosen the wrong parts of holy scripture to believe. There is absolutely no evidence, in either the Old or New Testament, that God turned his creation into an evolutionary process. That kind of thinking is purely a result of scientific knowledge today, knowledge that was not available to the writers of either the Old or the New Testament.

How does his first argument for finding faith in the rapist's bad act toward his daughter withstand any scientific test? The rapist was a bad person who just used his free will while the all-seeing, all-knowing God, who knew from the time of creation that this was going to happen, took no corrective action. The reason that God took no corrective action is, according to Collins, that such interference would create utter chaos.

Secondly, without any scientific evidence or reasoning, Dr. Collins comes to the conclusion that if faith is not just a cultural practice, but rather a search for absolute truth, we must not go so far as to commit the logical fallacy of saying that all conflicting points of view are equally true. He claims, "Monotheism and polytheism cannot both be right. Through my own search, Christianity has provided for me that special ring of eternal truth. But you must conduct your own search."

We are left to wonder on what basis he draws this conclusion. *There is no scientific evidence that there is even one God.* Nor, it must be said, is there any scientific evidence that there is no God at all. Those of us who do not believe in a God or supernatural creator believe so because our scientists' explanations of the natural world seem more persuasive than the various biblical texts. There is, of course, also no scientific evidence against the proposition that there could be several Gods running things. There is no evidence that this God would not be Thor from that ancient Nordic religion or that it is not the pantheon of Gods in Greek mythology that run things in our world.

Dr. Collins' conclusion, that monotheism and polytheism cannot both be right, is of course a correct observation with regard to a particular individual. There is no saying that declares it's not acceptable that some people believe in one God while others believe in several Gods. The belief in many Gods is still prevalent in some areas of the world today, as it has been throughout human history. Christianity believes in God the Father, the Son, and the Holy Ghost. Seems like more than one, but luckily, the three have been defined by Christian leaders as being just one, although they still seem to the untrained eye to be three. Since Christian leaders have explained it, we should be happy and take it as gospel truth. We should not think about it anymore.

Going back, in the beginning even the Bible was not at all clear that there was only one God. Dr. Collins' conclusion that, through his own search, Christianity has provided for him that special ring of eternal truth is very unscientific and doesn't do anything in terms of bridging the gap between science and religion, let alone show that they are compatible. At least he is generous enough to let the rest of us conduct our own search. The scientist in him does understand that your search could lead you to believe something entirely different, such as Hinduism, or perhaps nothing at all.

Dr. Collins bypasses the conflict between the actual biblical creation stories and current scientific knowledge by simply reinterpreting the biblical texts to have them mean not what they say but, instead, that God started evolution.

The third point we are now going to analyse is how Dr. Collins reasons around the origins of the universe, the planet Earth, and life on our planet. He starts this off very well, and he has his scientific hat on when he openly and clearly states that we know that the universe is approximately 14 billion years old. We also now know how long our own planet has been around and that the discovery of radioactivity and the natural decay of certain chemical isotopes provide an elegant and rather precise means of determining the age of various rocks on earth, a process that has, for obvious reasons, been given the name "decay clock". He describes how the oldest rocks that have been dated on the current earth surface are approximately 4 billion years old but that nearly 70 meteorites and a number of moon rocks have been dated at 4.5 billion years old.

Collins criticises the so-called young earth creationists who have reached the point of intellectual bankruptcy and have thus further widened the chasm between the scientific and spiritual worldviews. Collins points to Kenneth Miller who, in his excellent book *Finding Darwin's God*, discusses the claims that God might be a trickster who manipulated and transformed all the scientific evidence to mislead us and test our faith. By this argument, God would intentionally have designed the radioactive decay clocks in order to trick us. He would also have created all the fossils, all of the genome sequences, just to make it look as if the world was considerably older than the few thousand years that it appears to be according to the evidence of the Bible – and this is, it must be noted, a somewhat convoluted argument.

We can leave the actual age of the universe and the science to one side but acknowledge that Dr. Collins himself believes in the science. The important question that comes out of Collins' book is the following: "Would God as the great deceiver be an entity one would want to worship?"

And the follow-up question that is posed: "Is this consistent with everything else we know about God from the Bible, from the moral law, and from every other source – namely, that he is loving, logical and consistent?"

In fact, we are talking about a God who has no issue with taking revenge on human misdeeds for several generations and has no problem with ordering mass killings and torture. We are talking about a God who has nothing against slavery. We are talking about a God who has no problem drowning all creatures in the world except one family and one or seven pairs of each animal species.

Let us look at who the God of the Bible really is. Could that God be the great deceiver? Could He even be a deceiver who does no more harm than tamper with our instruments to trick us in terms of our understanding of how old our earth is? Is that really the worst He can do? Tricking us with our reading of instruments to make us believe that the earth is much older than the few thousand years according to the Bible does not really alter anybody's life. All it does is leave us ignorant as to the scientific facts.

But let us look at this with our scientific hat on. If Collins has no problem with worshipping the God who has drowned just about all the creatures in the world and ordered his human creations to commit outrageous acts, why would he have a problem with God's little deception game? So what? Among all the evil that God has, according to the biblical text, done to us on earth, is deceiving us by fiddling with our instruments really Dr. Collins, the scientist's, breaking point with God?

But if God is the great deceiver and has not only a good side but a very bad and even vengeful one, do we have any choice but to worship Him anyway? How unscientific it is to ask the question whether such a great deceiver could be an entity one would *want* to worship. By just raising the question the way Dr. Collins does, he is indicating that God is man-made and that we can therefore choose who and what we want to worship. God is God, and if you are a believer, He is who He is and you have no choice but to worship Him.

The way science works, if there were evidence for God's existence and He would show Himself to us in all his power, glory, vengefulness, jealousy, and vindictiveness, nobody would have a choice but to worship Him.

Could the answer to the question posed by Dr. Collins be that since Thor has never tried to deceive us regarding the age of the universe, we should worship him instead? Dr. Collins cannot produce one grain of evidence to show that Thor is not the only true God.

Is it really as easy as following? There is no evidence, or at least not enough evidence, to claim that God exists. There is of, course, no ultimate proof either that God does not exist. But if our scientific methods have taught us anything, it is that we need to go with the evidence wherever it may lead us. Our scientists have given us natural explanations for almost everything around us, so *currently the evidence leads us to the conclusion that there is no God.* Besides, in science, it is the one who claims that God exists who has the burden of proof. Being a scientist, surely this is something Dr. Collins fully understands.

I believe we are forced to conclude that Dr. Collins has not been able to explain himself as a scientist. His approach hardly seems scientific and his reasoning is convoluted. Occam's razor comes in handy at this point as it tells us that the more convoluted an answer to a question, the more likely it is to be wrong. It seems that Dr. Collins, in his younger years, was more able to keep the scientific approach separate from his faith and belief. Should our conclusion not be that there is no scientific way of searching for either God or His works?

It is time to move on to the writer who represents the religious side, namely the much-admired Pope Francis. It is interesting to study how the pope approaches science. Being the pope, he is not subject to the level of scrutiny that he ought to be subjected to. We find a level of adulation for anything he states that sounds reasonably scientific, especially if it is in tune with a progressive agenda.

We should not ignore the fact that in medieval times leading up to the Enlightenment, the most educated among Christians were often the priests and monks. The Catholic Church was not happy with ordinary people being able to read the Bible in their own language. Actually, they were so unhappy with it that the person who translated the Bible into English was burnt at the stake. With no direct knowledge of the holy texts, ordinary people had to rely on the priestly class for explanations, but at the same time that allowed monks and priests to delve into the sciences in a fairly accomplished manner. Ordinary people would never know, but they probably had good reason to believe. The priests could then easily go to the pulpit and explain to people whatever explanations happened to fit the purposes of the clergy.

There is no doubt that the pope can stand in for religious writers trying a scientific approach. He was much admired for his *Encyclical on Climate Change and Inequality*. In this encyclical, the pope states, "Although it is true that we Christians have at times incorrectly interpreted the Scriptures, nowadays we must forcefully reject the notion that our being created in God's image and given dominion over the earth justifies absolute domination over other creatures." This seems to be the religious entry point that later allows him to move into science and economics. With his words here, the pope clearly demonstrates that the scriptures are difficult to interpret by us mere humans. And, when he says that Christians have at times incorrectly interpreted the scriptures, I am sure he also understands that a future pope could reach the conclusion that Pope Francis himself was guilty of incorrectly interpreting the scriptures.

The pope, who in his encyclical endorses "technological innovations which can bring about an improvement in the quality of life", makes clear that there is a place for properly *regulated* markets – indeed, he stresses that the poor need more access to them. Pope Francis wishes for more economic equality and for the businesses of the world to pay less attention to the profit motive. The pope has found allies in, for instance, the French economist Thomas Piketty, who wishes to introduce a wealth tax that would confiscate 90% of the wealth above a few billion dollars. Another example of a concerned leader is Jamie Dimon, the head of J.P. Morgan Chase, which is the largest bank in the US. Dimon has also voiced concern over economic inequality. All of these economic pronouncements deserve investigation, and we will look into that in a separate chapter. In this chapter, we limit ourselves to looking into Pope Francis' relationship with science and scientists.

Having discussed the perils of humanity's mishandling of our environment, Pope Francis moves on to *climate as a common good* and starts becoming very scientific.

Pope Francis turns to science when he states,

> *A* very solid scientific consensus *indicates that we are presently witnessing a disturbing warming of the climatic system. In recent decades this warming has been accompanied by a constant rise in the sea level and, it would appear, by an increase of extreme weather events, even if a scientifically determinable cause cannot be assigned to each particular phenomenon.*

The pope calls on humanity to recognise the need for a change of lifestyle, production and consumption to combat this warming or at least the human causes which produce or aggravate it. We are not here analysing whether or not global warming or climate change is a result of or is aggravated by the human population on earth. We are just looking at how the pope reasons when he points to *a very solid scientific consensus*. He clearly points to science and scientific consensus for his conclusions and recommendations.

What is it the church is **not** doing? If it is the case, which it may well be, that overpopulation is one of the aggravating causes of climate change, perhaps the church should consider allowing the use of birth control. That seems to be a scientific approach. The church is already allowing for sexual pleasure without the use of birth control by trying to fit sexual intercourse into timeslots with the lowest risk of pregnancy. Is God that stupid that He cannot see that it is really the same thing? Various birth control methods allow for the enjoyment of sex for pleasure while minimising the risk of pregnancy. Having sexual intercourse according to the rhythm method, allowed by the church, is a form of natural birth control by avoiding sex when the woman is fertile. If one were to follow the teachings of the church, sexual intercourse should really only be allowed for the purpose of procreation. It is worth noting that the Catholic Church is not alone in this. Ultra-religious Jews are following the rule of not spilling their seed – at least at home. They end up having very many children, as God has told them to have, but unfortunately, God does not always provide the means to support their multitude of children. It is up to the secular working society around them, through taxation and welfare, to take on the responsibility of feeding many of these families while their men continue to study the holy texts.

Most of us know that prostitution is prohibited in Islam. But in Shia Iran, they must also feel that God is stupid. Instead of paying a prostitute, a man can approach a cleric, who, for a fee, will arrange a short-term marriage, perhaps for a day or two, with a prearranged divorce and the accompanying divorce settlement. The younger the girl, the higher the price. And if both young and virgin, it is an even higher price. To paraphrase Christopher Hitchens, religion really makes you do stupid things. The cleric who organises this would, by most decent people, be called a pimp.

Now we are aware that the pope is in favour of science and that, without hesitation, he cites scientific consensus. We, therefore, finally come to the really big question, which is whether the pope is equally inclined to cite scientific consensus in other areas closer to the heart of the church's belief system. I think we can reasonably assume that an even higher number of scientists would come to a solid scientific consensus about the fact that Jesus was not born to a virgin, that Jesus did not have God as his father, and that he definitely did not rise from the dead on the third day.

The act of getting a virgin pregnant has happened on earth very many times with only a man and a virgin woman engaged in the act. But this was an extraordinary conception as Jesus' mother Mary continued to be a virgin and obviously did not have sexual intercourse with the Lord. The belief that the Virgin Mary became pregnant via some godly intervention, with God Himself being the father of her son, Jesus, and that Jesus rose from the dead on the third day is so central to the Christian belief system that it is virtually impossible to call yourself a Christian without holding that belief.

A solid scientific consensus, regarding Jesus' not being born to a virgin and not having risen from the dead, by a huge number of scientists would have to be ignored by the pope as it would risk rendering a death blow to Christianity as such and perhaps even the church's existence. We can see that the pope is forced to cite scientific consensus only in regard to areas not central to the belief system of Christianity.

Pope Francis, who has no difficulty citing science, at the same time does not mind endorsing exorcism, which is, in short, driving evil spirits out of an individual or, better phrased, out of a poor soul who believes she is afflicted.

On Earth Day, Pope Francis said that nature would not forgive our trespasses. Perhaps God will be more forgiving. It was, after all, God Himself who set up all of creation and the entire future of His creation, knowing full well how it would turn out. Did Jesus not die on the cross for this particular sin?

Pope Francis cannot leave science alone. This time he concentrates on the limits of science. On September 4, 2020, he stated that the pandemic has taught the greatness of science but also its limits. Speaking at the forum of the European House – Ambrosetti, Pope Francis further stated, "In this tragedy that humanity as a whole continues to experience, science and technology have, of themselves, proved insufficient. What has proved decisive instead is the outpouring of generosity and courage shown by so many persons." Let us translate what the pope has couched in fine words to mean that we cannot expect everything from science. Of course, nobody expects everything from science, but we do expect a lot and have been supplied with scientific discoveries and inventions beyond our expectations. Anybody, and especially somebody my age, will recognise what an enormous contribution science has made to our lives. During my 72-year life span, medicine has improved immensely. Another area to which the pope was pointing is communication technology. When I was young, neither I nor anybody around me could even have dreamt up the enormous progress that scientists and innovators have delivered to us.

Let us turn this around and ask: can we expect everything from religion? Can we even expect anything from God?

We have a pope who prays to God to "stop the coronavirus with his hand" and an archbishop who wants the entire planet to pray in a worldwide exorcism to defeat the coronavirus. To be fair to the pope, it has been reported that in the summer of 2020, rabbis in Israel were praying at the Wailing Wall for God to stop the coronavirus. In both cases, it is probably useless to pray to God to stop a pandemic that He has already allowed to occur. Could we not agree that it would be much more useful to pray for Him to stop future disasters?

Perhaps we should conclude that, in the end, it is science that will at least do its best to solve our problems with Covid-19. It is science that, for instance, eradicated polio. Of course, science has its limits but reasonably far fewer limits than seem to be inherent in the solutions that faith and religion may bring.

CHAPTER 2

So far, God has seemed rather impotent, at least as far as the pandemic is concerned. But we must remember that God has not been more impotent at this point in time than He was when it came to other events of a similar nature. What did God do about the Spanish Flu or the Black Plague? God knew all the way back from our very creation that the Spanish Flu and the Black Plague would be coming but obviously did not care enough to just tweak His creation a little bit – which He could, of course, have done.

God could have listened and acted in response to the pope's prayer to stop the pandemic. The pope is, after all, the vicar of Christ and God's representative on earth. Did Jesus not teach us in the Sermon on the Mount that God already knows what you are going to pray for before you pray and what He is going to do as a result of your prayers? Does this not make relying on prayer less advantageous than relying on science, despite the limitations of science the pope rightfully mentions? Pope Francis must either believe or make us believe that prayer is, after all, helpful. If he did not believe that God could change His mind and tinker with His creation, any prayer for God to stop the pandemic with His hand would be meaningless.

A sinner, having committed violent crimes, may get absolution by simply confessing to one of the Catholic priests. Pope Francis has the power of Catholic priests to forgive the terrible sin of abortion. Further, a priest may not absolve a regretful sinner from a particular sin if he is going to continue the sinning. Violent acts will be forgiven if there is no risk of repetition of these acts.

So, will the church disallow absolution when a person enters the confessional to confess environmental trespasses? Jesus was sent to earth to suffer and die on the cross for our sins, past, present and future. Shouldn't the combination of God's sacrifice of his only son and a solid confession with true repentance do the trick? It may well be that earth will not forgive us our trespasses, but God might. After all, God was in a position to make a different creation that would not have led to environmental decay. He definitely knew what He was doing and, in the biblical creation story, explicitly expressed that He was pleased with whatever He had created on each of the six days that He spent creating the world.

Yet Jesus' death must be followed up with a true confession by a penitent and is only valid once the priest, having received the confession, utters the following: "God, the Father of mercies, through the death and resurrection of his Son has reconciled the world to Himself and sent the Holy Spirit among us for the forgiveness of sins; through the ministry of the church, may God give you pardon and peace, and **I absolve you** from your sins in the name of the Father, and of the Son, [sign of the cross] and of the Holy Spirit." It is imperative that the priest declares the absolving statement *I absolve you* or in Latin ***Ego te absolvo***. There is quite a bit of magic here as entire absolution becomes invalid without these three words.

There is, however, one sin for which the priest is allowed to refuse absolution and that is blasphemy against the Holy Spirit. There is hope that a person who has trespassed against our environment but is truly penitent may find peace in the church.

We can, therefore, conclude that when you approach science from the religious side, and try to fit religious beliefs and science together, that ends up a failure in the same way as when scientists try to fit science and religious beliefs together. It is difficult, if not impossible, to conclude that the pope has managed to close the chasm between science and religion.

Let us now turn to *The Encyclopedia of Bible Difficulties*, which is a very instructive book because it lets us know how to understand, as the title suggests, Bible difficulties. We should not come to the wrongful conclusion that there could be any faults in the Bible. Right at the beginning of the book, the author recommends a procedure for dealing with Bible difficulties. They include that "you must be persuaded in your mind that an adequate explanation exists, even though you have not yet found it." Another one of his instructions is that a reader should "consult the best commentaries available, especially those written by evangelical scholars who believe in the integrity of Scripture."

We are already starting to raise our eyebrows in the foreword by Kenneth S. Kantzer where he unabashedly states, "No doubt God could have given us the Bible in the perfect language of heaven, but then who of us would have understood it?

CHAPTER 2

He chose to communicate his will to us through the imperfect medium of human language with all its possibilities for misrepresentation and misunderstanding."

Stop for a moment and ponder what this means. What Kantzer is telling us is that the almighty, all-powerful, all-seeing God could not have communicated with us with complete clarity. He created us and He could have made us understand Him. Of course, He could have communicated with us with complete clarity, and He could have created and educated us to understand His message completely. That would certainly have made all our lives so much easier. God could surely have used the very clearest language possible, worded His message in such a way that we would understand every word of it and have it very easily translated into any other language. For God knew from the beginning of time all the languages that would be created for human communication.

There is a striking importance to Kantzer's statement. By communicating with us in a garbled fashion, God has created the possibility of so many different interpretations of what He wants from us, how He wants to be worshipped, and how we should conduct ourselves on this earth that even wars have come about because of this lack of clarity. Can we even begin to accept the notion that God could not have communicated with us clearly?

The book is quite a tome, with a total of 476 pages, of which 434 are devoted to the difficulties. Each page, from page 45 onwards, has two columns side by side, notably similar to how holy scripture is many times presented. Going back to the foreword, the very first words are: "Dr. Gleason Archer has written this encyclopedia to show that there is nothing in the Bible inconsistent with the claim that it is the inerrant word of God." The idea for this book is, in other words, to show that where there is something in holy scripture that might seem to us faulty, it is our reading of it that is wrong. The writing by God, or inspired by the Lord, is not at fault. The poor Lord finds no better solution, despite all His powers, than to write for us humans in our own imperfect language. God is, in effect, all-knowing and all-seeing and yet a really bad communicator.

In the preface to the book, our chosen author, Gleason L. Archer, picks up on the reason for his writing this work in the following manner: "The idea for this book first occurred to me in October 1978, in connection with the Summit conference of the International Council on Biblical Inerrancy, held in Chicago. At that time, it was apparent that the chief objection to inerrancy was that the extant copies of Scripture contain substantial errors, some of which defy even the most ingenious use of textual criticism. In my opinion this charge can be refuted and its falsity exposed by an objective study done in a consistent, evangelical perspective."

This early in his writing, Archer is already telling us that, to show that the Bible has no errors, there is a need for an objective study **but** one done in **a consistent, evangelical perspective**. He has already put an angle on the objectivity, which, to state the obvious, makes his writing lack objectivity. If you remove the angle or spin that is required to be able to find the holy texts to be without error, the errors may suddenly look different to us.

We are not going to go through the entire book. That is not necessary for our purposes. We just need to know why inerrancy is so important and how the author decides to refute apparent errors in holy scripture. The writer moves on to a recommended procedure in dealing with Bible difficulties where, among eight other points, he states, "Be fully persuaded in your mind that an adequate explanation exists, even though you have not yet found it. The aerodynamic engineer may not understand how a bumblebee can fly; yet he trusts that there must be an adequate explanation for its fine performance since, as a matter of fact, it does fly! Even so, we may have complete confidence that the divine author preserved the human author of each book of the Bible from error or mistake as he wrote down the original manuscript of the sacred text."

Again, there is a need for a filter in our reading of the holy text, so we must start with the premise that there is no inerrancy, no fault, even if there seems to be. In science, things are done the other way around. You start with the investigation, or hypothesis, and the research and/or experiment leads you to wherever it leads you. If you start investigating with a filter that leads to the outcome being certain, it is not a scientific endeavour. Judging by the book's name, *Encyclopedia of Bible Difficulties,* one could be forgiven for having

CHAPTER 2

expected, as I did, a clearer scientific approach to inerrancy in the Old and New Testament.

We now come to the question of why biblical inerrancy is so important, and the author has no hesitation in letting us know when he states, "Except for heretical groups that broke away from the church, it was always assumed that Scripture was completely authoritative and trustworthy in all that it inserts as factual, whether in matters of theology, history, or science. In the days of the Protestant Reformation, Luther affirmed, 'When the Scripture speaks, God speaks.'"

He goes on to let us know that, to all professing Christians, the authority of the Lord Jesus Christ is final and supreme. And this is a lead into the following, very clear statement by the author: "If in any of His [Jesus'] views or teachings as set forth in the New Testament He was guilty of error or mistake, He cannot be our divine Saviour and all Christianity is a delusion and a hoax."

Kantzer in his introduction goes on to tell us that without inerrancy, the scriptures cannot be infallible. He goes on to say that Jesus Himself affirms many of the miracles and concludes that there cannot, therefore, be any errors in the holy scriptures.

Let us stop here and take this in. The curious result of this writing is that he lets us know that if we do not put on the blinders and do not automatically regard any faults as just a misunderstanding, everything falls apart. Inadvertently, he helps us conclude that the scriptures are, in fact, full of errors and therefore not holy texts. Christianity cannot exist and Jesus is not our saviour if we do not accept Dr. Kantzer's preconditions for reading only with filters and blinders.

For those of us who insist on using the scientific method of study and choose not to put the conclusion before the study, his writing is easy to understand. Dr. Archer's book makes it clear that if one finds any error in Jesus' teaching, all of Christianity becomes a hoax. Dr. Archer and the writer of the foreword, Mr. Kantzer, are probably counting on your childhood indoctrination into your religion to make you prefer lingering hesitation between truth and fiction rather than leaving the faith entirely. If some people find it difficult to cast aside the preconditions for understanding scriptures, the choice is to remain in a state of doubt and in that state accept this author's filters and preconditions.

Assume for a moment that you were given a science book on gravity. In the introduction, you were given preconditions for reading the book. Already, in the first few pages, it is stated that Ms. Ceeall, who is a very holy person, has concluded that gravity does not affect humans, who can thus levitate. The fact that we seem not to be able to is because we have not understood that spirituality can conquer gravity. I think we all understand that if we accept these initial premises as directed by Ms. Ceeall, we really do not need to know the workings of gravity and can stop reading the rest of that book.

In the same way, once we have taken the blinders off regarding reading Dr. Archer's book, we are now left with several hundred pages filled with true biblical errancy which cannot be explained away.

Let us end this investigation into the compatibility between science and religion by looking into another faith, namely Islam. Followers of Islam are taught to believe that the Quran is the complete and ultimate guide for every aspect of life, including science. Muhammad was born around 570 CE and died on June 8, 632 CE. That is such a long time ago that a lot of scientific progress has been made since his time. What is required of a believing Muslim is that when, say, an observation is made in nature or discoveries are made in science, such observations and discoveries cannot be believed unless there is justification to be found in the Quran.

I think we can safely assume that it is not only Muslims who suffer this dilemma, but rather, it should be seen as a problem for many believers in other religions when there is a conflict between science and faith. But we must look at this clearly and honestly, and what we must surely conclude is that the chasm between science and faith continues to exist and cannot be simply explained away or otherwise dismissed.

Did Dr. Collins not fail in his objective of demonstrating how compatible science and faith are? Can the pope be allowed to cite scientific consensus when it suits him and disallow it when it doesn't? For instance, allowing contraception as a means to control population growth on earth might be advisable, thereby helping to minimise the sheer volume of humanity, a quantity that is being shown to add to the problem of climate change. The pope, after all, cited the scientific consensus that humanity bears some responsibility for climate change. Did the book about Bible difficulties perhaps inadvertently manage to demonstrate that *all Christianity is a delusion and a hoax?*

If the biblical stories were written today, it is very likely that they would look entirely different and would incorporate if not all, then at least some, of our scientific understanding of the natural world in our universe and on our planet. If these same old biblical stories were written today with the same content we find in the Bible, they would be found in publications such as the *National Enquirer* or together with headlines like "Aliens land in small town in the Midwest of USA and anally probe three toothless men" or "The ancient God Zeus comes to earth and impregnates a virgin; the son of God will soon be roaming earth" or even "Plot discovered: CIA out to kill all babies in small town to prevent one of them from becoming God on earth and ruling over us".

The fact that the biblical stories are a few thousand years old does not make them **more** true. Perhaps we should consider the reverse to be the case. The biblical stories were for very many years passed down the generations as part of an oral tradition. It took a long time for biblical texts to appear in the holy form we see today. A lot of errors over time could, indeed must, have entered the texts. A lot of deliberate inserts by self-interested parties could, indeed must, have entered the texts.

Let us end this with another Occam's razor question: if religion is so self-explanatory and is God's word, why is it that so many people feel the need to go to such lengths to convince us that scientific reason and religious belief are, after all, compatible?

CHAPTER 3

Why is it ... that Pope Francis' fine words about making the world a fairer place bring us no closer to closing the income and wealth gap?

In his encyclical on *Climate Change and Inequality*, Pope Francis suggests that climate change is more than just the failure of markets to internalise the true cost of carbon. It is the failure of a system in which profit is "the sole criterion to be taken into account." The pope is in favour of "technological innovations which can bring about an improvement in the quality of life". He also makes it clear that there is a place for properly regulated markets where the poor are given more access to those regulated markets.

We should start by looking at the reasons for inequality before we start to solve the problem. People who are very good-looking might end up in the modelling world and do much better than less attractive mortals. Very few make it to the top and are handsomely rewarded in financial terms. In the world of performance, very few make it to the absolute top, with even fewer having the potential to make up to hundreds of millions of dollars. Most show business wannabes barely make it. In the movie business, very few superstars get paid astronomical amounts; most hopefuls have to take several jobs while they try to gain entry to the business, and again, most of those will fail.

Many people have academic abilities, but very few of them will rise to secure the top pay packages. Some of us are born with leadership abilities and may end up like Jamie Dimon, running the USA's largest bank. There may be five or ten people to choose from when a position like running a top bank becomes available, whereas many $12-an-hour jobs could easily attract hundreds of applicants.

If this pandemic somehow made everybody over the age of 50 unable or perhaps unwilling to return to work, we would, at a stroke, find ourselves with fewer workers available for hire. The bargaining position of each worker would, as a result, increase, and very likely the greater proportion of all income created by the economy would suddenly be going to the working class, thus leaving less return on capital. It would mean a substantial shift from capital-owners to workers. In the long run, this may be how slices of the economy shift between capital and labour. It is a shift before redistribution. It is a shift based on natural distribution.

Some people are risk-takers, and very few of those will make it; most risk-takers will lose what they have. The few who do make it can in no way be said to compensate for all the enormous losses that we do not hear about. When we are informed about successful investors, we hear precisely that, which is to say we hear only the stories about the ones who have actually succeeded. The natural conclusion would seem to be that inequality is part of human life. It is impossible to create a system where everybody gets an equal share of everything created. The best we can do is to come as close as possible to giving everyone an equal opportunity to participate, even if that itself is also very difficult to accomplish.

Before we delve into the economics of the pope's inspiring words, it may be beneficial to start by looking at some statements made by Jamie Dimon. It would also be beneficial to look, at the same time, into the writings of French economist Thomas Piketty, whose solution to the thorny, perennial issue of inequality is to confiscate 90% of billionaires' wealth above €2bn. We can leave aside the graduated wealth tax that starts at 5% on those that have more than €2m. Since the Euro exchange rate is a little more than US$1.1 to the Euro, the €2bn arbitrarily chosen by Piketty as the number above which individual wealth becomes obscene is equal to a little more than US$2.2bn. (Should you be uninterested in the analysis of the arguments on greater equality put forward by our banker, Jamie Dimon, and our economist, Piketty, you should feel free to skip forward to page 53 where the pope's pronouncements on the matter are discussed.)

Let's start with Jamie Dimon, who in 2018 had a pay package of just above US$30m. He was not, by some distance, the beneficiary of the highest pay package even in the financial services sector. If he were to be compared to the really highly-paid movie stars or athletes, Mr. Dimon would look like a pauper. Just to still our curiosity, we note that for 2019 Jamie Dimon got a raise below 2% to $31.5m, and that was after his bank posted record earnings.

Some speculate that Elon Musk is the beneficiary of the highest pay package. There are reports that Mr. Musk was paid over $2bn for 2018, but those reports are denied by Tesla. Mr. Musk claims he had no remuneration for that year. Tesla is the electric car manufacturer founded and led by Elon Musk.

And, so that we are not left wondering about Mr. Musk, we can satisfy our curiosity by noting that in 2020 he reached one of the 12 benchmarks that could lead to a pay package of US$55 thousand million. If Elon Musk fails, he may come to be seen – by some – as a villain. If he succeeds greatly, he may be the hero who helped turn us from our ruinous dependence on fossil fuels and so perhaps deserves every single dollar that comes his way.

When Mr. Dimon was interviewed about the growing wealth gap between the rich and the rest of the United States, he stated, "I think it's a huge problem. I think the wealthy have been getting wealthier too much in many ways, so middle-class incomes have been kind of flat for maybe 15 years or so, and that's not particularly good in America," indicating his interest in resolving the issue. When later asked about his pay, which was somewhat above US$30m in 2019, he deflected the question by claiming the board of directors set his salary and that "I have nothing to do with it."

Mr. Dimon claims that greater growth over the last 15 years would have helped to resolve the problem of wealth inequality, and he puts forward solutions to that inequality which include changing the US minimum wage and lowering taxes for the poor and middle class. We take note of the fact that he is concerned about inequality in the US only. It is true that the wealth and income gaps in the US have increased. If we take a worldwide view, it is also true that very many of the poorest people in the world have been taken out of abject poverty. It is also a fact that there are many parts of the world with populations very much more dispossessed than the US poor.

We are disappointed, I believe, that Mr. Dimon does not want to take pride in his pay package but pretends that he has nothing to do with it. I do not think any of us truly believe what he says because we understand quite well that he is at one end of the negotiating table and at the other end are the directors. If he had nothing to do with his pay package, directors could have just offered him US$250,000 a year and he would not have taken the job. That, in turn, could have led to a less competently managed bank. I do not believe we need to begrudge Mr. Dimon his pay package. In a world where the Kardashians can rake in obscene amounts of money just by having many followers on social media, we cannot and must not believe that somebody like Mr. Dimon is not worth his pay. He is, after all, responsible for actually running the largest US bank. It would be better for Mr. Dimon's credibility if he were to own up to his pay package and claim that he gets this pay because he is worth it.

We do need to look into the quality of Mr. Dimon's suggested solutions. Do we really believe that raising the minimum wage for the very poor would make them wealthier or would it just allow them to get by somewhat better while waiting for the next paycheck? Do we really believe that lowering taxes for the poor and middle class would raise their wealth levels?

As far as the very poor in rich countries are concerned, they live on food stamps and other similar taxpayer-funded contributions, leaving them in a position to barely scrape by. They do not pay any tax in the first place, so lowering taxes would not make an iota of difference to their lives. As far as lowering taxes on the middle class is concerned, it may help them somewhat to pay off their student loans, mortgage loans, car loans, credit card loans, and mortgage payments, but very few would become notably or even noticeably wealthier. At the risk of stating the obvious, no one among the middle classes would, as a result of a lowering of taxes, reach the levels of income and wealth of Mr. Dimon himself.

While we are, of course, sympathetic to the cause of evening out income and wealth, we must ask ourselves the following: is it even possible to fix the problem of inequality by redistributing wealth from the ones who have to the ones who have not?

So, how difficult a proposition is it to use redistribution to try to fix the income inequality problem? Let's look at Jamie Dimon and all the employees at the bank that he is in charge of. If Jamie Dimon's pay package in 2018 had been distributed equally to every employee at the bank, each employee would have received around $130, which would not, in any way, have changed their lives, but the bank would almost certainly have become immediately leaderless, which could have created a far bigger problem in society. By not owning up to his salary, indeed suggesting that it had, in effect, been forced on him, Mr. Dimon loses credibility. It is, therefore, reasonable to conclude that he has also lost our trust regarding his very superficial solution to the problems of economic inequality. His proposed solution would not make much of a difference in terms of the inequality of either wealth or income, and we should presume that Mr. Dimon knows that. He is, after all, a banker. Is he perhaps just going through the motions of showing that he is concerned about inequality?

The French economist Piketty believes that billionaires are no good for the global economy. He maintains that the very rich should be stripped of most of their wealth. He wants to do that by putting a wealth tax in place that starts at 5% of wealth over €2 million and moves up to 90% of wealth above €2 billion. The obvious problem is that the very wealthy do not have that kind of cash, so it means that the various governments would have to take stakes in the corporations owned by the very wealthy and hold them for some purpose that Piketty must think would be better for growth and equality than the current system. Once the state holds what would presumably have to be majority stakes in all of the largest corporations, in whose interests should the corporations then be run? Should they be run in the best interests of the employees of that particular company? Should the corporations be run in the interests of the community/communities in which the corporations are doing business? Should the corporations perhaps be run in the interests of minimising economic inequality around the world? Which country should take the shares from the very wealthy shareholders? What about companies that are very big and multinational? There are many states that would like to have a say. And, once politicians realise that they control majority shareholdings, what would happen if they put each other on the boards and started running the companies in their own interests? Would we really prefer politicians to run our companies rather than exerting political control over them? Historically, when companies have been run by the state, supposedly in the interests of the people, the success rate in actually furthering the interests of the people has been consistently dismal.

It is unimportant and even uninteresting whether it is called a wealth tax, a gift tax, or an inheritance tax at the level of 90% of wealth above €2 billion. The result is the same, namely the summary confiscation of 90% of net assets above €2 billion.

Perhaps a little thought may be required here, that it may be better if it were, in fact, an inheritance tax, perhaps supplemented with a gift tax, so as to leave an entrepreneur alone in her lifetime to do the best she can with her company.

How practical would such a wealth tax be? To be able to impose such a confiscatory wealth tax, one would have to establish a value date and put in place a system of accepted valuation methods so that the tax, in this case openly being the confiscation of assets, could be collected.

When it comes to corporations listed on a stock exchange, this is fairly easy. The latest stock market price on valuation day would decide the amount of wealth to be taxed. What if the corporation is private? Wealth and inheritance taxes have existed historically and still exist today, so methods have had to be developed to easily calculate the wealth that is subject to taxation. In many countries, it would be the book value of the given company. The book value can be defined as the value of the assets in a company after deducting the debts and is often called net asset value. Book value could be substantially lower than what the shares would have traded at had they been listed on a stock exchange. Imagine that an inventor has just invented something that will bring in $500m a year in royalties. Her corporation is run from her flat, in which one of the rooms is her office. After the first year, the corporation would have an asset value of around $400 million, which would be the royalties after corporate tax. Had this company been listed, the market would have tried to decide for how many years the royalty was safe and therefore put a very much higher value on the same company.

Regarding real estate, assessed values are, in many instances, put in place for tax purposes, to substitute for market value. Normally, the assessed values would be somewhat lower than market value. The assessed value of the real estate minus the mortgages would be subject to wealth tax. Let us assume that the package of real estate has a fair market price of $12 billion, an assessed value of $10 billion, and a mortgage portfolio of $5 billion. That real estate package would be given a net value of $5 billion based on assessed value, or perhaps $7 billion if based on fair market price. Let us further assume that, in one instance, the mortgage portfolio is locked for 30 years at a 10% interest rate. That would not, in any way, change the value on which wealth or inheritance tax is calculated. But if we assume that the owner was much smarter and managed to lock up a 30-year mortgage at a rate of only 5%, the net income per year would, of course, be higher. If the real estate were held in a corporation, the shares of which were traded on a stock exchange, the second proposition would have a much higher value than the first.

Let's play with another idea, which is that a stock is subject to speculation and that one particular owner's holding has soared from €2 billion to €6 billion just around valuation date. In Piketty's world, her holding would be subject to 90% tax on €4 billion with shares worth €3.6 billion to be confiscated. The speculation would subside and a few months after valuation date, the shareholdings would go back to the original price before speculation and she would, without the imposition of the 90% wealth tax, have had her €2 billion

CHAPTER 3

left without being subjected to the 90% tax, since that tax only starts on net assets valued above €2 billion. This may be rather a lot to take in, but stay with me for a little while longer. The lady would have had 600 shares in this company worth €2 billion to start with. After the speculation, the 600 shares would, on valuation day for calculation of the tax, be worth €6 billion. The tax would take away shares worth €3.6 billion, which is equal to 360 shares.

When the speculation ended and the share prices fell back to the original price level, our investor would be left with 240 shares worth $800 million. Would we find this reasonable? Share prices would, of course, also be affected by the knowledge that the state would confiscate a large number of the shares in a stock exchange-listed corporation with only a few very wealthy stockholders. It would not only affect the very wealthy, but the ordinary person's pension plan, which is invested in listed stocks, could be very adversely affected.

The very wealthy will naturally not give up easily, and the mere fact that a French economist finds that a certain level of wealth is absurd and should be confiscated doesn't mean that the very wealthy will not fight it. They may want to divide up their wealth between family members before it goes up in value. They may want to take their assets and move to another country. Some may argue that we could simply refuse to deal with whatever country it may be that takes the wealthy investor in. That would, of course, be okay until she invents a pandemic cure that everybody would want to buy anyway, irrespective of her tax situation.

Hold on, we are only a few pages away from the papal pronouncements on equality.

It could also be a social media platform that everybody wants to use and for which everybody freely gives up their personal information, irrespective of the owner's tax treatment and wealth. Countries with experience of wealth taxes have found that they lead to owners of wealth being more occupied with avoiding the tax than running efficient corporations.

Would it not be interesting if we could find a country that at some point had had such draconian taxes on the wealthy? The fact is we can – and could go to Sweden, which in 1983 had an inheritance tax with a top rate of 70%. To pay the inheritance tax, the estate would have to sell the shares and also pay capital gains tax, so we do come very close to the 90% of high wealth that, according to Piketty, should be subject to confiscation.

The Swedish experience was that very many wealthy Swedes, including the owner of IKEA, left the country and took their wealth with them. The lesson here is a simple one.

The value of an asset is only what a buyer is willing to pay for it. And as a case in point, let us investigate what happened in Sweden in 1984. A widow by the name of Sally Kistner, whose deceased husband was one of the founders of the pharmaceutical company Astra, now known as AstraZeneca, will serve as a good example of perhaps unintended consequences of high confiscatory taxes.

When Mrs. Kistner died, she held a substantial fortune in Astra shares. The valuation date was the date of her death. The market instantly understood that a substantial number of Astra shares needed to be sold by her estate in order to pay the inheritance tax, which led to a substantial fall in the share price. The state wanted 249 million SEK to be paid in inheritance tax on an inheritance which, after the fall of the stock price, was only worth 230 million SEK. Her estate was bankrupted. Whether or not we find what happened to Mrs. Kistner's estate fair, we may need to be concerned about the unintended consequences of the draconian confiscation of wealth over €2 billion that Piketty is proposing. An experiment like that should not, we must surely hope, end up making the world economy poorer for everybody.

Let's look at the problem of inequality from a worldwide perspective. The example is intended to be extreme in the hope that it will help clarify the point of income redistribution. Let us consider what would happen if, under the United Nations, all countries in the world created a WRA (a World Redistribution Agency). According to Forbes magazine, in 2018 there were 2208 billionaires in the world. The total net worth of these billionaires, including the first billion, was around US$ 9.1 trillion. Let's put the number of people on this planet at

CHAPTER 3

around 8 billion. If it were possible to take every penny from all that have at least $1 billion and distribute that confiscated wealth evenly to every living body on this planet, each one of us would theoretically receive a bit over US$1100. But, as we have seen from the case of Sally Kistner, as soon as the markets know that so much wealth has to be liquidated, prices fall precipitously, and each one of us may get no more than a few hundred dollars.

For the absolutely poorest in the world, say in a village in India or perhaps in rural Africa, this would be an enormous amount of money and be spent quickly on items such as food, water, clothing, and perhaps accommodation. The purchasing pressure in these poorest areas might then create inflation.

For most of us in the rich world, it would make little or no difference except that pensions for ordinary workers would be in danger. We will, we must presume, never find out if such an experiment would damage the world economy in ways from which it would take a long time to recover. We understand how difficult it is in practice to solve the problem of world inequality. But we must remember that, to those really poor people living in an Indian or African village, the poorest of those living in the rich world look very well-off.

In Sweden, it was decided by a unanimous parliament, from right to left, to abolish the inheritance and gift tax and eventually, the wealth tax. Many of the wealthy returned to Sweden, among them the founder of IKEA, who died in Sweden. Even Piketty's home country, France, decided to abolish its wealth tax for the very good reason that the tax led to people of wealth making economic decisions more relevant to avoiding the tax than to growing the economy.

As opposed to Messrs. Dimon and Piketty, the pope may perhaps be granted a little leeway for his fine words. He is speaking from a spiritual corner and not as an economist. What does it mean that markets should be properly regulated? Who should regulate them and in whose interest? What does it mean when we consciously, deliberately step away from the profit motive, and how far away can and should we venture? There are organisations that are not for profit and they are – generally – called charities. They are sometimes called churches and religious institutions. Would we really want a world where charities run all corporations without a profit motive? I think we all instinctively understand that we would prefer to work for a very profitable company than for one that is consistently, even wilfully, money-losing. The long-term prospects of employment and rising wages are much better in a profitable company.

There is no CEO of a modern multinational corporation who does not also have to be a politician and understand corporate responsibility and survival for the long term. That does not take away from the fact that the profit motive is a reasonable guiding light for making investments and running a business. It is reasonable to conclude that companies can only make a profit for the long term after they have complied with laws and regulations.

The further problem is that when it comes to exploitation of the poorest countries, it is well-known that the church does its best "business" among the poor, ignorant and downtrodden. What does it mean when the pope says that helping the poor involves reaching outside of markets and thinking beyond the profit motive? We understand now, don't we, that running businesses for even partly non-profit reasons may perhaps lead to lowering the value of investments in the ordinary person's pension fund.

What one *can* reproach Pope Francis for is the matter of the credibility of the Catholic Church and the papacy when the pope puts forward the economic equality motive in a way that would tamper with markets and the profit motive. There is, for instance, the Vatican bank, which has been involved in money-laundering scandals. We can be fairly certain that the Vatican bank does not lend money to losing causes. Like every bank, it should lend money with the expectation of getting its loan repaid (with interest) so that other depositors to the bank will not lose their money. In other words, the Vatican bank is guided by the profit motive… and for good reason.

One can only wonder how the church has created its wealth over almost 2000 years if not by exploiting the superstitious, the ignorant and especially the poor. If we go back to the year 1517, Pope Leo X sold indulgences with the aim of gathering funds to rebuild St. Peter's Basilica in Rome. He was also a big spender, and we can be certain that some of the funds gathered by the papacy from selling the forgiveness of sins yet to be committed went for that same pope's personal spending.

Now, Pope Francis worries that if we make fossil fuel more expensive to discourage its use, the poor will be much worse off. That papal statement seems correct, and the solution will probably come from technology. As soon as other power sources become competitively priced, these sources will be used instead of fossil fuels. Our scientists are on their way to making the use of fossil fuel more expensive than more environmentally-friendly alternatives. The upcoming success in making greener power sources cheaper than fossil fuel is better for everyone, including the poor. Forcing the use of more expensive power sources instead of cheaper fossil fuels makes everybody worse off, including the poor. The solution seems entirely technological.

Without any reasonable explanation, Pope Francis moves on to claim that helping the poor would involve reaching outside of markets and thinking beyond the profit motive. This the pope says while Cuba, one of the few remaining communist countries, is moving most of its economy into the capitalist system based on the profit motive. Let us believe and assume that the pope is well-intentioned, but let us at the same time also understand that his pronouncements do not properly take into account the insight that if you tamper with economics in one respect, then something unintended may pop up in other respects. The pope could be seen as essentially ignoring the inevitable consequences of the very actions he proposes.

In democratic societies, there is political oversight over the big corporations. When corporate malfeasance is discovered, the courts may decide upon the imposition of substantial settlements against corporations found guilty of sullying the environment. Even in third world countries, substantial penalties may be imposed on corporations engaged in environmental misconduct. It is reasonable to assume that the managers leading these big corporations would like to ensure that the corporations survive in the long term and therefore that they must take into account the cost of misbehaviour which could ultimately wipe their business out of existence. The profit motive may still be paramount, but it is hampered by both political and legal oversight. We may conclude that companies can only make a profit, at least be profitable for the long term, after they have complied with laws and regulations. The question as to whether they comply with rules or regulations because of the profit motive or not lies in the realm somewhere between uninteresting and irrelevant. Comply with laws they must.

Many will find themselves tempted to agree with the pope regarding tinkering with the profit motive, but these same people will surely not be deterred from trying their best to increase the compensation they themselves receive from their employer. In other words, they don't mind, when their own bargaining power is low, forming trade unions to better their bargaining position to secure fairer conditions and higher pay, and most, if not all, of us may well sympathise with that. As much as one can see the value of – and perhaps the need for – a strong, fair trade union movement, one would assume that, deep down, employees would understand that an employer without a fundamental profit motive is probably not going to be a very good long-term employer. So, does Pope Francis, with his fine pronouncements, mean to say that companies should be run in the same way as charities, without any desire for profit?

The starting point for any wealth creation is that one has an income high enough to be able to save and invest. That is, of course, unless you are one of those very few movie stars who make many millions of dollars per year. That is, of course, unless you happen to invent something that many people want to use. That is, of course, unless you are a member of the Kardashian family, with wealth created by an incredible following on social media, which in turn has allowed them to make insane amounts of money. Becoming wealthy could be the result of somebody else's efforts and not your own doing. That could be the case when you inherit wealth from somebody who has herself succeeded in creating it. One could also become wealthy from, say, winning a large lottery jackpot. The ones who pay for this are all the ones who do not win but still continue to play.

Some may well feel that they would prefer to live in a more equal society, or even a more equal world, and that would be fine with them even if it meant – slightly or perhaps dramatically – lowering their own standard of living. One would have to decide whether this style of equality is in any way practical or realisable as, for example, employees in highly profitable corporations would initially get more than others and that would create a new level of inequality and requirements for further redistribution, and so on and so on.

The pope is very likely right when he moves on to claim that a great deal of environmental wreckage has been wrought by multinational corporations operating in developing nations in ways that would not be acceptable in the developed world. It would not be far-fetched to assume that these developing nations are exactly where the church is doing its "best business".

We should also not allow ourselves to forget that in the early stages of our modern economic development, at the time of the Industrial Revolution, what is now the rich world was also very dirty and very poor. We have to try to interpret the pope's words to see what would be required. Nobody is arguing that capitalism is free of fault. But what we can argue is that it has proven better than communism and similar state-controlled alternatives. Even China, which bills itself as a communist system, has some of the world's most freewheeling capitalism under party control and very likely with a substantial amount of political corruption. It is, to state the obvious, certainly not political corruption with which we would like to replace the profit motive. I do not think we should draw the conclusion that the pope is in favour of communism, but he does want to replace capitalism with something or at least replace the profit motive as the guide for corporate governance. If you disallow the profit motive, you may well, as we have discussed, end up with charities in which very few people would invest money but to which many wealthy people today already give money.

One could, somewhat unscientifically, claim that capitalism is based on the theory that everybody wants to do well for himself and, in so doing, drag others with him up the income and wealth ladder. That is what we have seen in the rich world, and what we are also seeing, in the midst of this capitalist drive, is great progress in eradicating starvation and poverty in developing countries. It is a fact that our capitalism, with all its faults, has reduced starvation and extreme poverty on a worldwide scale. Of course, the pope is right that there is a huge discrepancy in both income and wealth, and the question is whether or not we can do anything about that without creating unintended and damaging consequences. One of the unintended consequences of the Covid-19 pandemic is that we have seen inequality rise again on a worldwide scale. We can only hope – and try to identify policies to ensure – that the economic lot of the worst-off will continue in an upward trend once the pandemic has been defeated.

There may be many who feel that it is counterintuitive that the capitalist system that has created so much inequality has also brought so many people out of poverty. If you'd like to delve deeper into this in a more scientific fashion, I recommend the work of Prof. Hans Rosling. Prof. Rosling, who died in 2017, was a medical doctor and professor of international health. He knew how to work with statistics and developed his own methods to make complicated statistics easily understandable. There are two YouTube postings featuring Prof. Rosling that I recommend for viewing. One is "200 years that changed the world" at https://youtu.be/BPt8ElTQMIg, and the other, on why the world is better off than you think, is found at https://youtu.be/1vr6Q77lUHE. Those who want to delve even deeper should read the book *Factfulness: Ten Reasons We're Wrong About the World – And Why Things Are Better Than You Think*.

We should be hesitant about allowing religious institutions to run businesses, but we know from history that, for a while, the Catholic Church successfully ran bordellos. Yes, whore houses, where men could go and relieve their urges and then step into a neighbouring church, and even the Vatican, to ask a priest for forgiveness. In terms of pure profit motive, it is a notably good idea to be able to charge twice, the sinner first paying for the sin of fornication and then paying the priest for absolution.

Economic development is not an easy thing to accomplish. When I studied international economics at the University of Lund in Sweden, we had a professor who did some work for developing nations, and he taught us that if you wish to help a developing country, give them old technology that will employ many people. That will have the best overall effect on the economy as more people will have a steady income. A poor country has an abundance of available labour but is short on capital. Giving them the most modern equipment, for instance a plant that instead of requiring a thousand people would have one engineer simply pressing a button and overseeing the industrial process on his computers, would obviously not provide an income for many people. We should not indulge in the mistaken belief that we should compare – from the outset, at least – the income level of a very poor country with what we achieve in the rich world. The same people who claim to be unhappy with how poor the poor in the developing world really are may, at the same time, be against the outsourcing of, for instance, call centres to that part of the world. An outsourced call centre will bring at least some jobs and a certain amount of income to a few people in a developing country. Is redistribution meant to be only within our family or within our own countries? It is very difficult to get people to be rational about the issue of redistribution because, when it comes down to it, nobody really wants to give up what they have and individuals always seem to strive for more for themselves.

So, we must accept that choices that are not so good have to be made, especially in the really poor areas of the world. If you are hungry and thirsty, you may not care about using the earth in a potentially destructive manner since your immediate priority is to get hold of water and food, no matter the cost to the environment. Environmental awareness seems to be a thing for the affluent part of the world, and there is a marked trend that sees an increase in the standard of living being followed by an increase in measures to save or safeguard the environment.

The church would also have more credibility had it not made saints of people who have taken contributions from shady characters. We do not have to look further than the saintly, and now actual saint, Mother Teresa. Her friend Charles Keating was a swindler and one of the instrumental figures in the 1980 Savings and Loan crisis, a crisis that ended up costing American taxpayers at that time around $125 billion. Her charities received a contribution from him of about $1 million, which is the equivalent today of a little over $2 million. He also gave her access to a private jet during her US visit.

Mother Theresa was asked by a prosecutor to return these funds to the taxpayers since they could reasonably be seen as ill-gotten gains. She did not return the funds but, instead, intervened on behalf of Mr. Keating, pleading for a lighter sentence. She was known to be friendly with the brutally dictatorial ruling family of Haiti, in particular, Baby Doc Duvalier, who eventually had to flee and take up residence in France.

Historically, some US families established their fortunes in the slave trade, for which there is no excuse. It goes without saying that other countries around the world also participated in the profoundly immoral but biblically sanctioned slave trade. Eventually, in the US, fortunes were made or consolidated in banking, railroads, oil extraction and car manufacture.

We should now ask why some have become so incredibly wealthy in recent times. The answer is that nowadays most of the wealth is created because we, the ordinary people, make some innovators and corporate-owners wealthy, perhaps even obscenely wealthy.

The newest class of the very wealthy are people who have blazed trails in the world of social media, such as Twitter and Facebook (which now owns Instagram), as well as other tech giants like Apple, Google and Microsoft. To my knowledge, the pope and many in the hierarchy of the church are users of social media. If we were all to stop using social media, the wealth of the founders and shareholders of these companies would crumble. And the knock-on effect could be lower pensions for members of the working class since the pension funds are invested in those companies. The pope and the hierarchy of the church are especially big users of social media during periods of chaos such as the Covid-19 pandemic. Pope Francis' encyclical contains a lot of beautiful language and lofty goals. The problem is how, for instance, to put environmental protection into practice. Pope Francis would also have been more credible had he shown us that the wealth of the Catholic Church is being used to give the world's really poor access to local wells and drinking water.

CHAPTER 3

It is very hard to find anybody who believes she should have less compensation while most people still strive for more. I have found that when this is being discussed, it seems that it is always the people above a certain income or wealth level – which is higher than the income or level of wealth of the person one is engaging with – who should be subjected to higher redistribution charges.

Much of the wealth is created by the fact that so many of us are using the products or services created by the innovator. The best way to create, at a stroke, a more level playing field would be for we ourselves to immediately stop using, say, social media and stop buying products from companies such as Amazon if we believe that they are too powerful. It is, I hasten to add, not something that I would recommend. Like its millions of fellow users, I find deliveries from Amazon very useful and time-saving. But if we did stop using Amazon, there would be no reason to ask the government to cut them down to size. Of course, if we stopped using the services and products of these magnificent companies, we would ourselves also lose out. We use them because they are useful to us. But if we stopped using them, their shareholders would become much less wealthy and so there would be no need for worldwide cooperation to prevent the wealthy from seeking refuge, along with their money, in another state. The economy as a whole would suffer.

A case well worth studying is Walmart. In simple terms, the business idea of Walmart is to create a very large customer base for which the company has to buy large quantities of product, which, in turn, gives it substantial negotiating power to secure lower prices from suppliers. In a way, Walmart has done what unions do with employees, namely representing the many for bargaining power, but in Walmart's case, it has done this for commercial reasons and with a profit motive.

Walmart needs low costs for delivery throughout the entire chain from supplier to customer, including, it can be safely assumed, low costs for wages, in order to serve the great mass of its needy customers. Walmart is frequently criticised, perhaps for good reason, for not paying North American workers "livable wages". However, Walmart has made its founders very wealthy by providing reasonably priced products (clothes, hardware, even groceries) to its mainly poor and working-class customers. Furthermore, Walmart is one of the few remaining grocery providers that accept SNAP (Supplemental Nutrition Assistant Program) stamps in the United States. Walmart also employs approximately 2.2 million people worldwide. One could say that Walmart makes a profit by fulfilling the need of a substantial customer base for low prices. Walmart also takes a commercial risk. Purchasing a couple of seasons of products that find no favour among the customer base could wipe out all profits. The profits are also necessary in order to survive a downturn. Would the pope like to cut part or all of Walmart's profits? Do we perhaps believe that charities would do as good a job in delivering low prices to their customer base even without making a profit? We are not saying that Walmart is without fault. It has most certainly made mistakes, but isn't Walmart an example of where the many use products and services from a company that is obviously run with a profit motive but still manages to do good for the people who are in need of its way of doing business?

A reasonable guess is that it would be very difficult to replace Walmart and that they are very astute in their business model and manage to actually deliver what its customer base wants. Would we want to deprive Walmart's customer base of the ability to purchase reasonably-priced products because Walmart is also a business being run with the profit motive? It may well be reasonable to believe that the efficiently-run Walmart, in spite of making a profit, is able to deliver better-priced products than a non-profit organisation trying to do a similar job. In 2019, Walmart had 275 million customer visits per week, giving the company a profit of a little under $1 per customer visit.

In terms of social media, while the pope and the rest of us are complaining about the wealth that has been created by the owners and innovators, it is exactly these media that allow us to subject ourselves to **physical distancing** while **remaining socially close**. If you do not want the Kardashians to get any wealthier, just stop following them on social media. And once you have stopped following, all you have to do is hope that the government will follow up on Piketty's recommendation and confiscate some, or much, or perhaps all of the wealth created for them by you and subsequently redistribute it back to you.

We may take comfort in the fact that, in the really long run, one way or another, wealth gets circulated back into society. Neither Crassus from ancient Roman times nor the Borgias nor the Medicis control the world today, and we probably do not even know who their descendants are. In more recent times, the Rothschilds no longer represent anything but a smaller bank and have lost the financial clout they had when they not too long ago were formidable lenders to governments.

The people who come up with great inventions or create platforms that everybody uses and which make our lives easier perhaps deserve what they get. And they get no more than we award them simply by using their products. The scientists, some in large pharmaceutical corporations, have already found vaccines and may in time find a cure for the Covid-19 virus, and for this they may be greatly rewarded and for good reason. The winners will also be the people who hold stock directly in those companies and the pension funds of the ordinary working woman or man which may also hold shares in the corporations winning that particular race. Being the owner of stocks in a winning company could make up for all the losses from investments in corporations that failed to move with the times.

It is not only the income you show on a tax return or the wealth you declare that makes you stand out. Let's have a look at the opulent lifestyles of most of the cardinals and bishops and even some priests. It would take an awful lot of personal wealth for any person to be able to pay for an equivalent lifestyle. The Catholic Church and the pope would have so much more credibility if they started by giving away most of their assets and perhaps let their cardinals, bishops, and priests live in poverty. Some monks and many nuns have taken their vow of poverty seriously, but they are very much a minority.

In a three-minute YouTube clip, comedian Sarah Silverman plays with the idea that the pope should sell the Vatican and solve world hunger. The video clip is titled, "Sell the Vatican, Feed the World". It is a lighthearted and entertaining video which I would recommend watching. You can find it at https://www.youtube.com/watch?v=3bObItmxAGc.

Churches and other religious institutions are not subject to tax in most jurisdictions. Perhaps a good start would be to subject the various dioceses in the world to taxation. That would also go a long way towards the credibility the pope would urgently need before he considered asking for others to have their income and wealth redistributed. It is not only the Catholic Church that is sitting on substantial wealth, and what goes for the Catholic Church should go for other religious institutions as well. All of them might as well be transformed into ordinary taxpaying institutions. And, in their newfound status as ordinary taxpayers, they would be contributing to the redistribution of income and wealth they so dearly desire.

Regarding the economics of this, Pope Francis conveniently forgets that the New Testament is clearly not against poverty in this life. We would have good reason to believe that many of the wealthy at the time of Jesus would have been happy with the fact that they could stay wealthy in their lifetime, but remember that Jesus is (very often) quoted as having said in the New Testament, "It is easier for a camel to go through the eye of a needle than for a rich man to enter the kingdom of God." The rich would be punished for being rich by not having access to heaven. Again, we must remember since God has foreseen everything, he knew that there would be rich and there would be poor. I take it that many of the rich were and are now better educated and therefore not easily persuaded to give away their wealth so as to be able to enter heaven.

Pope Francis himself complains about the huge disparity that exists when it comes to income and wealth. We therefore must conclude that the rich take, as they have repeatedly taken throughout the time since Jesus, the *eye of the needle* threat with a grain of salt and have resolutely continued to hang on to their wealth while they are still alive. Pope Francis also conveniently forgets that slavery, which in some ways is the ultimate form of economic disparity, was quite okay both in the Old and the New Testament. Not only was it okay but, in the New Testament, slaves were encouraged to return to their masters, even if their master was mistreating them. The slaves would, they were reassured, receive their rewards in the next life. The pope also opportunely forgets that when Jesus tells people to get rid of their wealth, it is in order to follow him and forget about tomorrow. If you truly believe that following Jesus after giving up your possessions is the right thing to do, you should understand that there will be no growth, no income, and no pension.

In terms of corporate malfeasance, perhaps the pope should embrace corporate exorcism to prevent the large corporations from doing harm in the developing world. For those who believe that this is too far-fetched, even for the church, consider this: an Italian archbishop has called for the entire planet to pray together in a worldwide exorcism to defeat the coronavirus.

The pandemic has hit the Roman Catholic Church with cash-flow problems in much the same way that businesses have suffered the effects of the pandemic-induced economic contraction. These businesses are looking for taxpayer-funded handouts to allow them to survive. In the US, quite a few dioceses of the Roman Catholic Church have had to pay very large amounts in settlement as a result of sexual abuse by the clergy. Some dioceses have even sought bankruptcy protection.

When financial trouble hits the church, the pope and the clergy do not resolve it by praying to God for more funding, funding which, not incidentally, God could very easily have arranged. No, there is no asking God for more funding. There is a very worldly approach to securing more funding, namely by lobbying the US government to get an exemption from federal rules. The lobbying has been successful, with the various dioceses receiving payments of more than US$1.4 billion from the US taxpayer. This is money that could have gone to the least well-off but instead went to the hierarchy of the Catholic Church in the US. For those who want more information, it is available in an article by the Associated Press, published 2020.07.10 – AP: *Catholic Church lobbied for taxpayer funds, got $ 1.4 B.*

Many economists warn that the more improvements we make to artificial intelligence, the more ordinary work (and workers) will be made redundant. If that is the case, there will be fewer and fewer very well-educated people who will have a larger and larger share of the economic cake. Whether or not we believe that artificial intelligence will take over most of our jobs, we should at least acknowledge that it is complicated to level the playing field and when that is attempted, there might be unintended consequences, consequences that, frankly, we may not want to live with.

Inequality is, admittedly, a great problem. We may need to conclude that we have no adequate answer for how to deal with it. We must confront our feelings about financial inequality and answer a number of vital and difficult questions. Do we first want to redistribute within our own family? Do we first want to redistribute within our community or our country? Do we perhaps want to redistribute throughout the entire world since we who live in the rich part of the world are incredibly well-off compared to the poorest parts of the world? Do we mind very great inequality as long as our own standard of living increases? Is it so important to us to find solutions to creating a more level playing field in terms of income and wealth that we can live with an outcome that could mean a (perhaps substantially) lower standard of living for ourselves?

An Occam's razor question could be: if we are created unequal in terms of our abilities, how far can we reasonably go in creating a level economic playing field? We may even question why God distributed our abilities so unevenly. The God we read about in the Old and New Testament does not seem to be concerned with economic unfairness. Alms for the poor will normally do it. Freeing male slaves after six years of service is a step in the right direction. God could easily have fixed all those vexed issues that the pope finds the need to complain about. Jesus died for all our sins, even the ones yet to come. Do we not see that the pope finds himself engaged in an uphill battle, with very little help from the Lord?

CHAPTER 4

Why is it ... that we are afraid of being descendants of monkeys but don't mind being descendants of incest?

Let us start our discussion with a brief introduction to the way science currently explains how we came to be.

There is ample literature on the science of evolution, and I'm going to assume that everybody knows what DNA is. I must reiterate that this is not a scientific narrative. Anybody who wants to delve deeper into our current understanding of evolution can find plenty of reading, from the popular to the very scientific.

All life on earth evolved from a single cell. Many scientists believe that the single-cell organism was similar to a bacterium. The process of creating all life on earth from single-cell organisms has taken about 3.5 billion years. During that time, the single-cell organisms evolved into multi-cell organisms and, over time, into more complex life forms.

On earth, life began in the oceans. Somewhere around 2.5 billion years ago, some very simple life forms ventured onto the land. On land, these evolved into the myriad complex forms of life that exist today. 3.5 billion years is a very, very long time, and although it may be hard to fathom, that enormous time period gave ample opportunity for life to evolve, according to the environment on earth, from a single-cell life form to modern humans. In the womb, from conception until we are born, we are surrounded by a water-like substance called amniotic fluid. One could, perhaps somewhat unscientifically, surmise that in a short nine months from the time the sperm fuses with the egg, we have a shortened version of the journey of very early beings emerging from water and starting life on land.

I believe, and perhaps even insist, that it is important to remember that it is not that the environment on earth was created for us so that it could sustain life. It is much easier to accept that the environment on earth was what it was and that life forms developed into that given environment.

Over that enormous span of time, more and more complex life developed. It is interesting to consider that around 99% of all species that have ever existed on earth are now extinct.

So, let us move on to the monkey. It is not that science says that we have monkeys as ancestors. It is rather that many strands of complex life developed and that somewhere between two and six million years ago, one species that had evolved was the great ape. The humans that exist today are survivors from that great ape ancestor while other human species, such as the Neanderthal, are now extinct. Nevertheless, we do carry some genetic material even from the Neanderthals. The scientific conclusion is that humans and chimpanzees have evolved along different branches of a shared family tree from a common ancestor.

The question we now have to ask ourselves is: why should we believe this complex story?

Until we learned to sequence DNA, we relied mainly on the fossil record. Religionists complain that the fossil record is not complete and that there remain a few gaps. They raise the objection that there are gaps in the fossil record while, without hesitation, disregarding the fact that there are plenty of gaps in the biblical story of creation as well.

We are, once again, at that place where belief and science come into direct conflict. Science is here to be explained and re-explained. Science looks at the evidence at any given point and comes to the best conclusions until, perhaps, some new scientific evidence comes around to change our minds. Science is open to new explanations, something that we should remember and compare – and contrast – to religious beliefs. In religious terms, God created the universe, our planet, and us, and gave us holy books with explanations as to how all that came about. These explanations are harder to understand and, for some of us, frankly impossible to believe. Most importantly, the explanations of God's creation are not open to any revision based on new knowledge.

As opposed to religion, science is open to be proven wrong and will easily accept a different scientific idea or explanation if the evidence points in that new direction. Science further necessitates corroboration. A scientist cannot simply make a bold claim and allow it to go unchecked.

It seems to be accepted science that around 1% of the human genome could come from plants. We also share between 40% and 50% of our DNA with the banana. This does not mean that bananas and humans have the same DNA sequence but rather that some of our genes can be identified as having their equivalent in the banana. The chimpanzee, who comes from a common ancestor way back, shares around 99% of our DNA. We can even trace that we humans last shared an ancestor with the pig around 80 million years ago. If we were to compare ourselves to a fellow human, we would share 99.9% of our DNA, which, of course, makes us very similar to one another. Ricardo Sabatini, a physicist, has found a way to show us just how close we are to the next human. He has demonstrated that a printed version of a human's entire genetic code would be around 262,000 pages, equivalent to 175 large books. Only 500 pages (roughly 0.2%) of all this printed material would be unique to an individual.

With DNA sequencing now available, scientists have been able to follow our development from way back in time, and it seems a fairly reasonable explanation that we have evolved naturally with the most adaptable staying in the gene pool. Evolution is also a product of mutations and to a certain extent random events. Not only does the fossil record show the aforementioned, but our DNA sequence, traced backwards, also allows us to see at which points in our (very!) ancient history we separated from other strands of upright mammals, evolving from a common ancestor to become who we are today. This is where science leads us, and the conclusions are drawn from evidence, to repeat myself, from both the fossil record and from our tracing of DNA backwards.

You might now want to ask yourself: why don't monkeys start talking? There is no absolute answer to this except that even monkeys have developed and continue to develop to become better and better monkeys. The weakest monkeys get taken out of the system, and the gene pool creates successive generations of offspring that come from the strongest, and perhaps the smartest, or most cunning, among them. Thus, "better monkeys" is just a way of saying the most likely to survive and thrive.

In fact, that goes for all living creatures. The predators who survive are the best at hunting prey, resulting in their genes surviving. Among the prey, only the ones that get away are able to procreate. The hunt between predator and prey goes on not only in real time but also as a generational struggle of genetic survival.

Animals – obviously – communicate with each other. We call it instinct when a flock of predators together hunt down their prey. Our beloved dolphins have a dark side. We may not want to give them the kind of consciousness we as humans possess so it is difficult to call it "rape", but, for the sake of our argument, let's. What happens is that gangs of male dolphins isolate a female dolphin. They keep her locked in and slap her around and use her for forced sex, over several weeks, where the males take their turn. It seems to be very difficult to accomplish unless there is some form of communication between the dolphins and at least some form of understanding between the male dolphins that their individual turn will come and that the other male dolphins will continue to keep the female boxed in.

To go back to the monkeys, who knows whether, in a couple of million years, they will also be talking, if their survival mandates that they develop a need for speech?

We do not look like monkeys. We are definitely not that hairy, we walk differently, and we are able to communicate through talking. We do have one thing in common with our cousins, the monkeys, which indicates that we once had a tail. Over the long period during which we evolved from a common ancestor, we evolved to no longer need a tail for stability. Funnily enough, we have a remnant in the form of a tailbone that no longer protrudes outside our body. It is, perhaps, amazing and surely fascinating to find that we once even shared a tail with the monkeys that we are afraid to be descended from.

Here we are with evidence from the fossil record and DNA which allows us to go back not just generations but billions of years. It is still a bit hard to grasp, and so it is reasonable to ask: why can we not see this happening? We would find it easier to believe if we could watch it happening. Then, we would not have to simply believe what scientists have come up with in terms of evolution over billions of years, even if it is the best evidence available. So, can we see evolution with our own eyes?

I have said that this will not be a scientific work, but I will lazily answer the question by pointing to a chapter in Richard Dawkins' book, *The Greatest Show on Earth*, and specifically to chapter five in that book, *Before Our Very Eyes*. For those of you who wish to know more, and to have a substantial scientific explanation of what we can see before our own eyes, please read Dawkins' book.

A quick summary is sufficient for our purposes here. Dawkins writes that the vast majority of evolutionary changes took place before any human being was born. But he also states that some examples are so fast that we can see evolution happening with our own eyes during a human lifetime.

The starting point is the elephant. Elephants are being hunted for their tusks, that is, for ivory, and therefore the ones with the largest tusks are being killed. Larger tusks are an advantage when it comes to competition with other elephants, but that has to be balanced against the fact that larger tusks might get an elephant killed by ivory hunters. As the elephants with smaller tusks survive, their genes will pass on smaller tusks to future generations.

Although we might expect an evolutionary trend towards smaller tusks to take thousands of years to be detectable, it is possible to observe this within one human lifetime.

Dawkins shows data from the Uganda Game Department published in 1962 which refers exclusively to elephants legally shot by licensed hunters. The time frame studied is between 1925 and 1958. One can already see a trend, even over that short period of time. There is "a statistically significant trend toward shrinking tusks…". Dawkins points out that this is not in itself definitive proof of an evolutionary trend. But there is *"good reason to suspect the existence of strong selection against large tusks".* Chapter five in Dawkins' book has other examples, from lizards to bacteria, and on to a species of fish namely the guppy.

Regarding guppies, Dawkins relies on John Endler's work. Endler himself is an expert and the author of *Natural Selection in the Wild,* which is the leading book with examples of studies of natural selection unfolding in front of our very eyes.

The main thing male guppies have in common with the male pheasant is brighter colouring than the females. Humans have bred them to become even brighter to be nicer to look at in aquaria. The fundamental reason for the brighter colouring is to have a greater chance of being sexually selected by the females. When Endler studied guppies in various streams, he found that some were strikingly colourful while others were well camouflaged to fit in with the bottom of streams in which they lived.

Why is it so? When it came to attracting females, the male guppies would be selected for their bright colours; however, if predators were around, they would be easier prey.

In front of our eyes, and over a few years, it could be seen, studied and documented that when the guppies lived in streams without predators, the sexual selection was such that the most successful males were the colourful ones, therefore producing colourful offspring. Conversely, it could be seen that when guppies lived in streams with predators, the survivors were the least colourful and best camouflaged ones. This led to future generations of guppies with DNA that rendered them camouflaged.

That chapter – and of course the whole book – by Dawkins is worth reading, and I highly recommend it. For our purposes, we must now reasonably conclude that there is scientific evidence for natural selection. If, over a few years, we can see the guppies adjust to the surrounding circumstances, and over less than a human lifetime we can see the elephants undergo natural selection, it becomes more reasonable to draw the conclusion that so much more could have occurred over the last several billion years.

We humans are breeding cows to become better and better milk producers. We are breeding hens to become the best egg layers. We continue to breed dogs for fashion or for specific tasks. Humans have, over the last 15,000 to 40,000 years, bred the wolf into the remarkable variety of dogs we see today. We do this by picking partners for their genes to create the characteristics we wish to see prevail in the future generations of the species that we are manipulating. If humanity has been able to manipulate animals through the selection of traits over a fairly short period of time, why is it so difficult to believe that over billions of years this could have occurred randomly and naturally? There is no leap of faith required to believe in evolution. You just have to follow the evidence.

Now let's turn to creation as described in the Judaeo-Christian Bible. The Bible is, according to many believers, a piece of writing without errors. If one thing is wrong in the Bible, the whole set of biblical stories effectively collapses like a house of cards. Others believe that the Bible is inspired by God and that that explanation allows for some errors, although we may argue that God could, in the interest of clarity, have inspired better, more scrupulous and more accurate followers and interpreters of His will.

If you are prepared to read the biblical stories as stories, you could quite easily come to the conclusion that, on many occasions, not the least in regard to the creation stories, the Bible was subject to really bad editing. If you were dealing with any text other than a holy book that told you that the authors knew the names of the very first people on earth, you would be very hesitant to believe this. Scientology, for example, claims that Xemu, who was the dictator of the Galactic Confederacy 75 million years ago, brought billions of his people to earth. It is very easy for most of us to dismiss as absurd the notion that these believers know the name of that dictator, and it is therefore similarly easy to disregard the rest of the story – and indeed the entire religion – when the foundation is so self-evidently fragile and flimsy.

The first thing we need to make clear is that there are two inconsistent creation stories. In the first creation story, God created the world in six days and rested on the seventh, the Sabbath. In the first story, Adam and Eve were created at the same time, but in the second, Adam arrived first and Eve only later when Adam had to give up a rib for her. In the first creation story, animals are created before man, and in the second, God starts by creating man, places him in the Garden of Eden, which already exists, and then parades animals in front of him for naming. One could easily get the impression that the animals were created after man in this second creation story.

In the first creation story, God created everything out of nothing, but in the second, man is created out of dust. There is also no mention in the second creation story that God found it appropriate to rest on day seven. For now, it is sufficient to take stock of the fact that the description of creation consists of two somewhat different and inconsistent stories. That should not happen in a holy book, but it does.

We move forward, again, to the creation of Adam, which occurred on day six, the last day that the all-powerful, all-seeing and all-knowing God worked on his creation, according to the first of the two creation stories. God was spent and had to rest on day seven, something that seems to be a curious need for somebody all-powerful, but let's not dwell on that. Adam needed a companion, and he had to exchange one of his ribs for Eve to enter the picture, at least according to the second creation story.

Remember, once Eve was created, there were only two humans on this earth. Adam and Eve. They then had two sons and one of the sons, Cain, murdered his brother Abel. Making up for the loss, another son is born to the couple in the Garden of Eden and he is named Seth. Do we really believe that these names are accurate and that these people existed?

It is also stated that Adam and Eve had other sons and daughters. People who believe in the creation story have difficulty believing that we have a common ancestor in the great ape and that we have developed differently from our ape cousins. They do, however, believe that we know the names of the first people on earth because it is written in the book claimed by some to be inspired by God and by others to be the word of God without fault.

Those who deny evolution are happy to accept these two incomplete and inconsistent creation stories found in a holy book. Furthermore, without hesitation, the people who are happy believing that God created the world as per the biblical stories have no quarrel with incest. God had created Adam and given him a woman named Eve, and Adam and Eve had their sons and daughters. *How did they procreate?* It is unavoidable and self-evident that the only way they could have done so would be by incest. Any of the sons would have to have had sexual intercourse with his mother and/or sisters. And father Adam could have had sexual intercourse with his daughters.

We do know that it is genetically not a very good idea to create offspring with such close family members. Eventually, and for very good reason, incest became forbidden in the Bible. The excuse one often hears is that incest was not forbidden at the time of creation. That, of course, begs the question: did God not know better? Could he not have created a few different families instead of setting such a bad precedent?

We are left asking ourselves: which is the more plausible answer to how we came about on this earth? Did we come to be on this earth the way our scientists explain it, which is by evolving gradually over millions of years? Or did God create us on day six according to the first of the two creation stories in the Bible?

Some may find it difficult to grasp the scientific explanations for evolution, but at least these explanations are based on the best evidence we have and may be subject to tweaking, or even radical revision, in the future as new evidence perhaps comes forward. The biblical story leaves no room for revision. It is written in stone for all time and almost certainly by people who lacked any real understanding of the natural sciences.

The creation story requires a lot of faith and trust without evidence, or perhaps even in spite of the evidence and in spite of all inconsistencies already in the creation stories. I just want to add one little tidbit here: after Cain had killed his brother and was sent out of the Garden of Eden, he asked God for a token to protect him from being killed by somebody outside the Garden of Eden. This begs the question: who were the ones outside the Garden of Eden who might have killed Cain? According to the creation story, there was literally nobody but Adam's family and their incestuous offspring. This just scratches the surface, and the Bible is littered with such inconsistencies and impossibilities.

In terms of the faith-based explanations of our development into humans, I find myself needing to borrow from Dan Barker. He started his career as an evangelical Christian preacher until he "saw the light" and became an atheist in 1984. On YouTube, https://youtu.be/btJazTimH4M, "Dan Barker: God does NOT exist", you can find him speaking to the Oxford Union where he eloquently makes the argument that belief is not knowledge, belief is not evidence, and that any time you have to accept an assertion by faith, you are admitting that the assertion cannot be accepted on its own merits. Mr. Barker has written several books, including *Godless: How an Evangelical Preacher Became One of America's Leading Atheists*.

Science, in conclusion, follows the evidence wherever it may lead and is prepared for new evidence to prove current science wrong. Faith requires that you believe in something without evidence, and even in spite of the evidence pointing to the contrary. To take the leap of faith and disregard all scientific evidence for evolution is something all major religions want to make you proud of. Whenever you are prepared to suspend disbelief and take the leap of faith, you will be made to feel that you are worthy of admiration for being a believer. You may want to consider in whose interest the major religions want you to be proud of faith even against evidence. With an Occam's razor view, could it be in your own best interest to believe despite the evidence? Is it perhaps that making you believe in something, and making you proud of believing despite the evidence, gives religious institutions better control over your life? You also have to ask yourself how far you are prepared to go with your belief. If you had a child who was very ill, would you be happy with a faith healer or the blessing of a holy person, or would you revert to science and use a well-educated and knowledgeable medical doctor?

CHAPTER 5

Why is it ... that so much violence in recent times has come from followers of Islam while followers of Christianity have decreased their levels of violence?

Let us start by looking into what those who are Muslims are educated to believe.

Muslims generally believe that Muhammad is the last and final prophet and a perfect man. God used the Archangel Gabriel over quite a long span of time – 23 years, from December 609, when Muhammad had turned 40, until the year 632, when Muhammad died – to verbally dictate the various verses of the Quran to Muhammad.

Many believe, because of a passage in the Quran, that Muhammad was unable to read or write and that, therefore, dictating all the verses in the Quran to Muhammad for him to commit them to memory is itself a great miracle in its own right. Tradition has it that several of Muhammad's companions either wrote down or also memorised the verses of the Quran, having been introduced to them by Muhammad himself. After Muhammad had died, the companions put together the texts in what is now known as the Quran, and a Caliph named Uthman is given credit for having arranged the Quran in what is just about its current form.

The sequence of the process from God to the Archangel Gabriel to Muhammad and on to Muhammad's companions is important as it is believed by Muslims that the Quran is not just inspired by God but is the actual and literal word of God.

The Muslim faith has received a lot of criticism for the fact that Muhammad is seen as a perfect man and the Quran as a perfect book. Many critics take aim at the belief that a perfect man may even exist or that a perfect book may even exist.

Christianity is not that different as Christians are encouraged or perhaps compelled to conclude that Jesus, being the son of God and the Son of Man, must have the same quality of being perfect. We do not have to go as far as to the son of God for the purposes of comparison. In Catholicism, the pope is infallible. Can a person deemed to be without fault not be perfect? Furthermore, both Jews and Christians believe that their very many sectarian interpretations of the holy scriptures come, directly or indirectly, from God Himself. When it comes to the matter of messengers of divine revelation, or the perfect nature of holy scripture, there is not that much difference between the peoples of the various religions and the underlying sects of those religions claiming Abraham as their ancestor.

One can, of course, easily take issue with the fact that Muhammad, over 23 years, had to memorise all the verses in the Quran. Before we find this impossible, we should understand that there are people, even today, who are known to memorise the entire Quran. Even non-Arabic speaking Muslims have memorised the Quran as it is written, in Arabic.

If one does not belong to the Muslim faith, one might be tempted to wonder why God needed such a complicated path from Him to the archangel, from the archangel to Muhammad, from Muhammad to his companions, and from his companions to the perfect book. Allah could have just delivered it as a book written by his command. Allah could have done so but did not.

In every one of the Abrahamic religions, there is a convoluted way of getting the message across to the followers. One must be allowed to question whether that is because God was not involved at all and clever prophets made up stories to fit their own purposes in the name of God, perhaps even inventing God as they went along.

CHAPTER 5

Some Muslim scholars take issue with the notion that Muhammad was unable to read or write. The Quran, it is believed, is the only miracle of the prophet Muhammad. In Muslim tradition, the fact that he was illiterate made it even more miraculous. It also became an explanation for why Muhammad would not have read either the Jewish or Christian holy books and that all came to him fresh through the Archangel Gabriel.

Those of us who are not educated in Islam from childhood could easily argue that if Muhammad had such a great memory that over 23 years he could memorise, without any apparent problem, the 6,236 verses, he could also easily have memorised stories told from other holy books.

There are some writings in the Quran that direct Muhammad to *read* (from which the word *Quran* originates), indicating at least some knowledge of reading. In a particular verse within the Quran, people who rejected God as the originator of the holy texts in the Quran accused him of fabricating the stories. According to the Quranic text, they stated, "Tales from the past that he wrote down; they were dictated to him day and night." At least some early nonbelievers had the idea that Muhammad could write down the passages dictated to him, and ultimately, the question as to whether he could read or write is not entirely conclusive either way. Perhaps Muhammad could read or write just a little. Perhaps he was illiterate and a man with a preternaturally good memory. But anybody who is not educated in – and has not been indoctrinated from childhood into – Islamic beliefs must be forgiven if she were to question whether Muhammad just made it all up and even whether it was fabricated in Muhammad's self-interest.

Let us take just one example, which starts around the year 625 when Muhammad proposed to a cousin of his by the name of Zaynab that she marry his adopted son Zayd. She accepted and married Zayd.

There are various accounts as to the circumstances leading up to Muhammad's wanting the wife of his adopted son for himself, but the fact is he did want to marry Zaynab. His adopted son offered her to him, but he could not accept her because, in pre-Islamic Arabia, marrying the wife of one's adopted son was considered to be an incestuous relationship, even after the adopted son had divorced her.

All big problems must find a solution, and Muhammad, of course, did have a revelation leading to the illegality of adoption in Islam. This revelation nullified all previous adoptions. The revelation also meant that Muhammad could get his desired Zaynab to be his wife. After the revelation, it was no longer incestuous.

Those of us who are not raised in the Muslim faith could easily see this as self-serving. Nobody knew what the archangel had actually said to Muhammad. Nobody knows whether the archangel said anything to Muhammad. Those who are raised in the Muslim faith may still want to believe that Muhammad was a perfect man and that the Quran is a perfect book and therefore everything in it is the absolute truth.

What the true Muslim cannot do is say that perhaps this revelation about adoptions is a one-off revelation invented by Muhammad to solve a personal problem. If anybody who is a true believer were to acknowledge that the Holy Prophet had a convenient revelation, Muhammad would no longer be a perfect man and the Quran no longer a perfect book.

Those of us who are familiar with the Old and New Testament are used to having some form of chronological order of events found in the holy books. The Quran is divided into chapters, or *Surahs*, and verses, or *Ayahs*. The Quran is not a text that follows the chronology of events. The Quran does not even follow specific themes. The Quran is generally arranged with the longest chapters in the beginning and progresses to ever-shorter verses with the very shortest coming towards the end.

There are a total of 114 chapters in the Quran, of which 86 are connected to Mecca and 28 to Medina following the events in the life of Muhammad. We take note here that the chapters of the Quran the archangel delivered to Muhammad follow the prophet's life events and experiences, which may leave the revelations open to some criticism that it was actually invented by Muhammad around his own life experiences.

CHAPTER 5

It is also believed that the Archangel Gabriel visited Muhammad to have a final review of the Quran and let him know the order in which the various chapters and verses should go. It would, of course, have been less mysterious and more easily understandable had the chapters and verses followed either a timeline or specific themes. Here, as in the other Abrahamic religions, we again find how God has a need to be mysterious rather than precise and understandable.

In the Quran, one finds quite a number of the biblical stories used in somewhat different contexts. Let us take the example of the biblical story of Abraham's aborted sacrifice of his son, Isaac, by his wife Sarah. Until old age, Sarah could not have children of her own and urged her husband to visit her maid Hagar so that Abraham could have a child. Hagar got pregnant and had a son, Ishmael, for Abraham.

In the biblical story, Sarah remains childless until she is 90 years old, at which point God promises that Sarah will be a mother of nations and that she will bear Abraham a son. In his very convoluted way, God has to wait until Sarah is 90 before he promises that she will get pregnant and bear Abraham another son. When Isaac is born, he has an older half-brother, Ishmael. Sarah is anxious about her son's rights and makes Abraham send Hagar into the desert with her son with only a minimal supply of food and water. Another cruel biblical story that God could surely have handled so much better.

In the Islamic version, Sarah asks Abraham to marry her handmaiden, Hagar, since she herself has been unable to supply her husband with a child. Soon, Hagar's son, Ishmael, is born and he is obviously Abraham's firstborn son. In the Islamic version, God instructs Abraham to take Hagar and Ishmael to the desert and leave them there. Amazing how mysterious God's ways are.

As Abraham leaves her and the baby in the desert, Hagar asks if it is God who commanded Abraham to leave them there, and Abraham stops, looks back and answers yes. Hagar seems to be happy with that response and replies that God will provide for her and the baby.

Abraham journeys back to his first wife, Sarah.

While alone with his mother in the desert, Ishmael cries from thirst. Hagar tries frantically to find water in the desert, but she does not succeed. She returns to her baby and starts crying for God's help.

It is the Archangel Gabriel who comes to her and tells her to lift Ishmael from the ground; as she does so, she observes that the baby's feet have scratched the ground, allowing a spring of water to bubble up to the surface. It may be difficult for anybody not raised in the Muslim faith to believe in the absolute truthfulness of this story. In the Quran, we find the biblical story about Abraham and his sons but somehow turned on its head, making Ishmael the lead in the story instead of Isaac.

In Islamic teaching, Abraham visits his son several times and once finds only Ishmael's wife at home. Abraham decides to leave before his son comes home but leaves Ishmael's wife with a message to give her husband. The message is *change the threshold*. When Ishmael returns home, his wife tells him about his father's visit and the message. Ishmael understands the message and tells his wife that he has been instructed by his father to divorce her and find a better wife. Ishmael, wanting to be obedient to his father, follows his instructions. The next time Abraham visits, Ishmael is again not at home. Abraham speaks with Ishmael's new wife and this time leaves the message *keep this threshold*. We all now understand what that means, and so does Ishmael. Do we really know this to be true? How do we know that this happened? Who recorded this for future reference? Yes, we have to remind ourselves that this knowledge has come to us from the Archangel Gabriel via the prophet Muhammad.

It is not far-fetched to ask why this Quranic story shouldn't have more credibility than the earlier biblical story. If you are raised in the Christian or Jewish faith, you would tend to believe the biblical story. If you are raised in the Islamic faith, you would give more credence to the newer story in the Quran. If you are raised in none of the Abrahamic religions, it would be easy for you to conclude that perhaps neither story is describing a true event. Both versions could have been invented by man, conceivably to make a point.

CHAPTER 5

In many places in the Quran, one finds biblical stories, sometimes retold and sometimes turned around, with the people in the biblical story finding their way into the story in the Quran but with an entirely new twist, as with the story of Abraham above. The borrowing from Judaism and Christianity has led to accusations of Islam making use of stories from other religions and either repeating them or twisting them around for convenient use in the Quran.

Not only does the Quran reuse biblical stories, but it also makes true Muslims of many of the prophets in the Old Testament, and of course of Jesus in the New Testament. This is despite the revelation having come much later to Muhammad and despite the fact that Islam did not exist until after Muhammad had received the revelation.

It is part of Muslim belief that God had, in the olden days, revealed Himself to Jewish and Christian prophets before the Quran was revealed to Muhammad by the Archangel Gabriel. It is fascinating, isn't it, that Allah, via the archangel, went out of his way to "edit" both the Old and New Testaments. And, according to Islam, this latest edit was to produce the true and perfect Quran. Yet, as we notice, there are many interpretations of that perfect text, all of which makes us wonder: *can any perfect book be seen and be shown to lack clarity and yet still be considered perfect?*

Jesus is viewed as a prophet, and so are Abraham and Moses. Abraham is actually viewed as the first Muslim, although, if he did exist, he probably did not know that he would be considered the first Muslim or that he would one day be seen as the great-great-great-grandfather in Judaism and Christianity as well. Nevertheless, Abraham is revered as the first true Muslim, despite Muhammad's receiving the dictation of the Quran more than a thousand years after his time. The way this is handled in the Muslim faith is to explain that, over the years, both Judaism and Christianity had become corrupted. That same criticism is obviously, according to Muslims, not relevant to Islam. In terms of knowing the name of Abraham, we could challenge ourselves to see which of us would remember the name of our great-grandparents and then the generation before them.

The one piece of good news about the Quran's relationship with Jewish and Christian scriptures is that it gives Jews and Christians a special status as People of the Book. That relationship is, however, tenuous. It is not an entirely meaningless status because it gives these People of the Book the right to at least live in Muslim-controlled areas as opposed to people who are neither Jewish nor Christian, such as Baha'i. Jews and Christians are allowed to live in Muslim-controlled areas in a subordinated position as long as they pay the *Jizya*, a special tax levied on non-Muslim residents in such Muslim-controlled areas. Non-Jews and non-Christians have, in principle, no right to life at all. The People of the Book (and, later, those other than Christians and Jews) should pay the *Jizya* in humiliating conditions. There must be a price to pay for not believing in Muhammad and Allah.

In the Quran, we find the following text: "Fight those who believe not in God and in the Last Day, and who do not forbid what God and His Messenger have forbidden, and who follow not the Religion of Truth among those who were given the Book, till they pay the Jizyah with a willing hand, being humbled."

Is it perhaps that Islam recognises that when Muslims are the minority in a non-Muslim area, they would accept the fact that they are in an inferior position? The answer would seem to be no. Their answer is that some Muslims feel that they have more rights than others based on the fact that Muhammad is the last of the prophets that God has sent to mankind and, therefore, those who practise Islam are in possession of the absolute truth. The Quran is supposedly a book containing all truths. If one makes an observation in nature and cannot find support for that observation in the Quran, the observation must be wrong.

If one has been educated into such a strong belief in the absoluteness of the Quran, one could understandably acquire some arrogance based on the ingrained confidence of being the bearer of absolute truth.

We can go back to Thomas Jefferson and his war against the Barbary Pirates from Arabic North Africa. In March 1785, Jefferson and John Adams met Tripoli's ambassador to London. The ambassador was asked what right the

Barbary states had to attack American shipping and make slaves of both crews and passengers.

The answer from the ambassador was simply that "it was written in the Quran, that all nations who should not have acknowledged their authority were sinners, that it was their right and duty to make war upon whoever they could find and to make slaves of all they could take as prisoners, and that every Musulman who should be slain in battle was sure to go to Paradise."

Not only in recent times has the text in the Quran led to interpretations that allow for violence against non-Muslims on almost any pretext. Even between various Muslim sects, one finds ample animosity where both conflicting sides find justification in the way they read the same holy texts.

At the time of the importation of slaves to America, about 1.5 million Europeans were enslaved in Muslim North Africa. The enslavement of people, whether captured and purchased from Africa or as a result of the Muslim defeat of enemies, is of course equally unforgivable.

Eventually, there was a war between the US Navy and the Barbary Pirates which the Americans won. Is this perhaps because Allah had a somewhat different opinion from that of the ambassador from Tripoli? If the ambassador's interpretation of the Quran was that Muslims had a duty to make slaves of all they could take as prisoners, it is very odd that Allah allowed the Americans to win the war. However, the reward, according to the ambassador, was that every Muslim who was slain in battle could be certain of ending up in Paradise. Having defeated the Pirates, the Americans could freely use the waters for shipping and trade.

We have seen that the Quran often – and freely – borrowed from the Old Testament, and we also know that God in the Old Testament prescribes even genocide to make room for His favourite people on the land He promised to them Himself. The instructions are to kill all the inhabitants of the lands in question, and the tribes and peoples inhabiting those lands are identified in the Bible. The good fortune is that those ancient people no longer exist and there is, therefore, no reason to commit genocide based on God's direction in the Old Testament.

In Islam, however, it is prescribed that conversion to Islam may well – or perhaps even *should* – occur by force. The prophet of Islam said, "I was ordered to fight the people until they believe in Allah and his messenger." One should, therefore, not be fooled by a passage in the Quran that states that there is no compulsion in religion and interpret that to mean no one should be forced to become or remain a Muslim. It is believed that Islam is so plain and clear, and its proofs and evidence are so plain and clear, that people will naturally want to join. The problem occurs when someone is foolish enough not to see the light and either doesn't join Islam or wants to leave the faith.

If you decide to leave the Muslim faith, you are subject to the death penalty. After Muslim forces have had victory in battle, the defeated may be given the chance to convert to Islam or be killed. This is not too different from how Christians may have acted during the Crusades or the forced conversions of Jews during the Inquisition. It is also not too far from how, in South America, the conquerors forced the indigenous people into Christianity. It is also not too far from Christian missionaries who, from time to time, were engaged in a *food-for-Jesus* exchange as a means to convert the poor and hungry indigenous people in places where the missionaries held court.

The question we need to ask ourselves is the following: if a religion has to impose the threat of a death penalty as a disincentive for a person considering leaving that religion, or if people have to be forcefully converted, does that not mean that the religion isn't in itself attractive or convincing enough?

It is not that Christians cannot be violent. We have some modern examples of fundamentalist Christian believers who are adamantly opposed to abortion because it is the taking of a life and taking of a life is forbidden. Some of the same people, however, seem not to object so much when it comes to the killing of the doctors who perform the abortions.

And it is not as if there are no Jews who use violence in defence of their beliefs. Orthodox Jews are known to throw stones at cars passing their areas on the Sabbath, and at women who do not wear sufficiently modest clothing. The difference may lie in the severity and the scale of atrocities committed in the name of Islam as compared to other Abrahamic religions.

At this point, it may be advantageous to recall some of the more substantial acts of terrorism committed by people claiming support in Islamic teaching. There are many sources for the incidents listed below, but the main source is Wikipedia.

In 2001, there were the unforgettable September 11 attacks by Al-Qaeda. The attacks involved the hijacking and crashing of jet airliners into occupied buildings. Almost 3000 people were killed and over 6000 were injured.

In December 2001, a Pakistani-based Islamist terrorist organisation wanted to create chaos in India and wipe out the top leadership by organising a suicide attack on the Indian Parliament.

The following year, in October 2002, a tourist area in Bali was bombed, leading to just over 200 people dead and more than 200 injured.

In March 2004, the bombing of a Madrid train caused over 190 deaths and over 2000 injuries.

In September of the same year, hostages were taken in Beslan in Russia, leading to over 380 deaths and over 780 injuries.

On July 7, 2005, four suicide bombers mounted an attack on the London Underground and a double-decker bus during the morning rush hour, leading to over 50 deaths and more than 750 injuries.

That same year, bombings occurred in Sharm El-Sheikh, Indonesia and Amman, leading to over 200 deaths and more than 400 injured.

In 2006 in India, seven bombs exploded on a Mumbai railway, killing over 200 and injuring more than 700.

In the year 2010, there were several incidents, starting on March 29 with the Moscow Metro bombings. On May 28 came an attack on a mosque in Lahore, Pakistan. On July 1, another Lahore bombing. Finally, two more incidents in Pakistan on October 6 and December 25. The total number of deaths that year exceeded 175 and the number of injured exceeded 550.

If we skip over to 2013, we find, on April 15, the Boston Marathon bombings committed by two brothers near the finish line of that event. This led to three deaths and over 180 injuries.

Another substantial incident occurred on September 1, 2013, when a shopping mall in Nairobi was attacked, leading to over 65 deaths and 175 injured.

2014 was a horrific year, starting with a massacre in Nigeria on February 14 leading to over 200 deaths. In August, ISIL massacred 700 people in Syria. In November, another bombing in Nigeria killed 120 people and injured over 250. December 2014 had so many incidents that we need only pick a few well-known examples, such as on the 18th, when Boko Haram militants killed 32 men and kidnapped more than 180 women and children. That month also saw ISIL members kill 150 women in Iraq, women who refused to marry their conquerors. Some of the women were pregnant at the time.

2015 was another year marked by many appalling incidents, just one example being the January 8 Boko Haram attack on a town in Nigeria, which left 200 dead and a further 2000 injured.

2016 saw incidents all over the world, from Afghanistan to Somalia, from France and Turkey to the USA. On March 22, suicide bombers attacked the airport and the Metro in Brussels, leading to 35 deaths and more than 300 injured. Another incident was the mass shooting at Pulse nightclub in Orlando by a shooter who had pledged allegiance to ISIL. He managed to kill 49 and injure more than 50.

There was no lack of occurrences in 2017, in Egypt, Afghanistan, Pakistan, Iraq, Russia, the United Kingdom, Spain, Finland, and the USA. Perhaps the most widely covered of these was the March 20 attack in London, when a man drove a car into pedestrians on Westminster Bridge, leading to six deaths and 49 injuries. On April 7, a similar attack occurred in Stockholm when an asylum-seeker hijacked a beer truck and drove straight into a crowded high street. He managed to kill five and injure 15. The perpetrator's stated motive was to force Sweden to end its support for the fight against ISIL.

On May 22, the UK experienced the Manchester Arena bombing, which occurred at the end of Ariana Grande's concert with around 20,000 in attendance. This incident led to 22 deaths and more than 125 injured.

2018 was no different, starting with the Baghdad bombings on January 15, with 38 deaths and more than 100 injured. On January 27, the Kabul ambulance bombing resulted in more than 100 deaths and 235 injured.

Now, skipping grimly over many more occurrences, we move on to Morocco where, on December 17, two Scandinavian tourists, a Danish woman and a Norwegian woman, were killed, with the murderers filming their actions and calling the two women "enemies of God". Here, we see the same arrogance as displayed by the Libyan ambassador when he negotiated with the Americans on behalf of the Barberry Pirates. The murderers claimed that their actions were God's will. The ambassador from Tripoli claimed that if you are Muslim, the Quran allows you to do whatever you wish with infidels.

Let us pick just one day from 2019 – Easter Sunday, April 21. In Sri Lanka, three luxury hotels in the capital, Colombo, were bombed, and later the same day, explosions were heard at a housing complex and a guest house. Other cities were also targeted, and over 250 people were killed and more than 500 injured.

We would be remiss if we were not to mention the neo-Nazis marching and claiming to understand the only truth, but most of them do not invoke religion. They seem to hate others and respect only themselves. They would prefer the countries where they live to be white and free of Jews. Their "only truth" is that white non-Jewish people are a superior race and everyone else does not belong.

For those who believe that the Jews are engaged in some form of conspiracy in order to rule the rest of us, it must be disturbing that the non-Jews have been able to inflict so much damage on the Jews. If the Jews really ran the world, would they have allowed the continuation of a situation in which so many have been forced to live in secluded areas or ghettos for hundreds of years? Would they have allowed themselves to be excluded from certain trades and professions? Would they have allowed the conditions to continue whereby they were either forcefully converted or expelled from countries where they lived, for example, during the Inquisition under Queen Isabella? Why would they have allowed the Holocaust to take out six million of them? The Jews, even in North America, were forced to start their own law firms and banking firms since, at the time, they were not allowed into those controlled by non-Jews.

There seems to be very little in terms of the scale of violence directed towards others that can compare with what is perpetrated by followers of the Muslim faith. It is often claimed that Islam is a religion of peace, but, to paraphrase Sam Harris, if you follow Islam, you may very well end up with Al-Qaeda or ISIS. If we again borrow from Sam Harris, it would appear that Islam is the motherlode of bad ideas.

Not all fundamentalist Christian evangelicals who oppose abortions kill the doctors. Not all orthodox Jews throw stones at cars driving through their areas on the Sabbath or at women not dressed modestly enough. And, of course, not all Muslims are terrorists.

Muslims make up around 20% of the population on earth. There are different estimates, but of the approximately 1.8 billion Muslims, perhaps somewhere between 100,000 and a few hundred thousand could be viewed as militant extremists and fundamentalist Muslims. These extremists are prepared to find in the teachings of Islam either justification – or cover – for terrorist acts. It is impossible to ignore the sheer scale of violent acts committed by Muslims compared to non-Muslims. It should be impossible to ignore that so many terrorists find cover in their religious teachings. And just to clarify what *fundamentalist* means in all the various religions, it means to go back to the texts of the holy books and live by the word.

Support for terrorism in the Muslim world has been declining. However, several polls estimate that about 20% of the population of Muslim countries tacitly supports terrorism in the form of suicide bombings. That would bring the understanding of suicide bombings to a level very much higher than, for instance, the possible understanding of Christian fundamentalist killers of doctors who perform abortions among the broader constituency of their fellow believers.

CHAPTER 5

When evidence of a Muslim terrorist act emerges, instead of facing the truth, people often indulge in all kinds of conspiracy theories intended to cast blame on a combination of the Jews, Israel and Americans inflicting self-harm. To deal with an issue, one must be prepared to face the facts. This is a useful saying: *You are entitled to your own opinion but not to your own facts.*

A poll in 2007 found that one in four Muslims believed that the UK government had staged the bombings on the London Underground and then framed the convicted Muslims.

It is appropriate, also, to bring up a horrific domestic terrorist attack with no Muslim connection. Let us go back to Norway on July 22, 2011. A young man by the name of Anders Behring Breivik, a lone wolf, exploded a car bomb in the capital of Norway, Oslo. He placed a bomb inside a van and parked the van next to the office block housing the prime minister's office. That explosion killed eight people and injured more than 200.

Breivik followed this up by heading to the island of Utøya. The island is owned by a group connected with the Norwegian Labour Party, which was holding its annual summer camp there. Breivik, using a fake uniform mimicking that of a police officer, made his way to where 650 young people were enjoying themselves. He started shooting at individuals and continued until the police arrived about an hour after the first alarm call. He immediately surrendered, having killed a total of 77 people, 69 on the island and 33 of them under the age of 18.

Breivik was a terrorist deeply engaged in anti-immigrant issues and could probably be described as a neo-Nazi. In fact, while in prison, he identified himself as both a fascist and a neo-Nazi, even invoking the ancient Nordic god Odin. Although he had suffered abuse, mostly from his mother, and social services had failed to remove him from her, he was declared sane by the courts and given the maximum punishment. In peaceful Norway, this terrorist act was a profound shock. There were, at this time, among ordinary and peaceful Norwegians, conspiracy theories putting the blame on the government of Norway for having framed Mr. Breivik.

The truth is that conspiracy theories arise in the midst of any crisis and in the aftermath of almost every significant act of terrorism or political violence. The truth is also that many acts of shocking violence are being perpetrated around the world in modern times (and have been, throughout history), but there seems to be a markedly disproportionate number of these acts being perpetrated in the name of Islam.

To delve deeper into our understanding of Islam, we are going to listen to the voices of two women, Ayaan Hirsi Ali and Wafa Sultan, both of whom were raised in the Muslim faith but have chosen to no longer practise the faith of their childhood indoctrination. These two women are so well-known in their own right that they need no introduction. They are both accomplished authors and brilliant debaters. I recommend any of their writings, but a good starting point would be *Infidel* by Ayaan Hirsi Ali and *A God Who Hates* by Wafa Sultan.

Ms. Ali was born in Somalia. She was a Dutch politician and is now an American activist. She actively opposes child marriage and female genital mutilation. She is also actively against forced marriage and honour killings. In her view, "Islam is part religion and part political military doctrine, the part that is a political doctrine contains a worldview, a system of laws and the moral code that is totally incompatible with our constitution, our laws and our way of life." Ms. Ali further views Islam as a new breed of fascism and states, "just like Nazism started with Hitler's vision, the Islamic vision is a caliphate – a society ruled by sharia law – in which women who have sex before marriage are stoned to death, homosexuals are beaten, and apostates like me are killed. Sharia law is as inimical to liberal democracy as Nazism." She argues that violence is an inherent part of Islam and that it is a destructive, nihilistic cult of death.

This may all be true, but we must not forget that Christianity itself was, in its earlier days, quite violent, as during the Crusades and when women who were labelled witches were burnt at the stake.

Ms. Sultan was born in Syria as an Alawite Muslim. The Alawis have a strong connection to the Shia Muslim belief system which is mainly practised in Iran. Ms. Sultan tells us that she was shocked by the 1979 atrocities that were

CHAPTER 5

committed against innocent Syrians by Islamic extremists belonging to the Muslim Brotherhood. While she was a medical student, she witnessed the assassination of her professor, a world-renowned eye doctor. They sprayed him with bullets while shouting in Arabic, "God is great!" It was at that point, says Ms. Sultan, that she lost her trust in the Muslim God and began to question Islam.

She very bravely participated in an Al Jazeera debate on the "Clash of Civilisations", referring to the conflict between Western liberal belief systems and their equivalents in Muslim societies and among Muslim believers. She presented herself as a secular woman who could not hold the beliefs and condone the violence prescribed in Islam. This was a very brave thing to do as it immediately made her an apostate and thus subject to the death penalty.

I highly recommend that you have a look at the clip at https://www.youtube.com/watch?v=ISNpOkpcWqg, "Al-Jazeera Wafa Sultan Discussion on Muslim Belief and Clash of Civilizations, which has had more than a million views. In it, she says, among other things, that in Islam one is ordered to fight people until they believe in Allah and his messenger. She also states that the Muslims divided the people into Muslims and non-Muslims and called the former to fight the latter until they shared their beliefs – in other words, they started this clash and began this war. She urges a re-examination of the Islamic books and teachings, which are full of calls to fight the infidels. The naming of people is something else she brings up; people are given names that they have not chosen for themselves, sometimes being called "People of the Book" and at other times "apes and pigs".

When it comes to the infidels, she claims that they are not just the "People of the Book" but are **people of many books,** such as all the rather useful scientific books that we have today. Her bravery is shown when she claims to be neither Christian, Muslim, nor Jew; she claims to be just a secular human being who does not believe in the supernatural, in response to which the cleric in the clip accuses her of blasphemy and asks if she is a heretic.

When she talks about the Jews, she states that they come from the tragedy of the Holocaust and that they have "forced" the world to respect them with their knowledge, not through the use of terror; with their work, not as a result of their crying and yelling.

Ms. Sultan, now a medical doctor and psychiatrist residing in the United States, further claims that humanity owes most of the discoveries in science of the 19th and 20th centuries to Jewish scientists. She says, in that clip, that we have not seen a single Jew blow himself up in a German restaurant. And while Muslims have turned three statues of the Buddha into rubble, we have not seen a single Buddhist burn down a mosque.

Can it really be true that the hatred of Jews is still so powerful? Interestingly, we find an answer in Iran where a leading cleric has made it clear that if a cure for the Coronavirus were to be found in Israel, it would be okay to use it. This may sound positive, but what it means, in effect, is that, under normal circumstances, if an invention or a cure has been made by someone in Israel, it is not appropriate to use it.

It is difficult to argue with two women who have been brought up in Islam and have been subject to childhood indoctrination. They have worked their way out of their childhood beliefs to become rational thinkers who have embraced science.

Is the answer, then, that Islam is currently more violent than the other two branches of the Abrahamic religions, namely Christianity and Judaism? Judaism does not want any converts and actively makes it very difficult for a gentile to become Jewish. In the history of Christianity, mistreatment of non-Christians was quite common, and so was forced conversion. In Islam, hatred towards nonbelievers or infidels is still rampant if we go by what we have learned, aside from all the horrific terror incidents expressly committed in the name of Islam.

We should not allow ourselves to believe that we don't find a great deal of prescribed violence in Judaism and Christianity, particularly in the Old Testament.

Perhaps it is simply a fact that Islam is a newer religion and is found in states where rulers and the priestly classes work together on the indoctrination of their citizens? If you are indoctrinated in your childhood years, you may believe as true what comes out of that childhood indoctrination. If you are indoctrinated to believe that wearing a burqa is the right thing to do, you may do so in the belief that you are doing it voluntarily. If you indoctrinated from childhood in any belief, you may carry that with you even when you move to a place where you would find yourself in the minority.

Let us move on to the women who wear burqas and the men in their society. Supposedly, women wear burqas because it is their free will to do so in accordance with Islamic tradition and law. They feel they want to express that free will by wearing a burqa while they reside in Western Liberal societies. Would they be equally happy with Western women visiting Muslim-majority countries not wearing head or face coverings as an expression of their free will? I leave the answer for each one of us to ponder. For a non-believer, watching a woman walking around in a burqa on a hot summer's day, with her husband walking in shorts and drinking a cold Coca-Cola may seem the equivalent of offensive speech.

Why do we bring up burqa-wearing here in the first place? It is not a matter of terrorism or physical violence. It is a matter of indoctrination into a belief, one which becomes self-imposed, so the wearing of the burqa becomes a must. Burqa-wearing is obviously not an act of terrorism, but it *is* a form of oppression based on indoctrination and could, through western liberal eyes, easily be seen as gender-based violence.

If, perhaps, you are indoctrinated from childhood to believe that if your husband-to-be were not to beat you twice a day, that would mean that he did not love you, you may come to believe that as well. Some Christian and some Jewish denominations educate their women to believe that they must obey their husbands.

In neither Christianity nor Judaism did the priestly classes give up their power until forced to do so by secular education in the Western world. The fact that rulers in Muslim-majority states and their clergy cooperate, likely in the interest of furthering each other's hold on power, can easily be demonstrated through the controversy over the infamous Danish Muhammad cartoon, a story that erupted when a Danish paper published 12 cartoons of the prophet on

September 30, 2005. They did it to further the debate about how to examine and criticise Islam. It was a test in the world of free speech to investigate what, if any, self-censorship should be applied. In Islamic tradition, just publishing pictures of Muhammad is seen as blasphemy, and the publishing of the cartoons led to protests around the world and violent riots in several Muslim countries. The interesting part is that many Muslim countries got involved even at the level of government and wanted to force the Danish government to disallow free speech while threatening Denmark with economic retaliation.

Are Muslims perhaps equally careful not to offend believers of other religions? From our observations, it seems not to be the case.

There can, of course, be no change to holy texts that are written in stone and without fault. Change will, perhaps, come only when Muslim states educate their citizens to understand the natural sciences, become more enlightened and wrest power from the clerical classes. We can live in hope that, if and when that happens, Arab countries could once again lead the world in terms of scientific knowledge. They once had the finest medical scientists, the best mathematicians, and the top astronomers. Parts of the Muslim world still seem to live, to some extent, in a time bubble similar to when the Catholic Church denied ordinary people access to any scientific knowledge that contradicted the holy texts.

There is a danger when the clerical classes and the rulers enter a holy or, rather, an unholy alliance to control the masses. The royals and the church in Christian countries made many mistakes, including the Crusades. Is it perhaps that in many of the Islamic majority countries, the rulers and the clerics will not give up power and continue to rely on the same kind of – primitive? – indoctrination that led to the Crusades? There may be a lesson to be learned from the West where, over time, both the rulers and the clerical classes, against their very best efforts, inexorably lost power and influence.

The fact remains that there are enough Muslims who are willing to interpret the Quran in such a way as to allow the killing of nonbelievers. They also have a higher level of understanding for their deeds among the general Muslim population than would be afforded to potential Jewish or Christian terrorists.

CHAPTER 5

When former President Obama visited *The Tonight Show with Jay Leno* on NBC, he famously stated, "The odds of dying in a terrorist attack are a lot lower than they are of dying in a car accident, unfortunately." The statement is, on the face of it, true. What it does not take into account is all of the countermeasures that had to be taken against the risk of terrorist acts. What would it look like if we had not beefed up airport security? As irritating as it is to pass through all that security, we must remember why it is there. Passing through airport security means a delay when travelling, but it also brings comfort to a traveller who may otherwise not have dared to fly.

We also do not know how successful our security services are in monitoring potential terrorists and, behind the scenes, preventing terrorist acts. Do we believe that President Obama's statement regarding a lower incidence of terrorist fatalities compared to car accident victims would still be true had we, for instance, abandoned security checks at airports?

There is a cost for security and counterterrorism. We need to bear that cost because the alternative is too terrible. Since such an overwhelming percentage of terrorists and suicide bombers follow Islam, and so few follow other religions, it is no wonder that we have cause for concern. This is a concern we may share with the many peaceful followers of Islam who do not condone the violence.

In southern Sweden during August 2020, several attempts were made to desecrate the holy Quran. Let us note that, in liberal democracies, desecrating any holy scripture is part of free speech. It may be in bad taste, but it is allowed. There was a sudden flare-up in social media activity in the city of Malmö, with certain Muslims issuing terrible threats, including threatening to rape the perpetrator, his sister or his mother. The police in Malmö decided to forbid the desecration of a Quran, as well as any anti-Muslim manifestations, in the knowledge that they could not provide security. The perpetrator burned a Quran anyway, which led to riots in which several hundred Muslim men threw cobblestones at the police. All of these followers of Islam must have sincerely believed that they needed to do so to defend the Quran. They could, perhaps, have chosen instead to pray to Allah for Him to take care of the situation in a more peaceful manner.

If they really wanted a tit-for-tat, why not just burn a Bible?

Tariq Ramadan is a Swiss Muslim academic. He is a big defender of the notion that Islam is a religion of peace. We find him in debates taking the strong view that despite all the terrorist acts committed in the name of Islam, it is, essentially, a religion of peace. He puts the blame squarely on the reader of the holy texts of Islam. The people who commit violence in the name of Islam just don't read and understand the holy texts correctly.

We should analyse this further. When an ordinary human writes a book or an essay, it is the writer who is responsible for clarity and ease of understanding. Although we mere humans try our best, we are not perfect and often fail to deliver the desired clarity in our writing.

When it comes to the Quran, we understand that it is a perfect book. It is God's word transmitted via the Archangel Gabriel over many years in a cave to Muhammad, a perfect man who unfortunately, many believe, could not write but was equipped with a perfect memory. The Prophet would in turn dictate what he had heard to people who could write it all down and eventually this was put together as the perfect book we know as the Quran.

It seems odd, doesn't it, that a perfect book could be interpreted in so many different ways, ranging from being entirely peaceful to a series of commands to kill and to force the conversion of infidels in another. If Allah truly wanted to spread a message of peace, the perfect book would have made that message unambiguous and easy to understand.

Our conclusion must be that, if Professor Ramadan allows himself to argue the peaceful interpretation while other believers can find the opposite in the Quran, it is difficult to see it as a perfect book. Perversely, the only thing we can take from Tariq Ramadan's peaceful interpretation is that he represents one of many interpretations made possible. The Quran is, after all, the word of God and Allah has the ability to express himself in a way we would all understand clearly and equally.

CHAPTER 5

In October 2020, a French teacher was killed in France by an 18-year-old Chechen boy. The teacher had shown cartoons of the prophet Muhammad in a class on free speech. Prior to showing the cartoons, he had allowed students who were not comfortable viewing the cartoons to skip the class. The boy killed the teacher, Samuel Paty, by beheading him with a knife. The Chechen boy was assisted by two teenagers who identified the teacher. It is very likely that the killer was egged on by a social media campaign against Mr. Paty. The poor Chechen boy was, doubtlessly, filled with childhood indoctrination against the infidels around him. The people who sent him Facebook messages were, we can reasonably assume, not unaware of the radical views of the Chechen killer-to-be.

The response started off fairly rationally, and according to Arab News, the head of the Muslim World League stated that all religions opposed such acts of terror. In Arab News, it was also announced that Saudi Arabia led the Arab and Muslim world in condemning the terrorist murder of the French teacher. Muslims in France and their community leaders also condemned the killing and insisted that Islam ought not to be associated with such heinous acts. Unfortunately, here is where the good news ends.

In the Muslim world, many protests and other actions were seen. The protests were not against the killing of the teacher but against the showing of the cartoons and the French president's subsequent defence of free speech. France was quick to defend the right to free speech, and, in solidarity with the beheaded teacher, cartoons of the prophet were projected on various city halls.

In Bangladesh, around 40,000 activists took to the street in protest. Calls were made to boycott French products, and the French president was called a "Satan-worshipper". Protests also took place in Pakistan and Gaza. Iranian and Saudi Arabian officials then weighed in, denouncing the offensive cartoons of the prophet. In Malaysia, the opposition leader opposed the French president's comment on Islam being in crisis and called it offensive and unreasonable. He claimed, "With freedom comes responsibility." Is it better perhaps to have no freedom? President Macron was also attacked in Morocco, by the Taliban in Afghanistan and by Hezbollah in Lebanon. Chechnya's leader accused President

Macron of being provocative towards Muslims and equated Macron's stance on free speech with an act of terrorism.

President Erdogan of Turkey is not one to let an opportunity to demonstrate his Islamist leanings pass him by. The Turkish president called for a boycott of French goods and, at least initially, was not very keen on condemning the beheading of the French teacher; several times, he urged the French president to get his mental health checked. Do we find this a reasonable response in the circumstances?

Ibrahim Kalin, the president's chief counsellor, said, "Some may not understand how we love our Prophet more than ourselves. They may not get their heads around how we see an insult to him as an insult to us. They may call our affection 'fanaticism'. That is their misfortune. We will explain this to them persistently and in the best way possible."

After French pressure, the Turkish president caved and president Erdogan's spokesman tweeted this statement: "We strongly condemn the monstrous murder of Samuel Paty in France, and we reject this barbarism. There is nothing legitimate about this murder."

Should the West perhaps cave? One gets the impression that many Western governments and law enforcement agencies prefer not to allow offensive speech towards Muslims and Islam. The same governments and law enforcement agencies seem not to be equally upset when Muslim perpetrators of offensive speech make themselves heard.

In Sweden, the police had wanted to prosecute burning the Quran as a hate crime. The police had to, in the end, end their investigation after it was found that the burning of the Quran is part of free speech.

In Norway, a man wanted to show his sympathy for the brutally murdered Samuel Paty by putting up posters of caricatures of the prophet Muhammad in public places. The same evening, he was visited by four Norwegian police officers who explained to him that Muslims would be offended by his actions. The man, in turn, asked whether, according to Norwegian law, it was illegal to offend. The police had no choice but to answer that, while it was not illegal, society did not wish to allow such occurrences. He was accused of the crime of not having asked for permission to post the pictures. He asked whether he would have been visited by four police officers if he had instead posted pictures of Karl Marx, Buddha, or Jesus. The police officers' response was, "You can't know that." The next day, the local newspaper released an article about the police not having enough resources to attend to a car accident in the same area.

It seems, doesn't it, that many followers of Islam are easily offended on behalf of their religion. Does it not also seem that there is a significant number of Muslims who are quite willing to go from being annoyed to being violent against the offenders, their families, and even their societies?

The news continues to be abhorrent. Another killing occurred not long after the slaughtering of the French teacher. This time it was in Nice, France, where a Muslim man beheaded one person and killed two others outside a church.

The former prime minister of Malaysia, Dr. Mahathir Mohamad, deserves special mention. Only a few hours after the killings in Nice, he tweeted that Muslims have the right to "kill millions of French people for the massacres of the past."

Dr. Mohamad was referring to historical events when the French were responsible for taking many Muslim lives. The timing is not unimportant. The tweet came up just after the Nice killings. Although Dr. Mohamad deleted the tweet shortly after posting it, it does give us some insight.

Can we really support revenge in these modern times? It may very well be true that historically the French have caused the death of many Muslims. It is also true that Islamophobia places a lot of blame on and hatred towards Muslims. Is it at all reasonable that a Muslim leader such as Dr. Mohamad would support vengeful acts against innocent people simply because, at some point in history, Muslims were killed by people who may or may not have been ancestors of the people Dr. Mohamad wants to see killed?

The former Prime Minister also tweeted, "Since you have blamed all Muslims and the Muslims' religion for what was done by one angry person, the Muslims have a right to punish the French."

Do we not understand that Dr. Mohamad's tweets have certainly not helped to demonstrate that Islam is a religion of peace? This is a practical point and not just about what is written in the holy Islamic texts.

It is true that we find revenge prescribed in the form of an eye for an eye in the writings of the Old Testament. In practice, though, Jews and Christians no longer rely on the Old Testament as a call to arms to take revenge or to kill nonbelievers.

Those of us who are Muslim may need help to understand why so much violence is being perpetrated in the name of Islam.

Those of us who are not Muslim may need even more help to understand why we should view Islam as a religion of peace.

Can we be persuaded that all the people who are angry and violent in the name of Islam can be convinced by Professor Ramadan's view that they are just misreading the holy texts of Islam? Despite all the violence committed in the name of Islam, why is it that those of us who are infidels are required to agree that Islam is a religion of peace? And why is it that by just noting the level of violence perpetrated in the name of Islam one can easily be branded Islamophobic?

CHAPTER 6

Why is it ... that we accept so many errors in holy scripture that elsewhere would have made us stop reading?

We just have to read the first page in the New Testament to see that, right at the beginning of this holy book, the Gospel of Matthew does not exactly give credence to the story that we have been brought up with and indoctrinated in. Through our childhood education, we have been made to understand that Jesus' father is the Lord Himself, and that feels as if it is by now common knowledge. Remember, it would be common knowledge only to those who are Christian believers and are happy to put the blinders on and disregard the actual text. If you are Jewish, Muslim or Hindu, the story about the virgin birth of Mary's son, with God as his father, will mean little to you. In the same way, if you are Jewish or Christian, the story of Muhammad flying on a winged horse from Jerusalem may seem rather far-fetched to you.

The story we are to believe is that Jesus was the son of God and born to a virgin, who herself came about in an immaculate conception, and further that he rose from the dead on the third day.

Jesus' ancestry is found in two of the gospels, the one according to Luke and the other according to Matthew. Matthew's gospel starts off the New Testament with Jesus' ancestry. Is Matthew's line of ancestors compatible with Luke's? It would be reasonable to expect that the two versions are compatible, but this is not what we find.

The important things that both Matthew's and Luke's accounts have in common are that both clearly have only **human** ancestry in Jesus' line of ancestors and that both pass over King David. Both ancestry lines clearly pass over Joseph, a mere mortal, who, according to belief, is not the father of Jesus. If God were Jesus' father, the idea of having a line of ancestors presented in the way both gospels do, namely over Joseph, Mary's husband, does not make sense. The whole exercise, with a bloodline starting with Abraham and going over Joseph, seems to be an indication that at the time of writing these two gospels, there was no true consensus that God was, in fact, Jesus' father.

The believers amongst us might want to take the blinders off for a moment and wonder: could God, not even on page one, inspire better writing for a clear understanding of Jesus' divine origin? The follow-up question, which I will let you answer for yourselves is: what else is not right in the rest of the New Testament?

If you were to go through the exercise of putting the four Gospels side by side and comparing them, you would find that they are, to a great extent, incompatible and that they actually have different stories. The editing when the early Christian fathers picked what was holy text and what was not allowed into the New Testament became a really sub-par job. Take good note of the fact that the text of the Bible was chosen by ordinary people. They chose how to edit the text. They chose what was to be allowed in the Bible and what was not allowed to become holy scripture.

The early fathers of Christianity did not have much quarrel with the text and were quite okay with people living in a state of suspended disbelief without full knowledge of the text. The Catholic Church followed up by making sure that the ordinary people, those not of the ordained priestly class, would not be able to read the text in their own language.

One would be forgiven for assuming that throughout history, at least until the Enlightenment, church leaders had no fear that ordinary people would ever be able to read the holy texts and decide for themselves what those texts really said. But we know that it did not turn out that way. For some time in the liberal West, and increasingly throughout most of the world, people have been sufficiently educated to be able to read.

Over the years, religious hierarchies and organisations became paramount and wanted power and control over the ordinary people. They may well have been certain that they would get what they wanted, namely control over their ignorant flock, by keeping them ignorant and also by the use of Latin for Christian services, a language of which most ordinary people had little or no understanding. In Judaism, prayer is still conducted in Hebrew. It is not uncommon to be educated in the reading of holy texts and prayers in Hebrew without understanding what one reads. In Islam, the Quran is read in Arabic, even by and for those who do not have any understanding of that language. Many Muslims live in countries where the native language is not Arabic. Only around 20% of Muslims live in Arab countries. In Indonesia, one finds the largest Muslim population, close to 13% of all Muslims. Pakistan has the second-largest Muslim population with around 11% of all Muslims, followed by India with just under 11%. None of these three countries has Arabic as its official language.

From the time of the first written scrolls, the Jews had to learn to read in order to better understand the holy texts. Like people belonging to other religions, they were indoctrinated from an early age to believe that the stories of the Bible were true or, at the very least, inspired by God. The first part of the Old Testament consists of the five books of Moses, and the author is claimed to be Moses himself. The remaining parts of the Bible may have had different authors. Psalms, believed by some to have been authored by King David and King Solomon, made their way into the Bible. Various prophets added texts to the Old Testament. Authorship is by no means always clear regarding all entries in the Bible. We should, however, be assured of the essential fact that God inspired the various writers.

We must again remind ourselves that the stories that went into the Old Testament – which is, with very few exceptions, the same as the Hebrew Bible – had to be selected for inclusion in the holy texts. It was, ultimately, humans who had to pick what went into the Hebrew Bible, and other humans had to pick what went into its Christian counterpart, the Old Testament. Likewise, humans had to make the decisions as to what went into the New Testament and what was not allowed in.

Study of the Bible reveals quite a number of errors. *The Encyclopedia of Bible Difficulties* is a book that lists hundreds of pages of errors. The author of that book, Dr. Archer, had no intention of leaving us with the belief that these difficulties have no explanation. If you just believe, he claims, that God is right, and if you are still uncertain, seek evangelical advice and all the difficulties will be explained away. Nevertheless, all these Bible difficulties are listed in his book for us to study at our leisure.

There should, it must be said, be no difficulties in a book that is either God's word or inspired directly by God. It is, therefore, reasonable to at least ask the question: was the Old Testament really given to man by God or at least inspired by the Lord? Perhaps one may also ask: were the holy texts in fact written by mere mortals and then badly edited when put together in a book? It is difficult to believe that God could not inspire better, clearer, more accurate and more consistent work. It is difficult to believe that God's writing would be so full of errors. Is it not, perhaps, more logical to conclude that God may have had nothing to do with putting these holy texts together?

We have already discussed the inconsistencies in the creation stories in the Bible. The first part of the Bible, the five books of Moses, are often given the name the Pentateuch. As we noted above, believers claim that Moses authored these five books. But modern scholarship finds clear evidence for the existence of many writers throughout the Bible, and it is highly unlikely that Moses would have written the first five books, also referred to as the Torah in Hebrew. It is, anyway, far from clear that Moses was a historical person. If he was not, then of course he could not have had anything to do with the writing of the five books.

Nevertheless, what are known as the five books of Moses are, in order, Genesis, Exodus, Leviticus, Numbers and Deuteronomy. A little side note of interest here is that at the end of the writing, supposedly done by Moses, he

CHAPTER 6

describes some events that took place after his passing. A pedant may point out that writing about events that occurred after the author's passing may be an implausible feat, but we are, after all, in the realm of miracles here. The final chapter of Deuteronomy contains a record of Moses' death, and if we believe that somebody other than Moses wrote that, we may also ask: what else did Moses not write? Let us leave that aside for now and just bank it in the back of our minds as another compelling reason to take one's blinkers off and read the holy texts for what they actually say.

I feel that I have to delve into more of the actual text of the creation stories to get the point across and emphasise that the text is not always compatible with what you believe and what you hear in churches and synagogues. If you make the effort to read these texts on your own, you may find that they do not contain what you recall from your childhood learning or exactly what the priests, ministers and rabbis tell you when you go to worship the Lord.

To go a little more deeply into something we touched on earlier, there is one part of the creation story that is very ingrained in our knowledge base, and that is that the woman Eve, or in Hebrew Chava, was created after Adam in exchange for Adam's rib. The name Chava can be translated as "Life", but it is interesting that you can also find evidence of "Snake" from roots in ancient Aramaic. Prehistoric man, it seems, might well have been frightened of his desire for woman.

The two creation stories can, with a degree of good will, be seen as somewhat complementary. But we have to acknowledge that they are also somewhat contradictory.

The first story starts on page 1 of the Old Testament and begins with a description of God's responsibility for creating the heavens and the earth. The next sentence states that the earth was without form and void, and darkness was upon the face of the deep. The beginning of the world as we know it was that God had set in place a chaotic universe and needed to go further with His creation. For this English translation of the original text in Hebrew, I am using the English text in a Hebrew Bible, the illustrated Jerusalem Bible.

The first creation story now moves on to how God, day after day, over the next six days, creates the environment in which we, the human race, find ourselves. God, who can create anything with just a flicker of an idea in His mind (if one can even use such a turn of phrase about this supreme being) uses commanding words to trigger the events of creation. One would be forgiven if one curiously wondered: why did God need the six days for His creation and why did He need to rest on the seventh? He could surely have done all of this in an instant. Let us be generous and, for the sake of argument, assume that this was all done by God to lead by example and show us that we also need a day of rest at the end of our working week. The all-powerful God obviously does not need to rest and most certainly does not need six days to create everything in the universe.

On the first day, God decides that it is too dark in the chaos: "And God said, let there be light: and there was light." What comes next is somewhat surprising for an all-knowing and all-seeing God, and it is as if He did not know what His creation was going to look like. The text continues, "And God saw the light, that it was good: and God divided the light from the darkness." It must, in other words, have been a surprise to Him that His creation turned out the way He wanted it to turn out. The writer seems to be completely at ease with the fact that the sun has not yet been created but light could be seen. Is the fact that the light came before the sun perhaps another example of a lack of scientific understanding rather than this biblical story being God's word?

Finally, God names the light "Day" and the darkness "Night". The first day concludes with the text stating: "And the evening and the morning were the first day." In Judaism, the day starts in the evening when the first stars can be seen and ends the next evening. Christmas Eve, for instance – especially as celebrated in central and northern European countries – which starts the evening before Christmas Day is a reminder of the creation story.

On the second day, again by using commanding words, God divided the waters so that there was water below the firmament, that is, on earth, and water above the firmament, which is in heaven. And so, it became: "And God called the firmament Heaven. And the evening and the morning were the second day."

On the third day, as usual, using words to command nature, God gathered together the waters under the heaven in one place and let the dry land appear: "And God called the dry land Earth; and the gathering together of the waters called he Seas: and God saw that it was good." Obviously, God again surprised Himself by having created what He set out to create by His commands. "And the evening and the morning were the third day."

On the fourth day, God said, "Let there be light in the firmament of heaven to divide the day from the night; and let them be for signs, and for seasons, and for days, and years." Light had already been created on day one, but now it was time to create a greater light in the form of the sun to rule the day and the lesser light in the form of the moon to rule the night, and, while God was at it, He also created the stars. Again, the text says that God saw that it was good, and again God surprises Himself that He is capable of creating what He sets out to create. "And the evening and the morning were the fourth day." We do note that the moon was the lesser light. One would be forgiven for believing that in ancient times, they believed that the moon was its own light source. It is not a certain conclusion to draw from the text, but now we know that the moon only reflects light emitted by the sun.

I believe we now can draw one conclusion from the creation story, which is that the day is actually a day and a season is a season and a year is a year. God neatly ties time to the sun and the moon. We know exactly what that means. For a year, it means approximately 365 days, which is the time it takes for the earth to circle the sun.

It seems natural to us that early man did not come close to the scientific knowledge we possess now – and have possessed for hundreds of years – in terms of the sun being the centre of our solar system. As science progressed, people came to understand that our solar system was not built around the earth, with the sun and the moon created for ruling day and night on the earth. Even religious scientists such as Francis Collins now acknowledge that the earth is billions of years old.

The pattern of the six-day creation is clear: God issues a command and His command turns into creation. On the fifth day, He creates a variety of fish and whales, as well as "winged fowl" that were supposed to fly above the earth "in the open firmament of heaven". Heaven must have been very close to the earth in those ancient days of creation.

The pattern is repeated, and God is pleased with His creation; "and the evening and the morning were the fifth day."

On the last day of creation, God was busy: "Beasts of the earth after his kind and cattle after their kind and everything that creeps upon the earth after his kind: and God saw that it was good."

The creation He accomplished on day six is not finished because God also said, "Let us make man in our image, after our likeness; and let them have dominion over the fish of the sea, and over the fowl of the air, and over the cattle, and over all the earth, and over every creeping thing that creeps upon the earth."

The text goes on to explain that God created man in His own image; **male and female,** He created them. God blessed them and said to them to be fruitful and multiply. The Lord wanted to ensure that man was the master of the earth: "And have dominion over the fish of the sea, and over the fowl of the air, and over every living thing that moves upon the earth."

After some further admonishments, "God saw everything that he had made, and behold it **was very good** and the evening and the morning were the sixth day." It must be pleasing for us to understand that what He accomplished with His commands on day six He found not just good but *very* good. Humanity was created on that last day, namely day six, in the first creation story. As we can see, both man and woman were created on that day.

On the seventh day, God ended His work, "and he rested on the seventh day from all his work which he had made. He blessed the seventh day and sanctified it because he had rested on that day from all his work."

To claim that each day of creation really is an aeon of time would be to completely disregard the holy text that describes creation, day and night, and even seasons. It is only because of scientific understanding of the natural world that this reinterpretation to make a day an aeon of time has become necessary to explain away the difference between evolution that took billions of years and creation that took six days. This reinterpretation has only come about in recent years and is one of many examples where new explanations have had to be found and holy texts reinterpreted to fit people's growing, indeed evolving, knowledge and understanding. The Catholic Church is guilty of having fought tooth and nail to ensure that scientific knowledge would not filter down to the ignorant masses. The Catholic Church needed its followers to be ignorant.

The same issue surrounds the age of our planet which is, in biblical terms for Christians, somewhere between 6000 and 10,000 years. For Jewish believers, the earth is, as I write, in year 5781, a year which started on September 17, 2020. We note that with the same text in the Old Testament, the theologians of the two religions cannot even agree on the biblical age of our planet.

The second creation story concerns the Garden of Eden. God had created everything but there was not yet a man to till the earth. In this second creation story, God formed man from "the dust of the ground, and breathed into his nostrils the breath of life; and man became a living soul." In this story, Adam was not created by command out of nothing but out of the existing dust of the ground in the Garden of Eden. This seems not convincingly complementary to the first creation story where Adam and Eve were created together on day six.

There is a description of the Tree of Life and the Tree of Knowledge of Good and Evil planted in the Garden of Eden. A river in the garden is described as being there to water the garden, and there it was parted and became four heads. All the four flowing waters are named, and the first branch of this gigantic river encompasses the whole land of Havilah where there is gold. The second is named Gihon and comprises the whole land of Ethiopia. The third river goes towards the east to Assyria. The fourth river is the Euphrates. Are we not left with the distinct sense of this having been written so long after the creation that these countries already existed? Since there was nobody else but Adam's family and the Garden of Eden had just been created, there wouldn't have been any other countries needing to be named. There would also be no need to let us know where gold could be found. There was no intention to send Adam and Eve out of the Garden of Eden where they were supposed to live happily ever after. Only after Eve was tempted by a walking and talking snake and convinced Adam also to eat of the forbidden fruit did God decide to change the earth's first family's living conditions. As if God did not know that the snake was going to tempt Eve. As if God did not know that both Eve and Adam would eat of the forbidden fruit.

The text in the second creation story also describes rivers flowing to other countries and places full of gold. Since God had just created the earth and separated the water from dry land and created the Garden of Eden, we find ourselves with a problem. How could those foreign lands exist? It is likely a question of history being backdated. It seems obvious that country names outside of the Garden of Eden are from and about a later time, most likely once oral traditions had started to develop. Frankly, the explanation for how the second story made its way into the Bible in this form is not that it was inspired by God but more probably that it was a result of bad editing by humans. The editors at the time either did not notice the inaccuracy and the conflict with the first story or simply didn't care too much about it

Not to become too scientific, let us go back to the major difference between the first and the second creation story regarding the creation of humankind. It is worth a more detailed look. In the first creation story, as we know, man and woman already existed together, having been created on day six. But in the second creation story, the Lord God said, "It is not good that the man should be alone."

In this second creation story, God puts Adam into a deep sleep: "And he took one of his ribs, and closed up the flesh instead thereof; and from the rib, which the Lord God had taken from man, made he a woman, and brought her unto the man."

We can now see that already, in the first few pages of this holy book, God has either not been able to inspire the writer/s well enough to make the story clear or is deliberately deceiving us so that we do not understand his ways. One excuse we always hear is that God works in mysterious ways. That mysteriousness has led to a lot of unnecessary conflict between people who make their own interpretations of God's holy scriptures instead of being able to understand God's will with sufficient clarity that there simply couldn't be any ambiguity, disagreement or conflict.

We have gone through the text diligently and could have gone on much longer, but, as I promised, this is not a scientific work; some shortcuts have been taken when describing the two creation stories.

Let us now, for the sake of argument, accept that most of the Bible was written by human authors, including Moses, and that all the authors were indeed inspired by God. Let us even assume that God did not – for whatever reasons – wish to inspire the writers sufficiently for his message to be delivered to us mere mortals with crystal clarity.

So, let us go with the assumption that most of the Bible was just writing inspired by God but not God's actual, direct word. Let's even allow for Godly inspiration having gone slightly wrong since the biblical writers didn't quite understand the Lord. We know, however, that at least one part of the Bible was written by God Himself: The Ten Commandments. We now need to see whether God's own words bring greater clarity than the writings in holy scriptures that are, perhaps, merely inspired by God.

We move straight to the Ten Commandments in the hope that we will find the clarity that only God can bring us. We may be thirsty for His word because we know He wrote this Himself, as it is told in the Bible. We were raised to believe that the Ten Commandments are, in essence, what we today would call a constitution or basic law. We were also brought up to believe that Western culture bases its laws and morality on these Ten Commandments.

Whether the Bible, in the form of Old and New Testaments, or the Quran are actually good moral guides for our behaviour on this earth is something we shall have to leave aside for later discussion. We need to remember that we are looking into whether there is reason to believe that the holy texts are less holy than they seem and may, in fact, have been written, a long time ago, by mere mortals, perhaps even without godly inspiration.

These biblical writers certainly lacked the kind of scientific knowledge we have today and the understanding of the natural world that we have been brought up in. Is there any one who doubts that if these holy texts had been written today, they would have incorporated how modern science explains our universe and the natural world in which we live? If you, along with me, believe that the Bible would have looked different had it been written today with our current scientific knowledge it also follows that we believe that the biblical texts were written by ordinary people, and by modern standards, relatively ignorant ordinary people. The attempts to explain away the biblical age of our planet by turning a biblical day into an aeon of time without any justification in the actual biblical texts clearly demonstrate that there is an unease among theologians. Somehow, they feel the need to bridge the gap between science and biblical explanations.

Some of you who wish to continue to believe in the texts as being holy and representing the word of God must admit that God knew and has always known what scientific knowledge we would accumulate over time. He also most certainly knew that we would continue to develop our scientific knowledge into a greater understanding of both the natural world around us and how we ourselves truly function. God could have made sure that the writers of the holy texts would be inspired by Him to tell the biblical stories in a way that would match upcoming scientific understanding. He just didn't.

Regarding the Ten Commandments, there is no excuse about inspired or uninspired writers who might have misunderstood or misinterpreted God's message. We know from the biblical texts that God claims authorship of the Ten Commandments.

It is curious then, that there are two versions of the Ten Commandments. For the first set of stone tablets, Moses goes up the mountain, he sees the burning bush and God gives him the stone tablets written by the Lord Himself. When Moses comes down from the mountain, he finds that his people have made an idol in the form of a golden calf. Moses is so furious that he breaks the stone tablets, in spite of the fact that they are God's own writing.

When we hear of the Ten Commandments, we think of ten identifiable commandments that God has Himself written down for us. When we look at the actual biblical texts, we find that this is not the case. Even different religions and various Christian denominations have variations regarding how the division into Ten Commandments occurs. In the biblical text, we find just seven verses in Exodus which, somewhat differently depending on your particular denomination, get divided into ten, probably for easy reference. And that division of seven verses into Ten Commandments is subject to human interpretation. It is human interference in creating Ten Commandments out of seven biblical verses that moderates even God's own writing. Even what God has Himself written to be the Ten commandments does not show up exactly the same in the Jewish version as in the Roman Catholic version. And, as noted already, there are even some differences between various Christian denominations as to how the Ten Commandments are presented.

The mere fact that different religions, to any degree, can interpret God's own writing differently must be alarming. How can that be true, we ask ourselves? It could be true if God did not write the Ten Commandments. The Ten Commandments happen to match the number of our fingers. It is a number that is easy to remember. But the fact that there are somewhat different Ten Commandments or the same Commandments with different numberings depending on your religious denomination, is evidence that man must have interfered in God's work. How dare mere mortals edit God's writing?

In order, again, not to make this too academic and too detailed, we are now going to delve right into the major commandments and what God says about Himself in them. Remember, He wrote them.

There are a number of thought crimes, that is, crimes of your mind, within the Ten Commandments. I don't know about you, but very often I have difficulty controlling my thoughts. God requires you to have that ability without having created you with it as an inbuilt faculty. A thought crime is thinking about something even if you do not act on that thought. Some thought crimes, we find, are serious offences in commandment number ten in the Hebrew version, which we must consider to be the most original. So, you must not even think about wanting your neighbour's slaves, his animals or any of his other possessions. How do you prevent your mind from having jealous or envious or acquisitive thoughts? I think we all have to acknowledge that we may have had thoughts that we are not happy with, but they are still there.

In number Ten we also find that you must not lust after your neighbour's wife nor covet his house. Nowhere does it say that the wife cannot lust for the neighbour, but that is probably because women were seen as the property of a male or at least as close to being his property as you could come in the days when this was written.

Number Nine of the Ten Commandments plainly states that you shall not bear false witness against your neighbour. Here we have one commandment that makes sense and has become part of our judicial systems.

Number Eight of the Ten Commandments tells us not to steal. Property rights are important and have made their way into our legal systems.

Number Seven of the 10 Commandments shows us that adultery was an ancient problem. Let's face it, adultery must've been a problem since the beginning of man. In most Western countries, having sexual relations outside of marriage is no longer a crime. Adultery is, we have come to see, really no business of the state. And, when God created us, He knew that this would happen and could have created us somewhat differently by tweaking us not to have the desire to commit adultery.

Number Six of the Ten Commandments is the prohibition against killing or, more correctly translated, the prohibition against murder. Murder is when a person wrongfully takes the life of another, whereas killing could be done in self-defence. There are a great many exceptions to the prohibition of murder in the Bible. When God Himself orders mass murder or even torture or when God Himself kills, He cannot be punished since He is the ultimate creator. He is above His own law. Murder is, to this day, of course, prohibited in our Western liberal legal systems.

Number Five of the Ten Commandments tells you that you must honour your father and mother. *Hold on a moment*, you say to yourselves. Is that commandment really a reasonable part of any constitution? How far is one willing to go to follow this commandment? What if your parent was a serial killer or paedophile? What if your parents abused you? This is another one of the commandments that has not worked its way into Western legal systems. Should you choose to dishonour your mother and father, rest assured that this is not punishable by the state. And this commandment takes a turn for the worse in the New Testament. Under certain conditions, you do not really need to honour your mother and father at all. You are even allowed – and actually encouraged – to hate them in the New Testament on the condition you do this in order to follow Jesus. If you are God and the son of God, you can allow yourself some liberties.

Number Four is that we must remember the Sabbath day and keep it holy, which means that we must rest just as God did on the seventh day. In Judaism, a great number of rules have been created around what it means not to do any work and not create anything new on that holy day. For instance, you are not allowed to turn on the light on the Sabbath because turning on the light creates something new, in this case, the light that before turning the switch to "on" was not there. You are not allowed to carry items outside of your dwelling unless you find yourself surrounded by walls. City walls will do, so if you find yourself in a walled city, you may be allowed to do some carrying. If you find yourself in a forest without walls, the rabbis have come up with a clever solution. You can create a camp, and put a string or a rope around the camp and pretend that this is a wall, which immediately allows you to carry household items from one end of the camp to the other, just as long as all of this goes on inside the pretend wall.

If you have ever been on vacation in Israel and stayed in a hotel, you will have noticed that the hotels are obligated to keep the Sabbath. They are not allowed to serve you freshly-cooked hot food or even freshly-brewed coffee. You will also have noted that in at least one of the elevators, you are not allowed to press the button for a specific floor. So, the rabbis have come up with a fantastic solution, which is that you pre-program that Sabbath elevator to stop at every floor. An observant Jew can step in the elevator, take a long ride with many stops, and get off on his floor. We must ask ourselves whether God is that stupid that He does not understand that we have invented rules to circumvent the main commandment to rest on the Sabbath. All these secondary rules to make life more reasonable and liveable while we studiously pretend to follow the commandments are patently man-made.

If, at the time the elevator was invented, the rabbis had come up with the idea that it was so restful to take the elevator instead of trying to trek up 15 flights of stairs that such self-indulgence was allowed even on the Sabbath, that would have been the law today. There is a lack of authority in Judaism to change these rules, so the religious Jews are stuck with them and must continue to pretend that they are actually able to circumvent the rules and trick the, we must suppose, somewhat doltish Lord.

Indeed, all religions have instituted extra rules and regulations to make life more bearable while pretending that adherents are still following the commands of the Lord.

We should mention Christianity here. Almost all Christian denominations have decided to change the Sabbath, which is the Saturday, to the following day so that we are to rest on Sunday in memory of the Christ who rose on the third day. That shift seems to have been instituted without fear of being put to death for not honouring and keeping the Sabbath – Saturday – holy. It is perhaps reasonable to conclude that if you can change the day of rest from day seven, the actual Sabbath, to Sunday, which is day one of the week, you can make many – or even any – other interpretations to fit the hierarchy of your clergy and the needs of your brethren.

Number Three of the Ten Commandments states that you shall not take the name of your God in vain. If you just think about that for a moment, you will realise how many times people say, "Oh my God." We can agree that it isn't exactly God's name, but still, we must assume that God hears and understands. Even Christians who, in a moment of surprise, exclaim "Jesus Christ!" do this without expecting a bolt of divine lightning to strike them down.

The word games we play not only relate to God. Some words we find too foul to speak out loud, so we recast them slightly. People will happily say, "What the heck!" while they fully expect the hearer to understand that they mean "What the hell!"

Even your children, once they reach the age of around eight, will understand exactly what you are really saying. And of course, God must understand our word games at least as well as an eight-year-old child.

In Jewish prayers, the name of God, *Yahweh,* is never uttered and is substituted with Adonai (אֲדֹנָי), which, translated from Hebrew, becomes "My Lords" (plural, as with royalty). To be on the safe side, there is an even more holy spelling with the Hebrew letters יי (Yud Yud), which are also pronounced *Adonai* when they stand together, but individually each is pronounced as *Y* as in *yes.* They go even further: when you are not praying, you are supposed to say *Hashem,* which means "the name". God, of course, knows that there is no difference, and to Him it should mean exactly the same thing. If He is the creator of all on earth, the earth itself and the entire universe, then He cannot be so stupid as not to fully understand our little games with His rules and commandments. He also understands, all-knowing and all-seeing as He is, that our wordplay really does not matter. It all means the same whether we say *name* instead of the Lord or pronounce the name *Yahweh*. In Western legal systems, you can call God what you want. There will be no punishment from the state.

We now come to number Two of the Ten Commandments, and it simply says that you should make no graven images. No stone gods or pictures to worship are allowed. In Western society, nobody prevents you from doing that if you feel like it. Christianity believes in the claim of divine authorship of the Ten Commandments, yet allows – actively encourages – the worship of pictures and statues of the mother of Christ and statues and pictures of Christ Himself.

That too has been going on for a long time without the worshipper being struck by lightning. In Western society, you can pray to whatever you like.

In the Jewish numbering, number Two also contains the admonition not to have other Gods. Among the translations from the original Hebrew to English, one finds that you should have no other gods either *before* or *besides* Him. There is no way of explaining this as being a prohibition against worshipping idols, which is separately prohibited in commandment number two.

The Hebrew Bible's number One is a straightforward statement that basically says, "I am the Lord your God."

The Catholic version of the 10 Commandments combines the Jewish number One, "I am the Lord your God," and number Two, "You shall have no other gods before me," into commandment number One. In most Lutheran versions, number One is "You shall have no other gods before me." God could make all of this clear, between Judaism and different Christian interpretations based on the same stone tablets. God could have done better! A fluent Hebrew speaker who is also well-educated in biblical matters told me that he believes that a more appropriate translation of the biblical Hebrew would be "You should have no other gods instead of me." Even that interpretation in no way indicates that there is only one God. If God can state that no *other gods* should come instead of Him, He is clearly saying – in his own writing – that there are other gods. Even if we go with the translation "no other gods before or besides him", God is definitely telling us that there are other gods.

We must understand that God knows language better than anybody, knows every language that will come to be in any future, and knows how His writing will be interpreted in any of those languages. He is all-seeing – He knows all futures.

We have seen that the text itself, written by God Himself, leaves no doubt that there are other gods. The Muslims got this one right as they have only one God and their texts say so explicitly. What God says in the Bible is He wants to be number one of all the gods and the other gods cannot be either beside or before Him. They must be below Him. Shocking, we may think, that other gods are even mentioned by the Lord Himself. Once we continue looking at other parts of the holy text, we may find that the Bible, in many instances, makes references to gods other than Yahweh.

The God of the Jews and the Christians says, for instance, in Exodus that He will execute judgement *on all the gods of Egypt*. This is followed up in Numbers where it is written that God executed judgement against the Egyptian gods.

Then there is Psalm 82, for instance, which contains clear language about other gods. Yahweh had become disappointed with the other gods. They had not done their duty as instructed by Him. They were supposed to rule justly and especially look after the poor, the widows and the rest of the nations. Yahweh was very angry when He took his place at the divine council. We do realise from the text that at this council were sitting other gods, don't we? Yahweh would not be sitting with some stone or wood carvings, would He? Stone or wood carvings are, as we have noted in the Ten Commandments, separately dealt with as idols and not as gods. The judgement by our Lord is that the other gods must die as Adam did. And Yahweh assumes command over the entire earth and takes possession of all nations.

In Deuteronomy, God would Himself be in charge of Israel, but He has also created – and is in charge of – the other gods. Deuteronomy forbids the Israelites from worshipping "the sun, the moon and the stars, all the host of heaven". Those other gods may exist but are for other people and not the Israelites to worship.

One explanation as to why Yahweh wanted to be the number one – and only the first among gods – could very well be that at the time when the biblical stories were created, gods were seen to be territorial (and numerous). When somebody moved from one territory to another, where they worshipped other gods, Yahweh wanted to be sure that He was still number one. He might not have minded that the new immigrant in a different land also adapted to the local gods.

As the Bible progresses through chapter after chapter, the writing slowly moves towards monotheism. The belief in one and only one God takes hold.

In Deuteronomy, we find that very important Shema prayer wherein, finally, the Israelites make their declaration of one God. There are many ways of translating this, but in the fifth book of the Torah, Deuteronomy, the prayer could be translated as "Listen, O Israel, Yahweh is your God, Yahweh is one." *Listen* at the beginning of my quote could be replaced by *Hear* which is the more commonly used translation. In modern English, it is the prayer in which God tells his people: "Listen, all you tribes of Israel, I am Yahweh your God and I am one."

Let us take stock here. If God really were the only God, He could have made that clear to us very early on in the Bible stories. But He did not.

So, who is God? And how does God present Himself to us in His own words? He does so after having forbidden us to worship idols and, in His own hand, He must have written, "For I the Lord thy God am a jealous God, visiting the iniquity of the fathers upon the children unto the third and the fourth generation of them that hate me; and showing mercy unto a thousand generations of them that love me, and keep my commandments."

Let us go back to Francis Collins who asks himself, "Who would want to worship a God like that?" God has no problem introducing his vengeful side and his jealous personality. The biblical answer must be that God wants us to worship Him despite His having those terrible traits. Revenge by the Lord extends to future generations of innocents.

For most of us, it is probably surprising that the centrepiece of the five books of Moses, namely the Ten Commandments, do not seem to be what we were taught as children. After Moses had broken the first set of stone tablets, he went up to the mountain to get a second identical set. The second set is, however, not identical in the biblical texts. The differences are not major, but one would of course expect God, the author, to be infallible and clearer and not to allow any differences between the two sets of stone tablets.

We do not need to go into any great detail about the differences. That would be to go too far on our already long excursion into the Ten Commandments.

CHAPTER 6

In Christianity, if we take our blinders off, we find that there is God the father, the son Jesus Christ and the Holy Spirit. We, who understand numbers, count three divine entities here. That doesn't sound like one God, but there is, of course, a Christian explanation. The explanation is that these three entities are distinct but still are only the three parts of one and the same God. We can make of this whatever we want, and we may come to different ways of understanding the oneness of the three. Our explanations will range from some people concluding that the worship of one God, monotheism, is not part of Christian teaching to others coming to full acceptance of the oneness of the three.

Without blinders, one would come to the conclusion, prompted by Occam's razor, that three equals three. The convoluted explanations necessary to come to the right explanation make it more likely that the explanations are wrong.

In Catholicism, we are supposed to believe that the wafer and the wine in the Eucharist really are the body and the blood of Jesus Christ Himself. Stop for a moment, again, and think about this. Is the lady who goes to church to receive the Eucharist turning into a cannibal? Do we not understand Catholic teaching to be that the bread and the wine are what they appear to us only until we start drinking the wine and eating the bread? There is a fantastic word that describes to us what Catholics believe happens at that point, namely *transubstantiation*. Miraculously, the wine and the bread get turned into the body and blood of Jesus. If that is possible, then, of course, three different entities can also be explained to be one God.

As far as the bread and wine are concerned, today even the most religious Catholics are certainly educated enough to understand that the chemical substance and the very atoms in either the bread or the wine cannot be transformed into flesh and blood. A modern person would have great difficulty chewing and swallowing something they were convinced would turn them into cannibals.

So, what about ancient religions with the many gods of the Romans, the Greeks and the Icelandic or Nordic religions? We could here borrow from Islam. Muslims have no trouble believing that God has revealed Himself to earlier prophets of both Jews and Christians. Muslims also believe that they are, together with Jews and Christians, descendants of Abraham. Without any hesitation, they consider Abraham to be the first true Muslim. For a nonbeliever, as noted earlier, that seems somewhat far-fetched since this would have occurred a very long time before the divine revelation to the Muslims via the prophet Muhammad.

With that in mind, we could follow in the footsteps of those Christians who teach that the three entities – God the father, Jesus the son, and the Holy Spirit – merely appear to be three separate entities but are, in fact, one and the same God. In following Christian teaching, we could easily declare that all previous gods in each of the many ancient religions really were only one. After this, we can rest assured that, throughout our entire human history, people were, in fact, true believers in only one true God, although there appeared to them to be many. That conclusion would not be too far removed from the conclusion that God the father, God the son, and God the Holy Ghost may seem to be three but are really one and the same. If three entities can equal one, so can all the Greek gods.

Our point here is, again, the lack of clarity in the biblical stories. We must understand that if God was so determined for us to know the absolute truth, He could have made us understand it exactly the way He meant it to be understood. In any text other than holy writings, we would have come to conclusions based on the wording. As we have seen, God has not been able to bring clarity even in His own writing when He handed his words in the form of the so-called Ten Commandments on stone tablets to Moses. There are, as much discussed already, two versions, and, depending on how you divide them, there could be more than ten commandments. There could, equally, be fewer than ten if we choose to cut them back down to the seven verses of that first stone tablet. There are, as we know, discrepancies between Christian and Jewish versions of the Ten Commandments, which would not have been possible had there been ten clear commandments counted and numbered by the Lord Himself.

Is the answer simply – and conveniently – that God works in mysterious ways? Is it perhaps that several long-forgotten but eminently mortal and fallible men, substituting themselves for an invented God, wrote the Ten Commandments in

INTRODUCTION

the name of that same imaginary god? Did the men writing the holy texts create a God complete with very many not-so-desirable human traits?

These are Occam's razor questions which each one of us may need to answer.

CHAPTER 7

Why is it ... that we believe that we are in possession of the true religion when we don't really know what that is?

The Oxford Dictionary definition of religion is "belief in or acknowledgement of some superhuman power or powers (esp. a god or gods) which is typically manifested in obedience, reverence, and worship; such a belief as part of a system defining a code of living, esp. as a means of achieving spiritual or material improvement."

Faith can be seen as the belief in a certain religion, and if one is a believing Christian, one could say that that person is of the "Christian faith".

There are estimates that the total number of religions in the world comes to more than 4000. If one were to add up the various Christian faiths – and there are many – Christianity would be the largest religion in the world, with approximately 2.3 billion believers. Islam, in the same way counting all Islamic faiths, would be the second-largest religion, with approximately 1.8 billion followers. Compared to Christianity and Islam, Judaism, which is also an Abrahamic faith, is a tiny religion. Adding up all different Jewish denominations, only around 15 million followers can be identified.

Some religions have nothing to do with Abraham, such as Hinduism, which is the third-largest religion, with approximately 1.2 billion followers. Buddhism has just over 500 million followers, and there are many other religions, such as Baha'i, Sikhism, and Shinto. Jainism, an ancient Indian religion, has 4.2 million followers. The followers of Jainism are devoted to non–violence and are mainly vegetarian.

We should also note that there are probably between 500 million and 1 billion nonbelievers in this world. And let us not forget Devil worship (Satanism). Satanism varies between somewhat different traditions. Some Satanist groups worship in extreme opposition to traditional religions for the sake of freedom of religion (See *Hail Stan?* on Netflix).

It must be clear to us that if the Devil is allowed by God to exist, and if God can engage and interact with the Devil, worshipping the Devil could – arguably *must* – also be recognised as a religion. One well-known biblical interaction between God and the Devil was when God was making bets with the Devil over Job's faith. God knew that Job was a good and God-fearing man. All-seeing God surely knew the outcome of his bet with the Devil. Of course, God won the bet, but Job had to pay quite a price.

Those who are devout followers of any one of the Abrahamic religions will find worshipping the Devil an abuse of our free will; nevertheless, they cannot deny his existence. A Devil-worshipper may similarly find a God-worshipping person misguided.

Another word that frequently pops up is *mythology*. When we speak of the worship of ancient Gods, we tend to use the word *mythology*. All religions have a system of concepts or beliefs in supernatural beings or supernatural events. These beliefs can be described as the mythology of religion. When we speak of ancient Nordic or Greek mythologies, we are nowadays very likely not looking at the mythology in these religions but are using the term mythology as a way to distinguish the true Abrahamic religions from the mere myths of these ancient peoples. We do this at our peril because none of us has any evidence of who God actually is. We also have no evidence that He exists at all, or even whether the Greeks or Vikings got it right after all, with the belief that there are several Gods that involve themselves in human affairs.

There is good reason to also look into the word *theology*. Theology is the study of God, religious beliefs and holy texts. It is not an easy task to try to explain or perhaps even explain away the many contradictions that exist in virtually all holy texts. Many times, theologians are left wanting. Often, one finds theological writers and thinkers who require a reading of holy texts to be infallible, and where fault is in any way found, the explanation becomes that we just do not, as noted already, understand God's mysterious ways. The fact that we do not understand God's mysterious ways has given believers endless leeway and, at the same time, created an enormous number of problems in the world.

If we put our minds to it, we could easily conclude that religion does not exactly come from God. We could argue – with some justification – that it comes, instead, from our parents and the culture, the actual area in which we grow up. That doesn't mean, of course, that people who have left their parents' home or their native land for a different part of the world will not continue to adhere to their childhood faith.

Judaism was the first of the Abrahamic religions, followed by Christianity, and then by Islam. Starting with Judaism, there are many denominations, from the ultra-orthodox to the ultra-liberal. There are eastern and western Jews or, in Hebrew, Sephardi and Ashkenazi Jews. A lot of strife occurs between the orthodox and liberal adherents to Judaism. There are Jewish congregations with female rabbis, which is seen as totally out of bounds by the orthodox. There are liberal Jewish congregations that permit same-sex marriage and perform wedding ceremonies for them. That, again, is totally out of bounds for the orthodox Jews who believe that homosexual acts, particularly between men, are forbidden and, in biblical terms, subject to the death penalty.

In Israel, a Jewish majority country, the nonbelievers and the many liberal wings of Judaism constantly complain about the disproportionate influence wielded by the orthodox Jews, particularly over family law. As an example, under rabbinical law, a man can divorce his wife without any reason, but the wife cannot divorce her husband unless he consents. The rabbis cannot force the man to consent, although they may, on occasion, put a man in jail in the hope that this will persuade him to accede to his wife's request for divorce.

CHAPTER 7

What, then, is true Judaism? Let us go back to the time of the Second Temple. Let us also remind ourselves that, right up to the present day, Jews pray for the return of the Temple. God commands, in the Hebrew Bible, that the Israelites make offering and sacrifice to Him through the priests. In Judaism, a priest is not a person who has been educated in Jewish theology. A rabbi is a person educated in Jewish theology. A Jewish priest, a Kohen, is the bearer of an inherited title, just like nobility. The Jewish priest is seen as a lineal descendent of Moses' brother Aaron. Isn't that a nice piece of mythology for us? In fact, isn't the entire Exodus story a good piece of mythology for us?

After the twelve original Jewish tribes had been dispersed, Jews were – and still are – divided into three groups. The descendants of the priests who, at the time of the Temple, performed sacrificial duties, today still have the duty of blessing the congregation on certain holidays. A Jewish priest could be considered somewhat holier than other congregation members and is disqualified from performing his duties if he is, for instance, blind or has a crippled foot or hand, bad eyesight, or even – God forbid – crushed testicles, which one must assume is one disqualifier that is determined by self-assessment. We take note that biblical language is very direct. God's creation, it is believed, had to be perfect. All the while, we forget that God allowed some people to become handicapped. A Kohen is prohibited from marrying a woman who has had premarital relations with any non-Jewish partner. A Kohen is also prohibited from marrying the daughter of a Jewish mother and a non-Jewish father, although this woman counts as Jewish even among the orthodox Jews.

The Levites are of the tribe of Levi, the third son of Jacob and his wife Leah. The tribe of Levi were expected to be financially supported by the tribes who had land, and they were expected to give tithes in support of the Levites. The priests, Kohanim (the plural form in Hebrew of Kohen) were a smaller group inside the tribe of Levi. The Levites assisted the Kohanim in their religious duties. Going back to when Joshua led the tribes into the land of Canaan, the Levites would dwell in cities but could not be landowners. It was believed that God Himself was the only inheritance of the Levites. If you have heard the catchphrase "follow the money", this is an interesting anecdote. The Levites were supposed, as noted above, to receive a tithe, which is one-tenth of what the rest of the tribes made. Currently, the Levites make up about 4% of the entire Jewish population. We assume that in ancient times they were no more than 4% of the Jewish population and were given 10% of everybody else's income from their land. Since it is believed that there are ten lost tribes in Judaism, the Levites likely made up a much smaller proportion than 4% of all Israelites. Could there have been any self-interest in writing such a rule regarding this perpetual gift to the Levites into the biblical text?

Currently, the remaining Jews who are neither Kohanim nor Levites are called the tribe of Israel and make up around 96% of the global Jewish population.

God developed His personality and character over the course of the entire Bible. We do understand that personality and character are perhaps more properly used to describe human traits. We can allow ourselves to use human traits when describing the Lord since the Bible itself has no difficulty ascribing to Him human traits such as vengefulness and hatred. The Bible starts with God's creation of the world including us humans. In the beginning, God is one of several gods. In the beginning, God is very engaged in human affairs. In the beginning, God talks to his human creation. God later uses prophets to convey His message to everybody from kings to the ordinary man and, a few times, even to a woman. Later in the Bible, God becomes more distant and less engaged in human affairs. He stops talking to us. He stops performing miracles. And He is finally only one God, a mysterious God, to whom we should pray but, at the same time, a God that one can no longer be certain actually listens to us.

For those who wish to delve deeper into how God develops over the biblical texts from beginning to end, a good recommendation would be *God: A Biography* written by Jack Miles. In the book, Miles traces how the God of the Old Testament evolves over time. God is described as if He were a character in a regular piece of literature, which, in a manner of speaking, He is. God is therefore analysed as the hero of the Old Testament, which allows Mr. Miles to follow God's changing character over time without being blinded by belief.

God is mysterious. God's ways are mysterious. If something doesn't seem right to us, it is because God's ways are mysterious, and we just do not have the capacity to understand the true meaning of either God's words or His actions. When something goes wrong, it is expected that we should blame ourselves. The God to whom we pray is that nowadays distant and rather unengaged God, but a God who still leaves us with some – admittedly faint – hope that our prayers will be heard. We know that God is all-seeing and therefore knows all possible futures and all of our thoughts. We know that even Jesus gave us to understand that God knows what we are going to pray for and what He is going to give us in return even before we start praying. So, why pray?

Is it that mysterious distance between us and the mysterious God that allows enough doubt in our minds to make it worthwhile to believe in Him?

It is time, however, that we ask ourselves, *what is the true Jewish religion?* To answer the question, we must first remind ourselves – again – that Jews pray every day that the Temple in Jerusalem will be rebuilt. The First Temple was supposedly constructed by King Solomon and the Second Temple by King Herod the Great. If the temple were ever to be rebuilt, it would be the Third Temple.

In the year 363 CE, the Roman Emperor Julian ordered the rebuilding of the Temple to create more religious diversity and take some of the strength and influence away from Christianity. The rebuilding failed and the Jews continue to pray for the Third Temple.

So, how *did* God want us to worship Him? And how does God still want us to worship Him? God seems to like sacrificial worship. God likes the scent of burnt flesh and is happy to see blood as part of the sacrificial ceremonies. The temple was the only place where sacrifices were allowed, and people travelled far and wide to reach the temple with their offerings. The offering was handed over to a priest at the Temple, and his task was to perform the sacrifice in a ritually correct manner.

What God wants according to the Old Testament is one of five types of sacrifice, namely:

- a burnt offering
- a grain offering
- a peace offering
- a sin offering and
- a trespass offering

It is quite complicated to get the sacrifices right. We find the offerings described in Leviticus and they remain valid, just awaiting the rebuilding of the Temple. The offerings are to be either animal or grain. The offerings are split into either two or three portions, one for God, one for the Levites and Kohanim and, where there is a third portion, that goes to the sacrificing individual.

Some offerings are mandated while others are given voluntarily by the sacrificing individual, in good faith, so to speak.

The voluntary sacrifices include a burnt offering to show commitment to God and to atone for an intentional sin. You could burn a bull, a ram without any blemishes, or a bird. The meat, bones, and organs are to be completely burnt for God. The hide of the animal is given to the Levites, who could make some money by selling it. There is also a grain offering that can be in the form of a cake or bread. The grain offering requires a drink offering of wine, which is poured into the fire on the altar. This offering is intended to thank the Lord for having provided well for the individual making the sacrifice. The priests are – or were – given a portion but had to eat it in the temple by the tabernacle. The last voluntary offering is the peace offering. This requires an unblemished animal of any sort from the herd of the sacrificing individual which could be enhanced with – or perhaps substituted by – grains or bread. This is a sacrifice giving thanks to the Lord and is also made to honour friendship, and is therefore followed by a shared meal. The high priest is to be given the breast of the animal, and the priest performing the ceremony is to be given the right front leg. These offerings are to be waved over the altar during the ceremony. The fat and liver are burnt for God, and the rest of the animal is intended for the meal to be enjoyed by the participants.

One of the obligatory offerings is a sin offering. This is intended to allow the person offering the sacrifice to atone for sins and be cleansed back to a state of purity. For this offering, God requires either a bull, a male or female goat, a dove or pigeon, or a measure of fine flour. The individual giving the sacrificial offering has to choose which of the allowable sacrifices to bring forth, depending on their own status and financial situation. A female goat is to be offered by a common person, and fine flour is to be offered by a very poor person.

There are specific instructions as to what to do with the blood. The fat, kidneys, and liver are offered to God Himself, and the rest of the ram must be eaten inside the court where the tabernacle was located in the temple.

For our purposes, we do not have to investigate the other mandated offerings. We understand from the summary above what our God wants from us. We understand from the above precisely the nature of the burnt meat and blood that He wants. A poor person can get away with grain or flour.

On the day of atonement, Yom Kippur, special sacrifices are prescribed. The high priest, *Kohen Gadol* in Hebrew, has first to sacrifice a bull as an offering for his known, acknowledged sins and also to atone for whatever sins he may have unintentionally been guilty of throughout the year leading up to this Yom Kippur. He then has to take two goats and present them at the door of the tabernacle. It is decided by lot which goat will be slaughtered and sacrificed to Yahweh and which one is to be the scapegoat. The kid goat being sacrificed to God is a blood offering, and the blood is collected in a bowl. The Kohen Gadol sprinkles the blood seven times upwards and one time downwards. Later on, the same day, the other kid goat will have to listen to the high priest confessing the intentional sins the Israelites have committed against God. Kohen Gadol now symbolically places the sins of Israel on the head of the scapegoat and sends him out. The goat escapes with the sins of the people.

If it were only that easy. Those who are Christian believers and go to confession may still smile at the scapegoat running away with our sins. Any Christian, and particularly Catholics, should realise that the Old Testament is one of the holy books of Christianity. Any Catholic must realise that the scapegoat running off with the sins of the people has a similarity to the cleansing of one's sins after confessing them to a priest in person. The high priest would confess the sins of all the people and lay them on the goat. One could make the observation that what the Kohen Gadol performed was a group confession enacted for many people.

It is my hope that you notice that I am describing the sacrifices as if they were happening today. The sacrifices are prescribed in the Bible, and the only reason they are not performed in our time is that the third Temple has not yet been built. In other words, the true religion of the Jews is a religion of burning flesh and sprinkling blood for the Lord. This God likes the scent of burnt flesh and He likes to see blood sprinkled in His honour. Remember, the only reason that, in modern times, we are merely praying to God and not also sacrificing as prescribed in Leviticus is that we still have to wait for the rebuilding of the Temple. We may have to wait a long time since, as Emperor Julian found, the rebuilding of the Temple can only occur under the right conditions.

How much sacrifice did go on in the Jerusalem Temple? We do know from archaeological sources that it was quite substantial. The Talmud is a collection of authoritative rabbinical writings coming after the Bible and intended to help interpret the holy text's religious laws. Of course, when it comes to religion, it is never simple. We should understand that even the Talmud comes in two versions, namely the Jerusalem Talmud and the Babylonian Talmud. When one refers to the Talmud, it is normally the Babylonian version, written during the exile of the Jews from their holy land. The Talmud is the main source of Jewish theology and religious law. It is, therefore, interesting to find passages in Talmudic texts describing how priests were wading up to their knees in blood in the Temple. Other Talmudic texts describe 1.2 million animals being slaughtered in just one day. The Jewish historian Flavius Josephus, who lived between 37 and 100 CE, agrees that in the course of Temple worship, one would find a great number of slaughtered animals. Josephus' credentials as a historian of the Jewish people should be questioned because, if nothing else, he seemed to believe that the biblical stories about the Jews are true history. He is also seen as a traitor to his fellow Jews as he defected to the side of the Romans and acquired Roman citizenship.

Modern historians readily – and justly – come to the conclusion that these descriptions are a gross exaggeration while, of course, not denying that animal sacrifice on a grand scale went on in the temple. We can reasonably assert that it would be all but impossible to sacrifice 1.2 million animals in just one day. Even if the exaggerated tales are not factual, they inadvertently demonstrate the importance of what occurred at the Temple. The rabbis obviously did not mind that God required blood and animal sacrifice to such an extent that the holy Temple is described as, effectively, a slaughterhouse of some proportion. The exaggerated descriptions also prove what the rabbis were happy to portray, namely that a very large number of animals were slaughtered in one day and that the Temple priests were wading up to their knees in sacrificial animal blood. So, amid all the exaggeration, we do find one kernel of truth and that is that the true religion was very bloody. In fact, the true religion is still very bloody, just awaiting the rebuilding of the Temple. At the time when it was fully functioning, and even allowing for all that exaggeration, the Temple must have been a magnet for the businesses surrounding ritual sacrifice, such as money-changing, innkeeping offering the many travelers somewhere to stay, and the selling of animals to those individuals who had not been able to bring their own sacrificial offerings.

What about Christianity? We know that, as an infant, the Jesus of the New Testament was presented at the Temple in Jerusalem. His mother, Mary, and her husband, Joseph, came to perform the sacrificial ceremony to redeem Jesus, the firstborn son, and to allow Mary to undergo ritual purification after giving birth to Jesus. The Gospel according to Luke, in which the story about Jesus being presented at the Temple as an infant is found, ensures that Joseph and Mary are portrayed as ordinary and rather poor people. In Luke, Joseph and Mary are described as not being able to offer a lamb because of their social and financial circumstances and go for the option provided for the poor, sacrificing instead two young pigeons.

We know that, later in life, Jesus was upset with the money-changers and the ongoing business around Temple sacrifice. But neither Jesus nor his early followers showed any negative sentiment towards Temple sacrifice.

Was perhaps the Roman destruction of the Temple in Jerusalem in the year 70 CE a great gift to the future generations of Jewish – and perhaps also Christian – people? Had the temple still been in existence, God-fearing Jews – and maybe Christians too – would, even up to the present day, have to follow all the rules about obligatory and voluntary burnt offerings, blood offerings and the waving of these offerings with animal sacrifice. There would, if the Third temple were rebuilt in our time, be attempts made to explain why we no longer need – and should therefore discontinue – burnt offerings and blood offerings in sacrifice to God. Except for the utmost fundamentalist believers, it would be clearly understood what damage to religious adherence the reintroduction of animal sacrifice to God would do. Do we not believe that most people might be disgusted and, in fact, reject God's requirement to sacrifice flesh and blood to Him?

Some rabbinical sages have already come to the conclusion that animal sacrifice was only on the menu because God did not want to take the Jews out of paganism too rapidly. Isn't that just another convenient explanation? The text in the Bible is, however, clear on this matter. God wants his burnt meat and his blood. How many Jews and Christians would, in today's world, be willing to go through the very primitive and barbaric exercise of offering animals as burnt offerings to God? The fact that the Temple does not exist and the fact that sacrifice cannot be performed in any other place than in the Temple has made God the mysterious figure of the Hebrew Bible and the New Testament. This is a God that we do not really know, but He is, nevertheless, everywhere. It is a God we do not really understand because He chooses not to let us – or make us – understand either Him or what He wishes from us. It is a God who does at least – having taken away the burning of the meat and the sprinkling of the blood – not seem as barbaric as would have been the case had the Temple in Jerusalem still been standing.

There is the strong, and perhaps central, feeling in Christianity that the sacrifice of Christ was the last and final sacrifice and that, after his crucifixion, animal sacrifice was no longer necessary. The prediction, found in the Gospel according to Mark, and made by Jesus regarding the destruction of the Temple, was very likely made after the Temple had been destroyed in 70 CE. It was easy to backdate the prediction and make it seem as if it were a prediction pointing to the destruction of the body of Christ and his eventual resurrection. Had the Temple not been destroyed, who knows what would have happened with burnt offerings among Christians at that time?

If Jesus were to visit us now and look at the many ways Christians have chosen to worship Him, he might be very surprised indeed. He might even be surprised that there exists any religion other than Judaism, which is, of course, the religion that he and his brother James seemed so intent on reforming. We can only talk about the Jesus of the New Testament, and there is no way of knowing if he was a historical person.

The church with the biggest number of followers is the Catholic Church headed by the pope. The pope is the vicar of Christ and God's representative on earth, and Catholics believe that they are in possession of the true religion. The pope in his capacity as representative of Christ has a special authority over the church and its followers. The priests in the Catholic Church also have a very special role as a sinner can go to a priest and confess his sins. It is called the sacrament of penance and is one of the seven sacraments recognised by the Catholic Church. Church doctrine advises Catholics to go to confession at least once a year and, if it is just once, they should choose the Easter season. If anybody has committed a very serious sin, such as adultery or even murder, they should expressly not receive communion without first going to confession. This may seem a bit odd, and one can only wonder what Jesus would have thought about all of this.

When Martin Luther came along, he wasn't too happy with the pope's abuse of power and the greed of the pope and his church at that time. He rejected the papacy and instituted some doctrinal changes, and so the Lutheran church was founded. It led ultimately to the Protestant reformation. All of these denominations have a somewhat different view on how to worship God, His son Jesus, and even the Holy Ghost.

We also find a number of orthodox churches such as the Russian, Ukrainian and Greek Orthodox Churches. Other Eastern Christian denominations that are well-known are the Coptic and the Assyrian churches.

Calvin had his own way of interpreting Luther and influenced the formation of the Reformed churches. But there is no reason – and frankly not enough space here – to go over all the various Christian denominations or perhaps religions. We should mention that Mormonism counts itself as a Christian religion. Nowadays, the Mormons prefer to be called The Church of Jesus Christ of Latter-Day Saints, or LDS.

The Mennonites and the Amish have found their own way of worshipping the Lord and in some instances do so by avoiding technological innovation. What you have to believe if you are Amish is that fairly modern technological advances, such as electricity, could be seen as bad or perhaps even evil, while the invention of the wheel, which made transportation so much easier, is for the good. That may seem to us somewhat arbitrary, but it is still what the Amish believe.

Contrast this negative view of technological advancement with Pope Francis, who, in his Encyclical on Climate Change and Inequality, made it clear that he is in favour of technological innovations and especially those "which can bring about an improvement in the quality of life." Those who are Christians may have some difficulty explaining away such inconsistencies and arbitrariness, and we have already discussed the very particular issues connected with the notion of the Holy Trinity. Since humour is a good way to create understanding, I would direct you to YouTube: Video 125 – *First day at school* where Dave Allen brilliantly describes the experience of the first day in Catholic school. It can be watched at https://www.youtube.com/watch?v=YQ3dL5tJx6M.

It is, ultimately, impossible to escape or dismiss the complexities and inconsistencies inherent in all the Abrahamic faiths. Let's have a little Christian recap. The true religion of a Christian is the belief in Jesus being the son of God. It is true religion to believe that Jesus was born of a virgin, who herself was conceived in an immaculate conception, without original sin, and that the pregnancy was caused by God himself. It is true Christianity to believe that Jesus was sent by his father to earth to suffer for our sins so that God could forgive us. The Christian belief is true religion only when we ignore the fact that God could have forgiven us for our sins without sacrificing His son. We would never have known that God, just out of the blue, decided to forgive us. Humanity would never have known that God decided that humanity needed to be forgiven. Maybe we should ask ourselves the following question: *has there been any noticeable change in the life of humanity and our own lives on earth just because Jesus was crucified?*

Further, to be a Christian, the true religion requires you to believe that Jesus was resurrected on the third day after his crucifixion.

Those who are Roman Catholic must not mind being cannibals, as discussed already. Those who are Roman Catholic must agree that the true religion allows for exorcism. Priests perform exorcisms to drive out evil from a possessed human. In Italy alone, there are supposedly more than half a million exorcisms performed every year, and it is believed that Mexico leads the world in terms of the number of annual exorcisms. If the pope didn't like this barbaric exercise, he could have stopped it. Pope Francis is, after all, both royal and the dictator of the Catholic Church. Instead of banning exorcisms, he did not even criticise the practice when, in April 2020, an Italian archbishop made that call for the entire planet to pray together in a worldwide exorcism to defeat the coronavirus. Exorcism, it seems, now has a wider meaning than just expelling demons.

Those who are Roman Catholic must have thought about the difference between annulment and divorce. *Divorce* is not allowed, but *annulment* may be granted. Divorce is when the two parties in a marriage decide to go their separate ways. Annulment is the notion that the marriage never really happened in the first place. The church is against sex before marriage, so where does this leave the children that have been conceived while the parties have been married but before the marriage was annulled? The church claims that there is nothing illegitimate about the children of an annulled marriage.

We cannot help but ask ourselves that if the marriage never happened, wasn't the sex that produced the children illegitimate? We might add that since the children of an annulled marriage – a marriage that never was – can be baptised and even become priests, isn't annulment just divorce by another name?

Those who are homosexual and believe that they can find solace in either Jewish holy texts or through Jesus have not fully understood the true religion. The true religion of both Judaism and Christianity is expressly opposed to homosexual acts – especially male ones – with the prescribed penalty being death.

A practising Catholic woman, having gone through her pregnancy and looking forward to giving birth to her baby, finds that the baby is stillborn. What does the true Catholic religion say now happens to that baby? The true Catholic religion wants us to believe that baptism is necessary for salvation, and baptism can only be performed on the living. The grieving mother now has to find comfort in other ways to be allowed to believe that her stillborn baby will somehow end up in heaven after all. Although in recent years the Catholic Church has taken a more positive view on the chances of a stillborn baby reaching heaven, it is still a bit tenuous.

What does Roman Catholic baptism do? What it does is welcome infants into the Catholic faith and free them from the "original sin" that they were born with. Really? God is obviously so vengeful that He still cannot forgive all future generations stemming from Adam and Eve all that time ago. That alone is surely quite horrendous, that all of us suffer from the fall of man way back at the "beginning of humanity" in the Garden of Eden. Since humanity does continue to sin, confession has also been introduced to seek forgiveness for new sins that we are ourselves responsible for. And, remember, this is despite Jesus having already died for our sins. So, we must ask ourselves: do we believe that the main purpose of confession is to relieve the sinner of guilt or is it, rather, to create dependence on the structure of the church? Do we perhaps believe that baptism is better for the baby than it is for the church? Do we believe that either baptism or confession is effective in any way in the eyes of God? Do we believe that it would make any difference if a sinner turned directly to God without the interference of religious organisations that make themselves relevant with various arcane rites? Do we in any way believe that God Himself is bound by these rites which are made up by the church?

So, the baby has to be born alive to be baptised. Baptism is a ritual that includes at its ceremonial heart the sprinkling of some water on the baby. It is normally performed in church, and the sprinkling of this water, freshly blessed by the priest, is accompanied by the parents having to reject Satan and all his works and all his empty promises. Really? Why? Why not ask the bigger question, namely why God allows Satan to exist at all? Short of wiping Satan out – which would, of course, be the best Godly alternative – we ask: why does God ever engage with Satan and treat him as if he were an equal? That is exactly what God does, as we have noted earlier, in the book of Job in the Old Testament, when God makes a bet with Satan. Satan bets that he can turn Job away from God. Satan is allowed to do just about anything with Job except kill him, but Job does not turn against God. So, God wins the bet. Did we expect anything else? And yet, to our surprise, God has made a bet with Satan. With Satan! God Himself doesn't seem to renounce Satan at all, does he?

Here is a good place to ask ourselves, and perhaps even ask God, the following question: does God really need to allow the Devil to exist only to tempt us to be more evil than we are naturally capable of being?

Let us examine the situation with a stillborn baby a little more. We have an event where God obviously knows that the baby is going to be stillborn and yet He does not intervene. We have a situation where, after the baby is stillborn, further punishment is exacted, at least by the church, by sowing doubts as to whether the baby can reach heaven without being baptised. Let us assume – and this hypothetical exercise is unquestionably grim but not, sadly, purely fanciful – the baby is born alive but happens to pass away before the parents manage to get the baptism performed. That would also leave the poor baby in a sort of limbo. This situation must be dealt with. One idea would be to sprinkle the baby with some water immediately after birth to ensure that she has been baptised. Wow, one might ask, is that possible? The church obviously has an interest in keeping rituals alive to keep the flock dependent on the clergy who perform these rituals. In the end, it is God who decides what to do with the result of the rituals. But there is papal authority for anybody sprinkling some water on a person and magically rendering them baptised and Catholic. Pope Pius IX showed the way. During the year 1857, Father Feletti of Bologna came to know that a maid who had worked for seven years in a Jewish family's household had secretly baptised a toddler who was the Jewish son of this family. She was, in good faith one should assume, trying to save the boy from death while he was a baby and did so by baptising him. It was concluded within the church that the maid, having baptised the toddler, made the child Catholic. The church further concluded that it was forbidden to raise Catholic children in families of a different faith. This led to the final act where the pope himself had the young boy, Edgardo, kidnapped and taken away from his parents to treat him as if he were his own son and raise him to become a priest. The young Jewish boy would, against his parents' wishes, become – at least as close as one can get to be – the son of that pope. If the sprinkling of some water by anybody, even an ignorant nanny, can turn a baby into a properly baptised Catholic, then perhaps the church rituals are completely unnecessary.

For the stillborn child and its parents, the church has found all kinds of excuses. It can't be explained, so it must be explained away. The priest may let the grieving parents know that is not a bad situation after all. The grieving mother should take comfort in the fact that God is, after all, good and may choose to allow the baby into heaven anyway. Another explanation is that God, who knows everything, knows which of the babies would have chosen to live a good Catholic life and therefore be let into heaven. Also, the mother should speculate that, at the moment of death, the baby gets to choose to love and serve God or to reject God. As with the angels, one-third of whom rejected God, such a baby is therefore freely choosing hell. Stillborn babies must be given the free will to reject God. Finally, another explanation given to comfort the grieving mother is that she should understand that God loves this child far more than any of us humans ever could. What are we now saying about the true religion of Catholicism regarding stillborn babies? Do we find any of this in the slightest bit humane? And if God so loves this stillborn baby, why did He not intervene and allow the baby to live, which He could have chosen to do? Instead, the priest would let the grieving parents know that God might indeed act after the fact, the fact being that the baby entered the world stillborn.

In 2007, the Vatican announced that a papal investigation resulted in a re-evaluation of the concept of limbo. Stillborn babies no longer necessarily have to end up in a waiting room somewhere between hell and heaven, the limbo in question. The church has difficulty explaining what has happened to all the babies who were caught in limbo. We can go all the way back to the mid 300s CE and St. Augustine, who concluded that if the baby has not been baptised it must be burning in the fires of hell but with the "mildest condemnation". Thomas Aquinas, who lived in the 1300s CE, concluded that a stillborn baby would not go to heaven but did not necessarily have to suffer in the afterlife. They would not know what they were missing. Most of us understand that after we die, we do not know much about what will be going on around us anyway. Let us rephrase that and state that, once we are dead, we have lost contact with the natural world and know nothing about what is going on around us. The new Vatican doctrine is not entirely comforting for a grieving mother. It is clear that the church has changed its mind and a stillborn baby could go directly to heaven, but there is no certainty that that will happen.

In both Judaism and Christianity, women have no direct role in teaching and praying. In Judaism, there needs to be a quorum of ten men from the age of thirteen upwards to comply with certain religious obligations. In Christianity, women have been told to be silent in their congregations. That is the true religion, and yet we find Jewish congregations with female rabbis and we have female ministers in several Protestant congregations. Having female rabbis and ministers is in clear opposition to – if not violation of – the holy texts. There is nothing in these texts that allows us to interpret them so as to allow women to serve in those capacities.

Women priests and rabbis come only from *re*interpreting the holy texts to fit modern liberal views. God Himself doesn't care about modern liberal views. Once the various religious denominations decide that they can have female rabbis and ministers, have they not stepped away from the clear language in the holy texts? When religious congregations allow female clergy and gay marriage, have they not stepped away from holy prescriptions? The penalty for male homosexual lovemaking is, after all, death. By allowing gay marriage and female clergy, do such congregations not become an entirely social organisation and no longer a religious one? We do not mind, but it is difficult to tamper with – or, worse, go against – God's expressed will and then still claim to worship Him.

We know that the Jews do not send out missionaries to convert followers of other religions or nonbelievers. In fact, becoming Jewish requires a lengthy conversion process. If you are male, you have to finish that off with circumcision, which is a painful affair in adult life.

We know that many Christian denominations do try to convince followers of other religions and nonbelievers to join in the belief in Christ. If you die without having embraced the son of the Lord, you will end up burning in hell forever and ever. That is the true religion or, to be clearer, the consequence of denying the true religion.

Sometimes, Christians try to persuade their Jewish counterparts to become Christians through a form of trickery that would allow them to believe that they are still Jewish while having converted to Christianity. *Jews for Jesus* is an astonishing attempt to convert Jews out of their religion. One of the main differences between Judaism and Christianity is that the Jews are still awaiting the Messiah of the Old Testament. They may well be in for a long wait because the conditions required for the Messiah to arrive on this earth seem to be very far from being realised. In Christianity, of course, the Messiah has already arrived.

The son of God, Jesus, is, rather oddly, also seen as a Messiah from the house of King David. We know that the gospels traced Jesus' ancestry to King David over Joseph, the husband of Mary, which makes the kinship between Jesus and King David very doubtful. But the central fact remains that the Jews are still waiting for the Messiah and the Christians no longer are.

In simple terms, you cannot be Jewish and believe that Jesus is the Messiah in much the same way that you cannot be a Christian and wait for the Jewish Messiah to arrive as if Jesus had not already come as the saviour of Christianity. True religion would, in this case, mean that *Jews for Jesus* is the equivalent, the other way around, of *Christians against Christ*: both are equally impossible.

True religion never blames God for anything. When something awful occurs, it is either our fault or a natural event. In 2004, almost 230,000 people died when a gigantic tsunami hit various Indian Ocean coastlines. The tsunami was set in motion by an earthquake under the sea and very quickly created waves up to 40 m in height. The gigantic tsunami not only killed 230,000 people but turned coastal cities into debris. There was not a cleric who asked why God did not stop the tsunami, but the world went down on its knees in gratitude when a few survivors were eventually found in the rubble left in the aftermath of the destructive waves.

On September 11, 2001, Islamist Al-Qaeda terrorists hijacked four commercial aeroplanes to use them for maximum killing and destruction. The hijackers flew two of them into the Twin Towers of the World Trade Center. One hijacked plane was flown into the Pentagon, and one crashed after an onboard revolt staged by passengers and crew.

I remember seeing a television discussion with the participants being a Jewish rabbi, a Christian cleric and a Muslim cleric. To the best of my recollection, on the question of whether you should blame God for not intervening, the three clerics all agreed that you simply can't do that. They also agreed that you should thank God for the good that people did in rescuing others and thereby minimising the catastrophe and making it a smaller success for the terrorists than it otherwise would have been.

After a terrible occurrence, we are supposed to blame ourselves or accept natural causes but God is mostly there only after the event.

The media are quick to use the term *miracle*. On the afternoon of August 2, 2005, Air France flight 358 had landed at the international airport in Toronto. The plane did not manage to stop on the runway and crashed about 300 m beyond the runway. Of the 309 passengers on board, 12 were seriously injured, but all passengers and crew survived. All survived because of the diligent and well-trained flight attendants' good work. The crew organised a speedy and efficient evacuation effort that got everybody on the plane to safety before the burning plane exploded. On television, the journalist kept asking whether the rescue of all the passengers and crew was not a miracle. We know the answer. It was, as noted, good work by the very well-trained crew that got all on board off the plane. What would have been a miracle? It would have been if, after the plane had exploded, we saw passengers and crew disembarking in good order and still alive.

We have reason to ask ourselves whether religion is there for us ordinary people or rather in the interests of the institutions built up around the various beliefs. The Catholic Church, for instance, has an infallible pope who has, throughout history, made a remarkably large number of mistakes. The church has to be careful with apologies for mistakes because that would mean that popes are not infallible after all.

When one is given a gift, one should gladly accept it. I felt I was given a gift on 21 October 2020 when I was watching *Amanpour* on CNN. One of the guests was a Jesuit priest, Father James Martin. Father Martin is known for having lobbied his Catholic Church to show more understanding towards the LBGTQ+ community. He had appeared previously on CNN with Ms. Amanpour on March 13, 2018.

On October 21, I saw a very, very happy Father Martin. In a documentary that had just been released, the pope called for civil unions for same-sex couples. No wonder Father Martin felt so happy. His lobbying efforts seem to have borne fruit. The papal pronouncement was, in Ms. Amanpour's words, "a truly momentous move for the Roman Catholic Church". It did not take long for the pope to be condemned by many Catholic leaders. The pope did not make this statement from the pulpit. It is therefore not technically counted as infallible. But it is the pope, and, as father Martin pointed out, the church and congregants would have to listen.

First, let me make it absolutely clear that, personally, I do not care what sexual activity any adult engages in with another adult so long as it is consensual. We should be happy about the papal acknowledgement that same-sex couples may need to be in families and have legal rights in their relationships. That is, however, not what we are looking at here. We have no reason to doubt that the pope fully understands that same-sex couples may well engage in gay sex acts. Ms. Amanpour rightly asks Father Martin to clarify what the pope has done. She asks, "Has he broken from official doctrine? Has he created something new? Is he just clarifying views? What's going on?"

Father Martin answers that he thinks that the pope is creating a new space for LGBTQ+ people. The pope has now come to a different view from the 2003 document from the Congregation of the Doctrine of the Faith which was against same-sex unions. Father Martin continues, "It's momentous because he's saying it as pope. He said it before as archbishop of Buenos Aires. He's saying it on the record, and he's being very clear. It is not simply he's tolerating it, he's supporting."

In the interview, Ms. Amanpour rightly points out that "the official doctrine in the church still considers and states in black-and-white that homosexuality is a disordered state." She continues, "I believe Pope Benedict went further and, you know, aligned it with the work of the Devil and such."

So, what was the gift to me? We know that church doctrine is not freestanding and detached from the biblical text. We know that in the Old Testament, gay male sexual activity is subject to the penalty of death. We know that in the New Testament, lesbian sexual activity is subject to equal condemnation to its male equivalent.

The gift to me is that it helps me make two points. The first is that if the pope feels that he can make such a momentous declaration, he does so in clear and direct contradiction of the biblical law which forbids gay sex. Perversely, one can come to the conclusion that the pope has demonstrated that he can ignore God's law. Has Pope Francis not, as a result of his coming out in favour of same-sex unions, made it clear to us that the Catholic Church is a very large social club and not a religious institution? There was, I hasten to add, not a word about any of this from the happy Father Martin.

My second point is that religion, belief, faith, and religious leaders are all treated with deference. Pope Francis, who is hailed as a great reformer, is perhaps more than most handled with kid gloves. Ms. Amanpour is a seasoned interviewer. I have seen her tackle difficult issues and ask the necessary questions to get to the core of any issue. But, in her interview with Father Martin, she signally failed to go the distance. My point here is not to teach Ms. Amanpour the techniques of interviewing, but still, she might have asked father Martin: **Who is the boss?** Is it God or is it the pope? And, if the pope can reinterpret God's law in respect of civil unions which would lead to the acknowledgement and the official Catholic sanctioning of gay sex, why can he not reinterpret the entire Old and New Testament to fit with our Western liberal views?

We need to repeat and emphasise that we are not taking issue with the pope's being in favour of civil unions. We need to stress that there is no reason not to respect consenting adults in their right to engage in whatever kind of sex they may wish. It comes down to whether the Catholic Church finds itself forced to adapt to modern times and modern views. It comes down to this question: if the pope is not bound by the word of God, which believer should be?

If a woman has sought out a medical doctor to perform an abortion on her, she is to be excommunicated. The many priests who have sexually abused children in their care and even raped nuns seem to get away with a slap on the wrist or just suspension from duty. In many instances, the predatory priests are sent to other parishes to serve. It does not seem to be in the church's interests to excommunicate the misbehaving priests.

CHAPTER 7

We know, don't we, that the priests have gotten away with their behaviour for almost 2000 years and have only recently been caught by secular forces? Do we understand that we have become able to take on the priestly class only because we have finally mustered the secular strength? Very few of the abusing priests or church laypeople in positions that gave them power over the flock have been sent to prison, mainly because they have been moved around within the church, perhaps awaiting the various statutes of limitation to run out so that they could no longer be prosecuted. It seems to us, then, doesn't it, that the Roman Catholic Church looks after its own interests first. To the extent that there are other similar religious organisations – and there are – it is reasonable to assume that they also look after their own organisation first, and the followers of that *true religion* only secondarily.

All religions have a reason for their followers to remain in the fold. The Jews are the chosen people, chosen by God, to guide the rest of the peoples of the world. The true religion of those who are Christians is that at the end of your life it is only faith in Jesus Christ that will bring you salvation. That takes out most of the world's population, and the Christ-deniers or the ones who have never heard of Christ will definitely not go to heaven but instead be subjected to eternal torture after death.

The followers of Islam believe that Muhammad is the last and final prophet and a perfect man whose miracle is the perfect book, the Quran. The Quran contains all truth. Some followers of Islam thus maintain that they alone are the chosen knowers and bearers of the absolute and eternal truth.

In the middle of all of this, we find ecumenical efforts and interfaith efforts. Ecumenical efforts are to try to bridge the gap between the very many Christian ways of interpreting their holy scriptures and worshipping Christ. Interfaith efforts can best be described as an attempt to create and foster understanding between the various religions and especially between the three religions following in the footsteps of Abraham, namely Judaism, Christianity, and Islam.

So, what happens after an ecumenical effort? There is really nobody who leaves an ecumenical conference or an interfaith conference with the understanding that the other religion is just as good as their own. After all, their own religion is the only *true* one. After all the fine words of understanding and respect for each other have been communicated, nobody's true religion has really changed nor anyone's attitude to it. Interfaith love-fests change very little – if anything at all.

A very simple example will demonstrate the fact that each religion still believes itself to be the only true religion. In the summer of 2020, Turkey announced its intentions of converting the Hagia Sophia from a museum to a mosque. Hagia Sophia was once a very important Christian church. Turning a museum that used to be a church into a mosque does not sound that terrible to a nonbeliever. It is a fantastic building in a Muslim-majority country, and the people wanted it to be a mosque. That serves as evidence that their true religion comes first, irrespective of any hurt it may inflict on other true religions. The pope was upset because of the Christian heritage of that particular building and wished it to remain a museum. One might be allowed to suspect that had Pope Francis had the power to turn the Hagia Sophia back into a church, he would have done so. A true conflict between two true religions will never be solved through interfaith efforts.

With all understanding of other religions, religious Jews will not give up their belief that the Messiah has not yet come to visit us on earth and that Jesus was only an ordinary man.

Nor will Muslims ever give up their true religion, which holds that their holy texts are the last word on how to worship Allah, who is the same as God and Yahweh in Christianity and Judaism.

Evangelical Christians find in their midst many supporters of the state of Israel and its Jewish population. It is, however, a very tenuous relationship. The true religion of these true believers tells them that it is good that Israel's Jewish population grows and that the country of Israel expands to incorporate certain historically and politically sensitive geographical areas. Deep down, they know that there will be a war in the area and that that war may lead to Armageddon, which happens to be the precondition for the second coming of Christ. Once

CHAPTER 7

Jesus does arrive, the Jews of Israel, being former allies of the true-believing evangelicals, will be sent to burn for eternity. And they will be sent to burn together with the surrounding Muslims and, of course, the nonbelievers and Christian believers not in possession of the true religion practised by these evangelicals. Only the truest of the true believers, among whose number these believers must count themselves, will enjoy the rapture and be transported to heaven at the second coming of Christ.

It is, incidentally, common among Christians to ask what Jesus would say or to wish that he would return to this earth to give us good guidance. These true believers should be careful what they wish for. Jesus' second coming would be at the end of times when the very few true believers will be saved.

Let's leave that aside and assume that what they are really asking for is for Jesus to come back to earth without, at the same time, taking out most of the world's population. The second coming of Christ might otherwise make the pandemic of 2019–2021 look like child's play. Let us beware. Even you may, after all, be sent to burn for all eternity. You can never be certain that your way of worshipping Christ is the only way approved by Jesus Himself.

But, really, what are these true religionists wishing for? They are obviously wishing for the end of democracy as there would be no voting. There can, of course, be no democracy in a situation where the son of God, who is himself God, is present. He might want to reintroduce slavery and you may be on the wrong end of the stick and become a slave. If Jesus had picked you to be a slave, there would be no court to appeal to. You could pray to God, but Jesus is God.

You also need to be convinced that you are one of the really true believers and believe in Jesus in precisely the right way. You must be certain that you are in possession of the only true religion and that Jesus agrees with you. Remember that there are very many Christian denominations who have their own way of worshipping Jesus. Which one of these very many ways of worshipping Jesus will he find to be correct? It would be good to acknowledge that any one can be mistaken about our particular way of worshipping Jesus. God's ways and reasons are mysterious and He has, for mysterious reasons, chosen to express

Himself in ways that we do not really understand. You cannot be certain that Jesus agrees with your particular way of expressing your faith in Him, can you?

There are so many different religions and religious denominations that we must conclude that not all of them can be right at the same time. There are so many Christian denominations, or religions, that perhaps not even Jesus, were he ever to come back, would have recognised which one is, in his name, the true religion.

Which one of us can, under these circumstances, have confidence that we are in possession of the true religion? Which one of us can, with confidence, believe that we are in a good place with our true religion and will be saved by our God?

Consider this. If you tell the world that you hear the voices of Zeus in your head and he tells you to do things that you do not want to do, you may well end up in a mental institution. Why is it that if you are Christian and hear the voice of Jesus, you may be considered something of a prophetic hero destined, quite possibly, for sainthood?

In 1982, when I was a much younger man, I got a consulting assignment from the United Nations that took me to Vanuatu, formerly known as the New Hebrides. Vanuatu, which had become independent from joint British and French rule, consists of a chain of islands in the South Pacific, not too far from New Caledonia and New Guinea. A cult religion had developed on the island, and the followers were expecting a Messiah-like figure, John Frum, to come and magically deliver worldly goods to the believers. When American GIs came to the island during the Second World War, the cult followers could see how beer was taken out cold from refrigerators. This led to boxes being put in the forest overnight in the hope that some magically cold beer would appear in them too. The cult followers could also see military aeroplanes landing and delivering goods to the islands. This eventually made the cult followers clear areas of the forest for magical landing strips intended for magical deliveries.

If you're familiar with the Rogers and Hammerstein musical *South Pacific*, you will know that the song Bali Hai was inspired by the sight of Ambae island

CHAPTER 7

of the New Hebrides, now Vanuatu. After the war, the Americans were ordered to dump substantial amounts of military hardware into the ocean. The dumping spot became known as Million Dollar Point. There were tales in Vanuatu of illicit trading with military men, and very likely some military material was, against orders, sold in the area instead of being dumped.

It is easy to smile at the absurdity of the religion waiting for John Frum to arrive and bring worldly goods by magic. When I prepared for the trip to Vanuatu, I read up on the culture of the islands, and while in Vanuatu, I had the opportunity to speak to people for further inquiry. I came across the following story about a missionary who had approached a cult follower and wanted him to convert to Christianity. Of course, the missionary tried his best arguments, knowing full well that he was in charge of the true religion. He started by asking how it was that cult followers could still be waiting for John Frum, who had not yet arrived to deliver anything after about 40 years. We can bet that the missionary never expected the brilliant response which was that, as far as the cult follower was concerned, that is much less of a waiting time than the Christians who have been waiting almost 2000 years for Jesus to return. It is easy to conclude that the two individuals engaged in the conversation each believed that he himself was in possession of the true religion. Should we perhaps also conclude that, no matter what they believed, neither of them was right?

A good way to end this chapter is to ask a few questions with Occam's razor in mind.

Jewish believers must understand that their true religion is a religion of animal sacrifice to a bloodthirsty God. Jews must therefore ask themselves: are prayers any good when God really wants burned flesh and blood?

Muslims must ask themselves if the Quran really holds all truths for eternity. So much scientific progress has been made in the years since the Quran was revealed to Muhammad. Can it really be that any observation in nature that is not in line with Quranic text must be false?

Members of the Church of England, which has replaced the pope as head of the church with the royal head of state, have a few questions to ask themselves:

Is the Church of England's way of worshipping Christ a truer religion than Catholicism? Would there even have been a Church of England had Henry VIII not wanted to divorce his wife? Would there have been a Church of England had the pope found a way to perhaps fix an annulment of Henry VIII's marriage to Catherine of Aragon? Yet those who have grown up inside the Church of England may believe, insist even, that it is the true religion.

The Covid-19 pandemic is still ongoing as I write in the late autumn of 2020. Many religious people and quite a few leaders of all three Abrahamic religions are anxious to get their flocks into their respective houses of worship. God, who is everywhere, does not seem to be making much of an effort to hinder the spread of the virus outside of the houses of worship. One must, therefore, wonder why it is expected that God would do a better job inside churches, mosques, or synagogues. Our scientists tell us, incidentally, that the risk of contagion is substantially higher indoors.

One is left to suspect that it is in the interest of at least some religious leaders to keep their flock under control. Some ultra-religious Jewish leaders have come out in favour of their flock coming to synagogue to pray. It is very likely a selfish act by the leaders to retain control and prevent a number of their flock from discovering that there is a life outside of the synagogue and beyond the rabbi's congregation. However, the elderly in the congregation are at high risk of dying should they get infected by Covid-19 while in the synagogue.

In Judaism, there is one overriding rule that stipulates that one is allowed to break almost any biblical rule in order to save a life or lives. An example of this is the rescue team of deeply religious Jewish men who came to the capital of Haiti after the earthquake in 2010. They took a little time out from their rescue mission on the Sabbath to pray and then continued their work on the understanding that not keeping the Sabbath holy in order to save lives is completely permissible. Obviously, it is permissible to not keep the Sabbath holy in order to save non-Jewish lives.

Is it reasonable to assume that if Jesus arrived on earth today, he would fail to understand how, in heaven's name, all the various Christian denominations and their different ways of worshipping Him have come about? Would Jesus understand that the various Christian denominations have gone to war against each other because of the different ways of interpreting the holy texts of the New Testament?

> How do we even begin to know whether any of us, belonging to a certain religion or denomination, is in possession of the true religion in a world where everybody else's religion and denomination is, consequentially, in possession of the wrong version?

And one final Occam's Razor question: if there was true ecumenical and interfaith understanding, would there be any need for either missionaries or forceful conversions?

CHAPTER 8

Why is it ... that, in spite of best efforts, creationism does not make it into other than pseudo-science?

When we move to examine creationism, we must understand that it is an attempt to counter the scientific explanations regarding evolution. We must also recognise that when we examine creationism, we have moved away from the creation story, or even the two different creation stories, in the Bible. The reason that creationism has become a modern pseudo-science is very likely that it is difficult for educated people of today to wrap their heads around the biblical stories concerning how the universe was created. Most of us have been educated to understand that the earth is billions of years old and the universe even older. The six-day creation story, with God resting on the seventh day, doesn't quite fit in, and it definitely does not feel scientific enough for anybody who has had decent schooling. The people who have had decent schooling are currently interested in science and scientific explanations, in line with how and what they have been taught at school. It is for this reason that this strand of **pseudo-science** has come along to try to explain to us, in ways that at least superficially have a scientific feel, how the world came to be. In the first of the biblical creation stories, God created everything using commanding words. An example is "Let there be light." It also seems that God, after each step in his creation, was pleased with what He had accomplished because He "saw that it was good." We do take note yet again, don't we, that it is surprising that God would be surprised that His creation was good.

Creationism is, be in no doubt, a belief that belongs to the sphere of religion and not to science. We have been taught during our school years that science is there to be disproved and new science will replace old science forever and eternally. At every point in time, we believe only in the best scientific explanations available to us, knowing full well that there could be further discoveries and changes to these scientific explanations.

Creationists want to explain to us why our universe, our planet, life on our planet, and all human beings on planet earth could have come about only by acts best described as supernatural. This brings us back to some form of God figure who has created us and everything around us.

Creationists try to convince us that the universe and our earth are too perfect not to have a creator. Creationists also try to poke holes in the theory of evolution. Creationists have latched onto the fact that it is called the *theory* of evolution. The implication is that the word *theory* demonstrates that it is one of many possible theories. The argument that a scientific theory is just a theory is a deliberate misstatement, a wilful misunderstanding of how scientists define scientific theory.

What scientists want to show is that a scientific theory is the best explanation we have while still being open to further discovery. The National Academy of Sciences defines a *theory* in science as "a well-substantiated explanation of some aspects of the natural world that can incorporate facts, laws, inferences, and tested hypotheses." The law of gravity is a law as far as it describes the force of gravity. We know the force and we can calculate how long an object takes to fall to the ground from a certain height. We know that an object falling freely to earth accelerates at about 9.81 m/s^2. The explanation of *how* the force of gravity works is, together with other explanations of natural phenomena, called a theory. We need to understand that a scientific theory is not mere speculation. We should, instead, understand that a scientific theory is the best explanation available to us of what we can observe in nature... for now.

We are not going to go through all creationist ideas but, instead, concentrate on only a few in the hope that the discussion around a few of these arguments will show us to what extent we can accept creationism as science. Perhaps we will also want to see to what extent creationist arguments make a dent in evolutionary theory and other scientific descriptions of everything from how our universe came to be down to our solar system, our planet, and all living things on earth.

The first argument we are going to look at is that **everything must have a beginning**. As far back as in the thirteenth century, St. Thomas Aquinas, who lived between 1225 and 1274 CE, developed what he believed to be a way of showing that there must have been a God. He argued that everything in the cosmos must have a cause and if you go back in time, you may find a series of causes but there must have been a first cause. Thomas Aquinas concluded from this argument that the first cause is God and He is a necessary being. Having come to the conclusion that God is a necessary being, outside our space and time but able to act within our space and time, there is no need to explain God, and God therefore needs no cause.

What would we think is a proper way of countering that argument? Even Thomas Aquinas does not properly argue his case. He merely states that God needs no explanation. That is, we must stress, extremely unscientific. Just stating that something does not need explaining does not mean that no explanation is necessary. Only those who wish to believe in something without evidence can accept the argument of Thomas Aquinas. If you wished to employ scientific methods, you would need some evidence as to why everything else needs explaining but not the creator, God.

Stephen Hawking and Leonard Mlodinow wrote *The Grand Design*. In their book, the authors claim that it is reasonable to ask who created the universe. But if the answer is that God created the universe, that gives rise to the question, *who created God?* We can absolutely not let that counter-question remain hanging, unanswered. If the argument is that everything must have a beginning, then God must also have been created. And if the answer is that there was another God before Him, then we can go back as many steps as we like. If everything must have a beginning or a creator, then it is clear that God must also have been created. By whom? By what?

In more modern times, some creationists want us to believe that everything – from the universe to our earth and life on it – is so perfect that it cannot have come about by coincidences, natural causes or natural selection à la Darwin. Instead, they claim, there must be a creator.

The Big Bang Theory, which is the prevailing theory about how our universe was created, has yet to be fully explained and is therefore used by first-cause theorists as part of a first-cause argument. God created the Big Bang and brought the universe into existence. That the biblical creation stories give no evidence of such a creation is ignored. Modern creationists, some of whom accept evolution, still claim that the perfection we see around us comes from a creator, whether called God or not. They talk of a creator who just decided to set everything in motion and do nothing more but allow the universe to evolve on its own.

Our astronomers can explain that our universe came into existence around 13 billion years ago in something that could be described as a gigantic explosion, often referred to as the Big Bang. Our scientists find evidence in how the universe continues to expand and are able to trace this Big Bang back to a very, very small fraction of a second. Our scientists are not able to bring us all the way to the absolute beginning of the Big Bang. A very small fraction of a second remains thus far unexplained. In science, when you do not know exactly how something has come about, you say just that. If you invoke God or a creator (outside the biblical stories), then you have already made up your mind. Once your mind is made up that a creator set it all in motion and is responsible for that tiny, tiny fraction of a second to get the Big Bang started, you have set aside all other possible explanations. As soon as you have decided that there are no other possible explanations for an event you cannot fully describe, you have left the field of science. If you have decided that you know how it happened, you still have not explained how the creator came to be. After all, the necessity for a creator outside of our natural universe rests on the case that everything needs a beginning. Do we see the circularity in this argument?

The main difference we find here is that when scientists cannot explain exactly how the first tiny fraction of a second of the Big Bang occurred, they tell us. Believers in creationism make the case that there is a gap that needs to be filled and that gap needs a creator. It is a matter of taste whether that creator could be the God of the Bible or an undefined and unknown creator found in the supernatural sphere outside our universe. So, as is maintained by some creationists, God created the universe by interfering in that tiny fraction of a second. Here is a point for us to consider. *Why?* Why would a creator set the universe in motion and then stand back to see how it evolves? Perhaps the creator has set up different universes, some of which we do not see. Perhaps the creator regarded it all as a game just to see how their various futures would develop.

When some point to the necessity of a creator, they are stepping outside the natural world. That creator obviously has to be in a different space and time, and outside of our natural world, to be able to start up our universe. Our scientists would say that there is no reason to believe that there is not a natural explanation for what occurred in that tiny fraction of a second. The fact that they cannot yet explain the absolute beginning of the Big Bang does not mean that it may not come to be fully understood sometime in the future. Whether an explanation for the beginning of the Big Bang is found or not, it is still a step too far to say that the explanation must be found in the supernatural.

If we take the number 1 and divide it by ½, we come to the answer 2. If you take the same number 1 and divide it by 1/10, the answer will be 10. Again, the same number divided by 1 millionth becomes a million, and the lower the number you divide one by, the closer to infinity you get. Zero equals nothing, and if you divide one by a number next to zero, you end up with a number next to infinity. When you finally divide 1 by 0, the answer, somewhat unexpectedly, is that one divided by zero is undefined. Using our imagination just a little allows us to come to the conclusion that nothing, equaling zero, goes an infinite number of times into one or any number. Although there is no absolute evidence that the answer to the division one divided by zero is infinity, it doesn't defy human imagination. We may feel that it is too far-fetched to search for a creationist answer by looking for the gap between dividing one by an enormously small number and dividing it by zero. The whole chain points to 1÷0 being equal to infinity or, in terms of time, eternity.

There was a time when thunder and lightning were seen as the result of the action of the Nordic God Thor wielding his hammer. We have grown away from that one and many other supernatural explanations for thunder and lightning and now understand that it is a fully natural, meteorological phenomenon to do with electrical charges.

Some of us may wake up at night having had a bad dream. A man who has recently lost his wife may dream that she is talking to him. Most of us will understand that that dream comes from processes in our brain. A few may want to explain that something supernatural happened and that they were actually visited by the deceased spouse.

The world around us is complex, and we try to simplify what we perceive to be able to take it in. For instance, we see patterns where there are none. Many of us will have seen patterns or images in clouds when we look up into the sky. We could see a horse or a human face, but we know that neither horse nor face exists. It is just our brain trying to identify patterns. In this, we might appreciate our brain's ability to imagine make-believe relationships and should be content with leaving it as such.

At this point, it might be good to examine the universe around us to see what our senses tell us and what is actually going on. An understanding of what we see or feel compared to what we know the reality to be may help us to realise that a creator is, in fact, quite unnecessary.

When we sit down at the dinner table and put our plates, cutlery and glasses on the table, we are under the distinct impression that the table is solid. How could we otherwise put anything on the table? Let us scrutinise this table by magnifying it so that we can explore it down to the atomic level.

The first element, and simplest atom, is hydrogen, with the chemical symbol H. Hydrogen consists of a core, or nucleus, of one proton which has a positive electrical charge, and one electron with a negative charge that is making its way around the nucleus; perhaps one can somewhat unscientifically describe it as circling the nucleus. That one electron finds itself at a substantial distance from the proton. Let's scale this atom up and see how much space it would take up if the proton were the size of a golf ball. The answer is that it would be around 2.5 km or a little over 1.5 miles between the proton/golf ball and the electron. Everything in between is just empty space. Atoms of one element can form a bond with atoms of the same element or another one, and the combination makes a molecule and/or compound. When two hydrogen atoms log onto one oxygen atom, the resulting molecule is water, H^2O. Both hydrogen and oxygen are naturally, individually, a gas, but when combined, they turn into a liquid. Whatever material the table is made of, it consists of an enormous number of atoms, and each atom has within it an enormous amount of empty space.

Now let us scale this back down again and consider what the table consists of. There is almost nothing but empty space in the table (between and within atoms). The problem is that our senses do not pick that up so, in "our" world, that table is solid. How much empty space in any matter can be described by looking at our planet? If we assume that it would be possible to compress our entire planet by taking out all empty space inside each atom making up our planet, planet Earth would end up being approximately the size of a basketball.

We understand, here, that our senses may not always provide us with the most reliable information. Take something as simple as touching, for instance. Particles, by nature, attract other particles with an opposite charge and repel particles with similar charges. Every time we touch something, literally anything, we are feeling the electromagnetic force of electrons repelling other electrons. Which begs the question: have we really ever touched anything? Just something to keep in mind.

CHAPTER 8

Around 60% of an adult human's body is made up of water. Yet we can walk around, swim, and even jump up and down while the water stays in place tied up inside the body.

When we see sunlight on earth it is already eight minutes old. Eight minutes is approximately the time it takes for light emitted from the sun to reach us on earth. Whenever we look at the night sky, we see only the past and oftentimes millions and millions of years back in time. The sun is obviously the closest star to earth and is the centre of our solar system. The second closest three stars are in the Alpha Centauri system, and they are around 4.3 light-years from earth. That means that it takes about 4.3 years for the light from the three stars in Alpha Centauri to reach us. Compare that to the eight minutes it takes for the light from the sun to reach us.

A light-year is, of course, not a measure of time. It is a measure of distance, being the distance that light travels in one year, and we are talking about some serious distances here. One light-year is about 9.5 trillion km or close to 5.6 trillion miles. The space shuttle Discovery would take over 37,000 years to travel the distance of a light-year. The fastest human-made spacecraft would take around 18,000 years to travel a single light-year. To put this in perspective, we need to imagine that a spacecraft was sent out into the universe 16,000 years before Christ was born on a journey to a destination a light-year away from us, and that that spacecraft could quickly have reached and maintained thereafter the speed of the fastest spacecraft today. That spacecraft would, 18,000 years later, have travelled that one light-year and arrived at its destination sometime during 2020. A lot of history has flown by during what has been, in human terms, an immensely long time. 18,000 years ago, the world went through the coldest period of the ice age and there were probably fewer than a million people on the entire planet. The average temperature was probably 6°C to 10°C lower than now, and the Ice Age did not give way until around 11,700 years ago. From the end of the last Ice Age, there would still be 11,700 years left for that spacecraft to have hurtled through space to complete its voyage by 2020.

18,000 years is, let us remind ourselves, a very tiny span of time in cosmic terms. In terms of humanity, it is a very long time. Let us just again consider that as the ice age ended there might have been only between a few hundred thousand to around a million survivors on our entire planet. As we near the end of 2020, the population on earth is approaching 8 billion.

We try to make sense of our surroundings and our observations to fit our senses. It is hard to understand the enormous distances involved – in space and time –when we look at the stars. Some stars form constellations in the same way that figures appear in clouds. It is easy to believe that the stars in a constellation were put there together for some reason. Just as an example, let us look at the belt of Orion, which comprises three stars within the constellation that we know as Orion. Of the three stars, the one to the left is actually a three-star system, with one star orbiting the central one of these three stars, Alnitak, every 1500 years. What we see as the easternmost star in the belt of Orion is around 1260 light-years from earth. It is the enormous distance from the earth that makes us see the three stars in the east of the belt as one.

The middle star in the belt is Alnilam. Alnilam is a gigantic single star about 2000 light-years away from earth, and it is close to 400,000 times brighter than our sun. The star on the right is Mintaka, which is about 1200 light-years away from earth. Mintaka appears to our naked eyes as one star but is also a system of several stars. When we look at Orion, on a clear, starry night, the stars in the belt of Orion really have nothing to do with each other, but we want to believe that they are part of the constellation of Orion, probably because it makes sense for our brains to categorise what we see. What we are seeing is light from stars in very different places in the universe. What we see is light that has travelled 800 light-years more from the star furthest away from Earth than the light from the star closest to Earth. Is there any reason to believe that the constellations have been created for our viewing pleasure? Is it more reasonable to believe that we make sense of random stars and find patterns we can recognise?

There is so much in our universe and in the world immediately around us that seems inexplicable to us. It is hard to believe that if all the empty space in our planet were removed, the earth would be about the size of a basketball. The explanations seem solid and are the best scientific observations we have. There is no need to cry out for a creator to make sense of what can be explained. It makes no sense to call out for a creator, even if we accept that future observation may alter our understanding of the natural world.

The universe is full of leftover astronomical bodies such as comets hurtling around. Sooner or later, our earth will be hit by a comet, and it has happened before. Our sun will one day burn out. Our planet consists of a thin solid crust surrounding an inner layer of magma. The magma is a result of the intense pressure inside the earth which heats the rocks inside our planet to such high temperatures that the rocks melt. In some ways, one can describe the outer crust of our planet, the thin layer on which we reside, as floating on the magma. From time to time, we see some of this magma spewing out from volcanoes. Several simultaneous and substantial volcanic eruptions could spew so many particles into the air that they could, in turn, block sunlight and even create an Ice Age. The earth is ripe with natural disasters, from incredible winds to tsunamis. Many people die in natural disasters every year, and as we all know, there have been incidents when more than 200,000 people have died in just one tsunami.

The human body is frail and deteriorates from illness, from ageing, from the environment, from bacteria and viruses. As I write, we are all suffering from a pandemic in the form of a virus called Covid-19 that, in the autumn of 2020, is still spreading and continues to kill many people.

Modern creationists want us to believe that creation is so perfect that only a creator could have organised our universe and the tiny speck that is the planet on which we reside. We know from the above that the world in which we live is an imperfect one. Why would a creator who could do so much better create such havoc? It is really only in the span of a human lifetime that everything, or at least many things, seem to us to have been organised. We will, as noted already, one day again be hit by a comet that could, at a stroke, wipe out all life on our planet. We could end up fighting future pandemics without success. Diseases such as the Black Death and the Spanish flu have swept the earth and killed a very large proportion of the inhabitants in the afflicted areas. Ebola remains a prominent issue in some regions of the world. When the Spanish conquistadors arrived in South America, they brought with them diseases that almost wiped out the indigenous populations. Does that seem to be something a creator would have wanted to set in motion? Can it be that the creator established life on our planet with no care for what might happen after the initial creation?

Modern creationists would also want us to believe that the creator organised for us a planet with exactly the parameters needed to sustain such life as currently exists on earth. In claiming that there has to be a creator, it is conveniently forgotten that more than 99% of all species that have ever existed on earth have become extinct. What is so perfect about such a creation? Doesn't it seem as if life on earth is a game of trial and error where the fittest species survive? There is very little reason to believe that we humans will be the last survivors in the really long term. How good a creation is that? Surely, we now realise that we managed to make our way to life on a planet that had already been created and we grew into an earthly environment in which we could exist. Had the climatic circumstances been different, other life forms than the ones we now know might have sprung to life. It is really not the case that planet earth, which has existed for a few billion years, was created for our existence. Life has been on earth for a rather short time in comparison to the time the planet has been in existence. Let us go back to Occam's razor and ask ourselves: is it more likely that a creator was needed to set the universe with all its stars and planets in motion or that it happened by a chance occurrence and that life on earth also came about by chance?

If we are driving a car on an icy road, we would tend to drive the car carefully so as not to lose control. Suddenly, despite our careful driving and feeling that the car was fully under our control, the car starts spinning around. We would say that it was because of the slick road surface, but we might have difficulty explaining exactly how it happened. Would we say that some greater being outside our reality had interfered to start the car sliding? It would be a great excuse in our own minds, but would any of us want to tell that to the policeman investigating the accident?

Let us assume that, in the dead of night, with nobody present, an explosion occurs in a big factory. In the fire marshal's investigation, they would be able to pinpoint the spot where the explosion started by tracing back the items hurled out in all directions. They would very likely be able to establish the time when the explosion occurred. They may be able to establish the ingredients and the particular circumstances that made it happen. But even if they were not able to establish the initial or first cause, they would not go to supernatural explanations.

We must realise that not everything in the natural world is necessarily what it seems at first to be. Stars are scattered millions to billions of kilometres away from earth. The universe is still moving as if it had started with an explosion. Everything we feel is solid is really nothing but hollow space. Even earth itself could be reduced to the size of a basketball if all the empty space in all the atoms that make up the earth were removed. There is no perfection in our lives as our bodies are frail and subject to disease. There is no perfection on earth when it is subject to natural phenomena such as volcanic eruptions and earthquakes which may very quickly destroy what we have built up and even life on earth itself. Do we want to believe that all these natural events that seem to hit us randomly are the result of an Intelligent Designer's efforts?

We now move on to the second creationist idea, namely **irreducible complexity**. Now, there is a pair of well-chosen words for us. *Irreducible complexity* leaves us with the feeling that it belongs to the field of science and not to the field of faith or belief.

Simply put, evolution is the scientific theory that maintains that all life forms on earth are related and gradually evolved or developed over time. For instance, over time the humans most equipped, most fit for the environment where they live, are the most likely to survive. They would, therefore, be the ones who would have human babies to inherit their genes and thereby also inherit the characteristics that made themselves and their forefathers more likely to survive. There is also an element of sexual selection. The strongest males in most species get to control the females in their group and try to ensure that other males are not able to mate with them.

As described earlier in the book, the male guppy, normally a very colourful fish, can demonstrate evolution in front of our eyes. A male guppy who finds himself in a stream without predators will display his colours vividly for sexual selection. Once predators are found in a stream with guppies, the display of colours would only help the predators locate the guppy prey. From an evolutionary point of view, the guppy has a genetic choice between being sexually selected or devoured by the predator. Over a fairly short period of time, what will happen is that the colourful guppies will indeed fall prey to their predators. Over the same short period of time, the guppies who are less colourful and have adapted their colouring to match the bottom of the stream will have a greater chance of surviving. We can witness that in streams where there are predators, the genes of the less colourful, camouflaged guppies will be passed on.

The combination of the fossil record and the DNA record so overwhelmingly points to the truth of evolution. Do not fall for the idea that because it is called a scientific *theory*, it cannot be fact.

We humans have, through selective breeding, been able to make our cows produce more milk and turned what was once the fierce, predatory wolf into the many kinds of dogs we see today. Humans have done this over a very short period of time in the grander scheme of our planetary history. The theory of natural selection tells us that, given the millions of years that have been available for evolution, it can happen naturally and even randomly.

It is not only that we humans change because of genetic mutations over time, but we are also affected by the environment we inhabit and the availability of an adequate food supply. Where food is in short supply, people can either starve to death or, in certain circumstances, their bodies can adapt somewhat. We can look at North Korea where the population is substantially shorter than in neighbouring South Korea. North Korean men are on average around five cm shorter than South Korean men. North Korean preschool boys are already four centimetres shorter and pre-school girls around three centimetres shorter than their South Korean counterparts. We can rule out genetic differences between North and South, as both Koreas have the same genetic population. North Korea has had several famines, and it is estimated that up to several million North Koreans died directly from starvation or hunger-related disease. That is a substantial number out of a population of approximately 26 million. North Korea's resources are spent on the military and keeping the ruling family in place. Too little food for the population is the result of this militarisation of the economy. Perhaps the people who survive can better handle low-calorie diets and pass on their genes. In sharp contrast, the South Koreans have had very good economic growth and ample food. As a result, South Koreans have access to a good diet that meets all their caloric needs.

In the rich world, we now have an abundance of food available and no longer have to do hard labour to sustain our lives. Obesity seems to be the unintended result, and we should worry that obesity may be passed on to future generations.

Believers in the biblical creation stories know that we all come from Adam and Eve. People who believe in evolution as a fact point to DNA evidence that shows that we all come from Africa from where we migrated to different parts of the world. What we see in the world is that people have, over time, evolved to have different skin colours depending on the geography they settled in. The Inuit, previously referred to as "Eskimo" ("Eskimo" is widely regarded as no longer appropriate, although some smaller tribes still identify as such), have evolved to have shorter limbs for less exposure to the cold climate around them.

In one of the coldest parts of Siberia in Russia live the Chukchi. The Chukchi are genetically related to America's indigenous people. As opposed to the indigenous people in America who live in warmer climates, the Chukchi have evolved similar physical traits to the Inuit peoples. Does this not mean that even those who believe in the creation stories in the Bible must admit that some form of evolution has occurred and will continue to do so in the future?

For those who believe in evolution, it is much simpler. For us, the natural conclusion is that those most adaptable to their surroundings have been and will be the ones who survive and will be able to pass on their genes for long-term survival in the various areas to which our original African ancestors migrated.

The theory of evolution is a factual description of how life has evolved from the simplest life form to the many complex life forms currently in existence. All of the different life forms on earth are somehow related. All of this evolution occurred naturally, and there is no need for supernatural intervention.

Irreducible complexity enters the picture as a further attempt to show that there is a need for a creator to explain how complex life forms have developed. In simple terms, what the theory of irreducible complexity tries to explain is that there are biological systems that cannot have evolved gradually. Many creationists believe that life is too complex to have evolved naturally and, particularly, that some biological systems cannot have evolved slowly over a long time from less well-functioning systems to better-functioning systems through natural selection. Some biological systems, they maintain, will simply not work if they do not have all their current components and they needed all these components right from the beginning. Michael Behe authored a book named *Darwin's Black Box*. In it, Behe tries to define irreducible complexity: "… a single system which is composed of several well-matched, interacting parts that contribute to the basic function, and where the removal of any one of the parts causes the system to effectively cease functioning."

It seems simple enough. What Michael Behe is saying is that some biological systems are so complex, with all the components depending on each other, that they cannot have evolved gradually. These parts could not have been added little by little.

Believers in evolution maintain that any biological systems could be formed by natural selection even if they are complex, and Darwin made the following statement in his book *On the Origin of Species*: "If it could be demonstrated that any complex organ existed which could not possibly have been formed by numerous, successive, slight modifications, my theory would absolutely break down."

Michael Behe uses the common mousetrap as a way to demonstrate what he means by irreducible complexity. In 1996, Behe made the claim: "If any one of the components of the mousetrap (the base, hammer, spring, catch, or holding bar) is removed, then the trap does not function. In other words, the simple little mousetrap has no ability to trap a mouse until several separate parts are all assembled. Because the mousetrap is necessarily composed of several parts, it is irreducibly complex."

John H. McDonald, of the Department of Biological Sciences at the University of Delaware, took Behe's statement on in the following way: "It is not my purpose here to point out all of the philosophical flaws in Behe's argument; this has been done thoroughly elsewhere (see Talk Origins and Talk Design to get started into the literature)."

Let us concentrate on what I believe to be the most interesting part of what McDonald states about the mousetrap as an irreducibly complex feat of engineering: "…instead, I wish to point out that the mousetrap that Behe uses as an analogy CAN be reduced in complexity and still function as a mousetrap. The mousetrap illustrates one of the fundamental flaws in the intelligent design argument: the fact that one person can't imagine something doesn't mean it is impossible, it may just mean that the person has a limited imagination. Behe's evidence that biochemical pathways are intelligently designed is that Behe can't imagine how they could function without all of their parts, but given how easy it is to reduce the complexity of a mousetrap, I'm not convinced."

For our purposes, it is enough to acknowledge that there are other ways of creating a mousetrap. For instance, in a simple form, a mouse could venture into a trap where a box would be triggered to fall over the mouse, with the box falling just because of gravitational pull.

It is better we move over to an example of biological systems that Behe believes cannot be reduced in its complexity. We are talking about the human eye. We should start by acknowledging that the human eye is indeed very complex. But is it so complex that removing any component of the eye would make the eye entirely useless? The eye can get damaged and function less well, but still function. It is reasonable to assume that if something can function with less perfection then it could also develop more perfection, as it were.

We know from science that there are very simple organisms that have been fitted with light-sensitive cells. These cells would not have the ability of the eyes to see but would be able to distinguish between light and darkness. These cells could have developed so that they could sense direction by picking up shadows. Eventually, further development would have turned them into the complex eye we now have.

Could our eyes perhaps develop further given enough time? We know that we can improve our eyesight with laser eye surgery called LASIK. The vision correction is accomplished by using lasers to reshape the cornea, which is the front surface of our eyes, enabling the eye to focus better. If laser surgery can re-form and perhaps reform the cornea, it should be possible, over thousands and thousands of years, by the force of natural selection to have the eye develop improved capabilities, together with the rest of the human body.

We do know that the human body has been subject to natural selection. If we were created as humans from the beginning by a creator, there is no way that that creator would have found reason to supply us with a tailbone. The only reason we even now have a small tailbone is that we have evolved from ancient ancestors who needed a tail for balance. Over time, as we stood up and walked upright on our feet, the tail became less necessary. Eventually, the tail had to become an impediment or at least a nuisance and our ancient forefathers with the shortest tail adapted better to their environment. Even further down the evolutionary path, the tail no longer protruded outside our bodies and we were left with just that tiny remnant of a tailbone.

Are our eyes now the best possible? The eagle has developed eyesight that is between four and eight times better than that of the average human being. The eagle is much smaller than a human, but its eyes are almost the same size. The eagle flies high above the ground and needs to have extraordinarily good vision to see its prey below. There is no reason that the human eye could not develop further to see things more sharply, to get better night vision and perhaps to pick up a broader spectrum of light.

CHAPTER 8

The argument that all the eye's components are absolutely necessary for the eye to function as it does now does not mean that each component could not evolve to become better adapted to new circumstances. Let us imagine that five gigantic volcanic eruptions occurred at the same time and spewed small particles into the sky. Assume that this would lead to a darkening of our earth because sunlight has difficulty penetrating the particle dust encircling the globe. Assume further that the resulting state of darker days and even darker nights would persist for a very long time. Do we not believe that, over a very long time, through natural selection, our eyes would evolve to better cope with the new circumstances?

If we wish to believe that such an adaptation would require a creator or God to interfere, we must ask ourselves why God would first allow the earth to be darkened and then decide whether He wanted to give us vision better adapted to the new circumstances.

If circumstances change and we do need better long-distance vision, it would be nice if our eyes evolved more towards what the eagle already has. Perhaps that is not impossible. It is reasonable to ask ourselves the following: if a creator is able to give the eagle such incredibly good vision, why could he not have given that to us humans as well? Is it really that the eyes are so irreducibly complex that we must have gotten them just the way they are, from a creator? But if a creator gave us our current eyes, could he not have done a better job so that our eyesight at least would not deteriorate with old age? Could the creator not at least have given us eyes that provided us with good vision throughout our lives? A creator who is able to create our eyes could have created them any way He wished, and, obviously, and for mysterious reasons, He did not wish us well enough.

We are back to asking a few Occam's razor questions. If a creator or God created our eyes, why did He not give us eagle-eyes? As a matter of fact, some of us do have close to eagle-eyes. Some indigenous people in Australia have been found to have vision around four times better than the average Australian. Do we really need more evidence than that to understand that the eye is not irreducibly complex and can evolve over time to become even better? The alternative explanation could be that somehow the creator prefers aboriginal Australians and has thus given them better eyesight while still, in other physical aspects, creating them to be as imperfect as the rest of humanity. Does the theory of irreducible complexity rise to the level of scientific fact, or is it, to borrow from John H. McDonald, just an unscientific theory based on a lack of imagination as to how things could work?

If there were a creator, He could give us the ability to smell as well as a dog. If there were a creator, he could have given us the ability to see five primary colours like the butterfly can, rather than just the three that our human eyes can differentiate. Are we saying that our creator would not want us to experience all of the beauty in the world with better senses than the ones he created for us? Our creator could even have given us the ability that some lizards have to reproduce limbs. Why didn't He?

We know from the real world that throughout our lives we have to compromise. Neighbours have to compromise to coexist. Within the family and between families there is the need for compromise. The need to compromise exists within societies and between societies as well as within and between countries. On a societal level, we are all competing for the limited resources of the world in which we live. Evolution can be described in a similar fashion. All our bodily parts and bodily functions compete for energy and space in our brains. We survive fine without eagle-eyes. A good way to see our evolution is that we have evolved to be adequate but not perfect. If a creator engineered us, we, the result of creation, should have noticed and experienced perfection in how we function.

The third creationist point that we are going to discuss is the **watchmaker argument**. If one finds a watch in the desert and picks it up and sees that it works, one has good reason to conclude that the watch has a creator. The watchmaker argument is an intelligent design argument, but we all understand that a watch is not irreducibly complex. There are many ways of making a watch, and, over time, even the art of watchmaking has incrementally evolved.

CHAPTER 8

Very much has been written about the watchmaker argument for creation so we will concentrate on one specific point, namely that we are comparing simple human engineering with a creator who has the capacity to create the entire universe including the stars, the planets, and life on very likely many planets in the universe.

Should we not expect from a creator with such abilities a creation that would demonstrate his extraordinary abilities and not leave us with the need for natural explanations?

As humans, we experience illness because of, for instance, bacteria which God has also created. God willingly left us to wait for thousands of years after the creation for a scientist to find a cure by accident, which is how Alexander Fleming discovered penicillin in 1928.

As humans, we experience that our bodies deteriorate with age. We also experience, say, tooth decay and problems with our backs. To be able to distinguish what a God can create compared to a human engineer, one would want to see, among other improvements to the creation of humans, perhaps some of the following.

Would it not be nice if our teeth were made of white titanium? It does not matter if titanium is white or not – God could do it.

Wouldn't it be nice if our entire skeletons were made of stainless steel and not subject to decay? The objection that steel might not work as well as the bones we now have would demonstrate a disbelief in God's abilities. God could do it. The objection that we might not be able to grow during our lifetimes from babyhood to adulthood is not acceptable because God could have programmed it to work.

Wouldn't it be nice if we could live in an environment that we did not need to sully? God could have made us so that we could live on air alone and did not need any food for sustenance.

In the olden days, at the beginning of the Bible, people lived for up to a millennium. With the death of Moses at the age of just 120, God obviously decided he did not want us to live longer than that. He could have programmed us to die at a certain age, having lived a productive and healthy life right to the end. He did not.

And, by the way, if God really made a covenant with Abraham and thereafter made the Jews his chosen people, he could have organised it somewhat differently. Circumcision is not compulsory in Islam but highly recommended. It is believed that Muhammad was born without a foreskin. Good for him, as surgical removal of the foreskin became unnecessary. When the early Christians broke with Judaism and introduced Christianity as Judaism-light, the Jewish dietary rules, kashrut, were abandoned, together with circumcision. Since we wear clothes, it is not obvious to others whether or not they are looking at a person who continues to fulfil the Lord's covenant with Abraham. Once the Lord chose to make the Jews his chosen people, could he not have written with fire in the sky 'I love the Jews!'? He could have done that and have avoided millennia of persecution. A Jew could, of course, pull out his penis and show that he is circumcised, as agreed with God, but it wouldn't have quite the same effect as a godly message written with fire in the sky.

We now come to an inspection of creationism with the aid of Occam's razor. Which is more likely? Is it that over millions and millions of years of evolution we have come to be who we are, even by pure chance, and incrementally adapted to our environment? Or is it that there must be a creator who set everything up, in our universe and our planet, including us, with such perfection that it rendered evolution meaningless? Or is it that a creator set the entire universe in motion by creating the original Big Bang and then stopped caring what happened to his creation? And if your view is that there must be a creator, the follow-up question is: why did this perfect, omniscient, omnipotent God not do a better job?

CHAPTER 9

Why is it ... that so much anti-Semitism from Christianity and Islam has been directed against the Jews when, at least in Christianity, the Jews must be acknowledged to be God's chosen people?

There is no doubt that God declared the Jews His chosen people in the Old Testament. In Deuteronomy, the last of the five books of Moses, God clearly states (as translated in the illustrated Jerusalem Bible 14:2), "For thou art an holy people unto the Lord thy God, and the Lord hath chosen thee to be a peculiar people unto himself, above all the nations that are upon the earth."

The Lord has promised His chosen people a lot of things, promises that He has decided, for mysterious reasons, not to keep. He has changed his mind about them so many times, let them live in slavery for hundreds of years and finally decided to take them out of slavery, but that is for another chapter. He promised Abraham that his descendants would be as many as the stars in the sky. The Jews who have taken this as God's promise to them find that they are only a tiny minority of the people in this world. If we add the people of all Abrahamic religions, which would include all Muslims and all Christians, God's promise gets a little closer to fulfilment. The stars in the sky are unimaginably numerous, something which God knew when He delivered His promise to Abraham, but we will let that pass as a figure of speech.

God has let His chosen people be persecuted and eventually subjected to genocide by the Nazis without intervening. Going far back in time, God acted in the biblical story of Esther to save the Jews from a similar fate.

If you are a pious Christian and believe that God's word is without fault, and that is how the Bible should be read, then you must wonder how it is that God's chosen people have been so hated and persecuted throughout history, at least since the time of Jesus.

Even if you do not believe that the Bible has no errors, it is still very clear that the Jews are God's chosen people. Should they therefore not be given somewhat more respect?

If you have no belief at all and you are an atheist, you probably understand that no God or religious organisation has asked you to treat people of any faith or even nonbelievers in an immoral way.

Jesus himself had a Jewish mother, and when she called him in Hebrew, she would call him Jeshoa or Joshua. The name Jeshu would be the nickname, which became translated as Jesus. There is no doubt that the Jesus of the holy New Testament was Jewish. There is also no doubt that He lived in a Jewish land where the majority of the population was Jewish.

We acknowledge that Jesus lived in a Jewish land, a Jewish land partly occupied and partly controlled by the Romans, through the dynasty of King Herod. History teaches us that the Romans were harsh governors. We also know that there was plenty of revolt in the air and there were several people who claimed that they could lead the Jews out of their Roman occupation. Many self-proclaimed messianic figures and false prophets roamed the land. Those who believe in prophets and prophecy will understand that a false prophet is one who really does not speak for the Lord. For those of us who are non-believers, every prophet is false. Not one of the prophets, other than Jesus, managed to create an enormous future following. In the name of Jesus, several new Christian religions or denominations were created.

Jesus himself, being Jewish, would not have been the first in line to create the anti-Semitism that arose after his passing. We should remember that the four Gospels in the New Testament were written at least 30 and maybe up to 80 years after Jesus' death. A lot of true history could have easily been lost. A lot of new interpretations became possible.

In the New Testament, we find that Jesus made statements about upholding the laws of Moses as written in the Old Testament, but we also find passages where he is in favour of breaking the law. James, one of a few of Jesus' brothers and sisters, was one of the early Christian leaders. James, following in Jesus' footsteps, was in favour of adherence to the law of the Old Testament. The early Christians were Jewish, and one could probably not even call it Christianity at that time but rather a small sect inside Judaism in the Roman-controlled Jewish land.

In the Gospel according to Matthew, one understands the importance of following Mosaic law. It is insisted in this gospel that the Ten Commandments were still valid and should be followed. In the very famous and much venerated Sermon on the Mount delivered by Jesus, he indicates in Matthew 5:17 that he has not come to destroy the law or the prophets. "Do not think that I have come to abolish the Law or the Prophets; I have not come to abolish them but to fulfill them," he is quoted as saying. I think for further study you should look up the Sermon on the Mount and read it for yourself.

I hope not to tire the reader by picking up Matthew 5:19, where Jesus warns that if anyone breaks one of the least of these commandments, "he shall be called the least in the kingdom of heaven." The opposite, according to Jesus, is that whoever shall follow the commandments and teach them shall be "called great in the kingdom of heaven". So far, Jesus seems to be hanging onto his Jewish roots. He states fairly clearly that the Ten Commandments are all to be obeyed. He then affirms five of the Ten Commandments and does not say anything in particular about the other five. Our initial interpretation may well be that Jesus has affirmed all Ten Commandments, but he does leave some wiggle room in that he has come to "fulfill". That could mean some changes and improvements are, in his mind, allowed. Jesus does, in fact, break some of the rules. He teaches on the Sabbath. He wants everybody to forget about the future and give up everything to just follow him. Imagine if everybody did that, gave up work, family, economic planning for their life and the life of their society just to follow Jesus. Would there be any food, any pensions, any healthcare? Would there be any children?

Giving everything up just to follow Jesus would be fine if it truly were only for a short time before this world was going to end anyway. That was what was believed at the time, but it is now almost two thousand years later. Still, there are Christian leaders who preach the same message about giving up everything just to follow Christ. Is that the message for the next few thousand years as well? Start by imagining what the world would have looked like if the advice to give up your daily chores for Jesus had been followed by all Christians over these almost two thousand years. I hope most of us would come to the reasonable conclusion that there would be no reasonable circumstances to sustain life if people did not go about what they needed to do for society to function. By the way, how could God and Jesus be wrong about the timing of the End of Times by, as it seems, at least two thousand years?

Jesus does not care much for the commandment to honour your mother and father, since he states that if anyone comes to him and does not hate their father and mother, wife and children, brothers and sisters – yes, even their own life – "such a person cannot be my disciple."

It is quite clear that he allows himself, in the words written for him many years after his death, to skirt the law. Yet he had himself stated that the law must be followed. Jesus states that whoever does not follow even one of the Ten Commandments would be called the *least* in the kingdom of heaven. Even God, Jesus, does not seem able to get it right.

Perhaps Jesus actually believed – or it was believed for him – that he was not just figuratively a God but literally so. That is what you perhaps get to understand from Peter, his rock.

Let us look into the other side of the argument. Jesus was called the Son of Man. We should go back to Hebrew where the term is *Ben Adam*. Translated, that means *son of Adam*, or the last name *Adamson*, but also means a descendent of Adam, which, in turn, means to be human. Hardly a *Godly* description of a man. Also, Jesus often talks about His father in heaven. In Hebrew, *father* is a term used frequently in Hebrew prayers such as Avinu Malkeinu, which translated means *our father our king*. Even the Lord's prayer, as put forth by Jesus himself, talks about *Our Father*, and, in reciting that prayer, every Christian talks to his father.

Let us, for the sake of argument, stipulate that Jesus and some people around him believed that he was the embodiment of the Lord on earth and was a literal God himself. We should remember that at the time there were no newspapers, no radio, no television, no Internet and no social media. He would not have had a huge following, and his teachings would have been mostly unknown in his lifetime.

His fellow Jews would probably have continued worshipping the Lord and sacrificing in the Temple as if Jesus had never existed. It is reasonable to conclude that the majority of the population in Judea and Galilee either did not know of Jesus or had no reason to believe that Jesus was a or the God. And, if you do not know that someone is a or the God, how can you be responsible for killing God? Can God be killed against his will, even by somebody who does not know that he is God?

Neither the Jews nor the Romans nor Pontius Pilate had reason to believe that they had a true God in front of them or in the midst of them.

We know from history that Pontius Pilate was the fifth governor of the Roman province of Judea and that he served under the Emperor Tiberius. He served from about the year 26 CE until the year 36 CE. In the Christian world, he is best known as the Roman official under whom the trial of Jesus was held and as the man who ordered his crucifixion.

Historical sources inform us that Pilate was sent back to Rome by the legate of Syria, and it is assumed that he was returned to Rome because of his harsh rule over his province. He was known to have experienced several incidents of tension with the Jewish population. Historians are divided in that some believe that he was a brutal ruler and others surmise that his ten-year tenure as governor should be seen as an indication of competence. There was, of course, not necessarily a contradiction between brutality and competence in the eyes of the Roman emperor at that time.

One could be forgiven for assuming that it must have been an extraordinarily brutal incident that finally had Pilate relieved of his governorship. The historical Roman governor Pilate was not a person who would be bothered by small things. It is also reasonable to assume that the trial of Jesus before Pilate is a work of fiction. The very brutal ruler would not have bothered with a mere Jew. There is also no historical evidence that before Passover the people got to choose between various criminals, which one should be crucified and which one should be freed.

The events leading up to the crucifixion start with Judas Iscariot identifying Jesus so that he could be arrested and brought to the Jewish Sanhedrin for trial. He is asked many questions and answers most of them well, but, in the end, he is deemed to be blasphemous. The story moves rapidly forward, and Jesus is seen by Herod Antipas, the son of Herod the Great, who rules with Roman consent outside of Judea. The king is in charge of the Galilee. The king sends Jesus back to Pilate for trial and judgement.

While he is sitting in the seat of judgement, Pilate receives a note from his wife that she has had a dream. We are left to wonder how we know that. But in his wife's dream, she was made to understand that Jesus was innocent of any crime. She does not tell this to her husband right away; she reacts only once Pilate is sitting on the seat of judgement in the public square. Why did she wait that long? The dream must have bothered her and seemed urgent. Anyhow, she waits until her husband has started the trial of Jesus and only at this point does she send the note to him. In this note, she tells her husband not to have anything to do with that innocent man, for she has suffered a great deal that day in a dream because of him. Who found that note to record it? For the sake of credibility, we would like or need to know.

Pilate is now supposed to have taken his wife's note very seriously and asks the crowd what he should do with Jesus. The collected crowd – who are, of course, Jews in a Jewish land, with Jesus also being Jewish and subject to Pilate's judgement – shouts back, "Crucify him!" Pilate is said to have asked the crowd in turn what crime he has committed, well knowing, from his wife's note, that he is innocent.

You must, again, remember that all of this is written quite a few years after Jesus' death. The writer now has Pilate washing his hands to show the mob that they are responsible for the fate of Jesus. And they accept responsibility for the killing of Jesus by shouting to the governor, as in the translation from the King James Bible (which is just one of quite a few similar translations): "His blood be on us and our children."

What a fantastic story, told as if it were historically true. The really brutal governor, who cannot have had a clue or any reasonable belief that Jesus was God, would not even have been bothered with such a trial. Yet, in a gospel, he is made to wash his hands to demonstrate his innocence of the killing of someone who, for him, was just a nuisance in the shape of a common criminal. The mob of Jews standing around the public square are made to scream that Jesus' blood should be not only upon them but also upon their children. This requires us to stop and think. Did they have any idea that Jesus was God? If it were God standing in front of the crowd, He could obviously have saved Himself, and, if He would not, then His father, the Lord Himself, could have saved Him.

Let us now add to our understanding of the trial and what the mob was screaming to Pilate regarding Jesus. Jesus was, unbeknownst to either Pilate or the crowd, born of a virgin with God as his father. He was sent to earth to be punished, suffer and die for our sins, past, present and future. What God was doing was sacrificing his only son in order to forgive us. Do we really want to believe that this is the only way God would be willing to forgive us for our sins? God is all-powerful, without any limitation, and all-seeing. He could have chosen to forgive us for our sins without Jesus being sacrificed. We would not have known the difference, but if the historical Jesus existed, it would at least have saved him from a lot of unnecessary suffering.

Was Jesus, the son of a Jewish mother, a historical person? The evidence is sketchy. The Jewish-Roman historian Josephus Flavius makes a brief mention of

Jesus, but his credentials as a historian are not that great. He also believed that the Bible stories contained the true history of the Jews. Tacitus wrote in CE 116 about how the Roman Emperor Nero persecuted the Christians after the Great Fire of Rome that burned down much of the city in the year 64 CE. Tacitus has more credibility and is another non-Christian source. We should remember, though that his writing was many years after the time when Jesus was crucified around the year 33 CE. Tacitus wrote this only in the year 116 CE.

Many scholars believe that Tacitus' one line about the execution of Christus who gave the name to Christianity is sufficient evidence for Jesus being a historical person. We could just as well find it likely that his sources were the persecuted Christians who carried the belief of the crucified Christ.

Since Jesus' family was moved from the Galilee to the city of King David, Bethlehem, in order for Jesus to be born there, one would have reason to suspect that there was a family in the Galilee that needed to be transported to Bethlehem. Otherwise, the story could just have had Joseph and his wife Mary come from Bethlehem. They would, then, simply have stayed in their home town and given birth in the city of King David. By the way, the name Bethlehem in Hebrew means House of Bread.

We have reason to be at least doubtful about Jesus being a historical person since the story about why Joseph and Mary had to go to Bethlehem from the Galilee is, in the New Testament, based on a Roman census that is not historically accurate. Further, it is based on moving Joseph and his wife Mary from the Galilee, ruled by a king and not under direct Roman rule, to the Roman province under the rule of Pontius Pilate where Bethlehem was located. How would the Romans know that Jesus had ancestry going back to King David and therefore had to come to be counted for tax in a Roman province?

Let us translate the story about moving Joseph and family to Bethlehem to modern times. The equivalent situation would be that a family that has resided in Canada for two hundred years descended from one of the settlers in the US that came over on the *Mayflower*. The US would now, in the year 2020, require current descendants of this family in Canada to go to the US to file a tax return. The biggest question here is how would the US Internal Revenue Service know about this Canadian family? And even if they knew, how could they make them go to the US to file a tax return? Replace a US immigrant arriving on the *Mayflower* in the year 1620 with King David being the Bethlehem ancestor of Jesus, and we understand the difficulty. King David, according to the Bible, died around 970 BCE, while the crucifixion of Jesus was around a thousand years later. That is leaving aside the fact that, as discussed already, for obvious reasons King David cannot have been Jesus' ancestor. Two Gospels in the New Testament showed Jesus' ancestral line going back over stepfather Joseph with whom Jesus had no biological connection. It is worth repeating that Jesus had only one father and that is God himself. There cannot be a male line of ancestors going over his stepfather, Joseph. It is easy to be sceptical regarding the biblical story about Jesus' mother and stepfather having had to go to Bethlehem, falsely identifying a Roman census as the reason. But to Bethlehem they went in order to give birth to the son of God. The writers of the two Gospels must have felt that it was important for the credibility of the claim that Jesus was the Messiah to make his birthplace Bethlehem, the city of David. In writing about the census and the birth of Jesus in the manger in Bethlehem, they conveniently left aside that Jesus' ancestry going over Joseph back to King David must be false. It is worth repeating – God was the father of Jesus, and so Joseph was not.

If Jesus existed and was the great miracle worker he is supposed to have been, there should have been more writing about him outside of the holy texts.

In terms of creating anti-Semitism in the New Testament, it is definitely not helpful when, in the Book of Revelation, one finds references to the *synagogue of Satan*. The context here is not as clear as when the Jewish mob are shown screaming, "May his blood be over us and our children." The context here is a passage pointing to people who say they are Jews and are not. The context here is about pretend Jews, and it could perhaps even be interpreted as a positive statement about those who are truly Jewish and not just pretending to be. The author, John, was himself Jewish, as of course was Jesus. It is difficult to come to a clear conclusion about the meaning of the pretend Jews being the *synagogue of Satan* but it is not helpful. If you are inclined to be anti-Jewish, you will find comfort in the fact that *synagogue* normally refers to a Jewish house of prayer and *synagogue of Satan* would need no further investigation.

Let us take an Occam's razor view on this. Some seventy or so years had passed after Jesus' death, and the writers of the texts in the New Testament discovered that the remaining Jews had stayed with their Jewish faith. They had difficulty believing that the Messiah had arrived without the preconditions set out in the Old Testament for his arrival having been met. They would, of course, have had even greater issues with believing that Jesus was the son of God. Christians, a few generations after Jesus, had started to make inroads among non-Jews, especially after introducing Judaism-light, which allowed you to skip circumcision and the burdensome dietary rules. It was a time to convince the pagans to follow Jesus. We should remember that the New Testament's chapters were chosen to fit what early church leaders wanted us to believe. There were other Gospels and writings at that time which were declared to be heretical. Among other Gospels and writings, some could be found where Jesus was described as a mere mortal. Even in the Gospels of the New Testament, it is hard to pin down language that definitely turns Jesus from human to God.

Is it perhaps reasonable now to assume that the story of the trial before Pontius Pilate is simply a made-up story with the intent of showing the innocence of the pagan world and the guilt of the Jews in the killing of the son of God? All this, perhaps, to allow the pagans of the ancient world to embrace the new religion, while having somebody to blame for the death of the son of the Almighty Lord?

The Muslims have a view on the crucifixion and that is that God manipulated the situation to make it seem that Jesus had died on the cross. According to Islam, Jesus is by no means the son of God but merely a prophet who, instead of dying on the cross, ascended to heaven.

It was not until the year 325 CE that the council of Nicaea, called by King Constantine, was made to vote on Jesus' divinity. There would not have been any reason for such a vote had there been unanimity in the Christian world about Jesus being an actual God. With an overwhelming majority, in which only two voted against the proposition, Jesus was finally declared a true God. Knowing this, one should be able to forgive both Pontius Pilate and the Jewish mob at the public square for their collective ignorance.

1800 bishops in the Roman empire were invited to the council of Nicaea, but a much smaller number showed up. The two dissenting voters at the council were banished, and it would not be hard to believe that at least some of the ones who were dissenters, and would have voted no, did not show up for fear of what they expected might become their fate.

Was the trial of Jesus a historical event or was the trial a fictional tale written to show the innocence of the Romans with Pilate's handwashing and the guilt of the Jewish mob and, by extension, the Jewish people? I think you would agree that you could find a mob screaming, "Crucify him." I also think you would agree that it is all but impossible to find a crowd that would actually scream, "May his blood be over us and our children." That would require that the crowd knew that they were killing God and that they would willingly take the blame for it, not only themselves but also the next generation. Had they had any reason to believe that Jesus, about to be condemned to crucifixion, was God, one can be certain they would have been asking Pilate to spare Jesus, or they would have at least remained silent. If Jesus was not God, what would be the point of screaming for his blood to be over them and even over the second generation of the mob at the square that day?

I hope you believe with me that the Occam's razor answer is that the story about the trial of Jesus before Pilate is not historical but fictional. By the way, can anybody kill God? Can even everybody together kill God? The mere fact that the killing of God has been described in the New Testament may seem to us to be evidence of a lack of faith. This all-powerful being we are supposed to believe in, being the all-powerful God that has created everything in the entire universe and us, could not reasonably be killed by mere humans. If God is to be killed, it is more likely that he be killed by reason than by crucifixion.

The anti-Jewish sentiment created here has led to the most horrific crimes against the Jewish people with the blessing of the Catholic Church, but not only the Catholic Church. From the sermons on Sundays, in the cathedrals and churches where Jews were blamed for the killing of God, to the Inquisition, to the quiet cooperation with the Nazis (giving the pope at the time, Pius XII, the nickname "Hitler's Pope"), the Catholic Church bears a very great responsibility for allowing anti-Semitism to penetrate society. In 2011, Pope Benedict XVI finally declared that there was no basis in scripture for the argument that the Jewish people were responsible for the death of Jesus Christ. Officially, the church abandoned the belief in the Jewish blood libel back in 1965, but it remained contentious between the church and the Jews, and there are likely many conservative Catholics who still blame the Jews for the death of God's son, being himself a God.

The church took an awfully long time to come to a reasonable conclusion, but a conclusion that is not textual, that is to say, the text still leaves us with the impression that the pagan Pontius Pilate, symbolically washing his hands, was innocent and the crowd of Jews were screaming for Jesus' blood.

With our Western view on guilt, both Pontius Pilate and the mob would have had to know that they were killing God. Pilate, after washing his hands, sent Jesus off to crucifixion, after all. More importantly, and I know I'm repeating myself, Jesus was sent to earth born of a virgin mother with God as his father to absolve us from our sins. In other words, God is responsible for the death of His son by manipulating earthly players, mere mortals, to fulfil his plan for allowing himself to forgive us for our sins. Not even Judas Iscariot can be blamed since he was only a pawn in God's scheme.

Let us not forget that Jesus himself is believed to be God. Perhaps it was suicide by Roman crucifixion to fulfil his and his father's reason for sending him down to us. John, in the New Testament, seems to be certain that Jesus is the son of God. He says, "for God so loved the world, that he gave his only begotten son, that whoever believes in him should not perish, but have everlasting life."

CHAPTER 9

The Gospels, however, have conflicting stories, with Jesus himself being evasive and wavering between being, on the one hand, a mere mortal, a learned man and rabbi, and, on the other, being of a godly nature. You can read the entire New Testament and come out in favour of either interpretation. There is, in other words, no absolute clarity that Jesus is – or perhaps, better, sees himself as – a God.

Let us assume that there was a historical person named Jesus. To the Jewish mob on the square screaming for the blood of Jesus to be over them and their children, Jesus was an ordinary man. He spoke Hebrew, he knew how to read Hebrew as all Jewish boys were taught, so that they could participate in the reading of the five books of Moses. He was known by his Hebrew nickname, Jeshu. There was no reason for the crowd to scream for an ordinary man's blood to be over them, and if it were known to them that Jesus was a God, I doubt they would have dared to scream for his blood to be over them and their children. No reasonable person can believe that a mother would want her own children to be punished by deliberately cursing them in the manner of the blood libel.

If we are still not convinced that all the actors involved in Jesus' crucifixion are innocent, we must find a good explanation for why a God can be killed by mere mortals. We must find an explanation for why Jesus was sent by his father to die for our sins and yet, when he is killed, as God has wished him to be, the blame falls on ordinary men and, perhaps, women. Since Jesus was sent to earth by his father, God, to suffer and die for our sins, we have no option but to conclude that all human actors who might have been involved in this crucifixion are innocent. The list of innocents would include the Sanhedrin with the high priest, the mob that screamed for his blood to be over them and their children, Pontius Pilate himself, King Herod and the Roman soldiers who physically crucified him. We would also have to ignore the two ancestral lines for Jesus in the New Testament that wrongfully go over Joseph.

Hold on, we might say here, *we know Jesus' bloodline*. God is his father and his mother is the Virgin Mary. There is no human ancestry to follow here, except perhaps over his mother, but in those days, women did not rise to the level of importance that justified tracing their ancestry. Jesus' paternal bloodline is not mortal. A few generations after Jesus' crucifixion, when the Gospels were written, it seems they were not, even at that time, quite certain about Jesus' godly bloodline.

Let's start with page 1 in the New Testament where we find the Gospel according to Matthew and *The Genealogy of Jesus*. Here we should be really surprised that there is a need to find a bloodline of mortals for Jesus.

Oddly enough, the two ancestral lines in the New Testament – the one by Matthew and the other in the Gospel according to Luke – do not match. They do not follow the same ancestry and are in the main incompatible. Matthew starts with Abraham and finds his way over King David to the 39th in the bloodline called Jacob, the father of Jesus' stepfather, Joseph. In this line of ancestors, that position would be Jesus' stepfather's father or his step-grandfather.

Luke starts with God, goes over Adam and in number 35 in the bloodline comes to King David. In both bloodlines King David is central. Luke's number 75 is Jesus' earthly step-grandfather Heli, which is a different name for the father of Jesus' stepfather than Matthew's Jacob for the same position.

It is amazing, isn't it, that even the writers of the Gospels could not get Jesus' nature as God right. It is also amazing that the gospel writers could not even get to the same name for Joseph's father. It is clear to us that if God were the father of Jesus, neither Joseph his stepfather, with no biological connection to Jesus, nor Joseph's father, whether named Jacob or Heli, nor anybody else in the entire line of ancestors has a place there.

What is this? we ask ourselves. Is Jesus, after all, human? Why else would there be a human bloodline going over King David? Several attempts have been made to try to explain away the fact that the two bloodlines differ in terms of the name of Jesus' step-grandfather. One far-fetched explanation is that one of them would be the adoptive father of Joseph and the other one Joseph's biological father. Looking at genealogy, though, the bloodline should go over Jesus' biological father anyway. God is his father, but I feel uncertain that one can use the term *biological* in relation to God's fatherhood.

CHAPTER 9

Jesus' bloodline going over King David seems to have been important to the two gospel writers. The Messiah was going to come from the house of King David according to predictions in the Old Testament. Stop again and think. If Jesus was the son of God, and himself God, there would be no need to construct a human bloodline which would obviously, in both instances, be mere fiction. That is not only my opinion but that of many modern Christian scholars, such as John Dominic Crossan, who believe that both gospels were invented to ensure that Jesus had his bloodline over King David so that the claim for Jesus being the Messiah would have merit. Just as an aside, if this central proposition of the New Testament can be reinterpreted, what else might also be mere invention?

Jesus' paternal bloodline goes only one step up to God himself. If the writers could not get this straight, there is good reason to believe that much else might not be right or true in the texts of the New Testament.

Let us reiterate that the real crux of it is that both bloodlines go over Joseph, the husband of the Virgin Mary. It is extremely difficult to explain this away because the whole bloodline would not make sense unless Joseph was the father. But if Joseph is the father, God is not! No matter what we want to believe concerning the ancestry of Jesus, his nature as God is already contested on page one in the New Testament where we find the Gospel according to Matthew. A few generations after Jesus was crucified, the Gospels of Matthew and Luke were considered by the early Christian fathers true enough to be included in the New Testament. If neither Matthew, nor Luke, nor the early church fathers who put the New Testament together could get Jesus' Godly character right, how could a mob screaming on a square many years earlier have been expected to understand who Jesus was? We must, at least, be very surprised that God appears in neither of the two bloodlines. The genealogies are entirely populated with mortals, and both genealogies go over Joseph to Jesus. If Joseph were not the father of Jesus, the two ancestry lines described in Mark and Luke would make absolutely no sense.

Besides, being the son of God must trump anything else including having ancestry dating back to King David. Do we not now understand that the true genealogy of Jesus, being himself God and the son of God, must be very short? **Jesus is the son and God the father**. There is no other father of Jesus than God Himself. Every attempt to create another ancestry, which both Luke and Mark tried, without being able to agree on the line of ancestors, does nothing but cast doubt on Jesus being God and the son of God. There should be no such doubt in the New Testament, which, after all, comprises the stories that make Christians worship Christ.

Having reviewed Jesus' ancestry, we are still left wondering what Jesus' last words before dying on the cross are supposed to tell us. Before dying on the cross, Jesus is supposed to have cried out, "My God, my God, why have you forsaken me?" Or in Hebrew: *"Eli, Eli lama sabachtani?"*

There could be two contrasting interpretations, the first of which is that Jesus, being an ordinary human or Son of Man, cries out to God, the father of everyone, because he has abandoned him. The second interpretation could be that, if Jesus was both the son of God and God himself, what he cries out seems very out of place and, to paraphrase Professor Zizek, could be seen as an ultimate form of atheism wherein God no longer believes in Himself.

We now move on to Martin Luther. He decided that the papacy was no good and wanted to create a different kind of Christianity without a pope as its head. Luther was born in Germany on November 20, 1483, and died on February 18, 1546. He was ordained to the priesthood in 1507. He started the Protestant Reformation, breaking a substantial part of the Christian world away from Catholicism. In 1517, Martin Luther pinned 95 Theses to the door of his Catholic Church, and he rightly denounced the church's sale of indulgences. Amazingly, the Catholic Church had made substantial income through extortion of the ignorant by selling indulgences, which is an advance pardon for sin not yet committed and thus an easier path to heaven. Luther also questioned papal authority and was excommunicated.

At the beginning of his ministry, he was hoping to be able to convert the Jews to his new faith but was disappointed when they did not accede. He did, as one of his main points, state that the Bible was the ultimate truth and yet, obviously, did not believe enough in the fact that the Jews were the chosen people to let them live in peace. He obviously did not believe enough in the Ten Commandments, either, to honour the Sabbath as the day of rest. The Lutherans continue to keep Sunday as the day of rest.

Luther's anti-Semitic writings in many ways dwarf what the Catholic Church accomplished. He called for severe punishment and persecution of the Jewish people. The Jews, he said, being the chosen people, should not be allowed to teach their heresy. To let his Protestant followers know what to do with the Jews, who, in his view, were both condemned and rejected, he stipulated the following:

1. "First, to set fire to their synagogues or schools ... This is to be done in honour of our Lord and of Christendom, so that God might see that we are Christians ..."
2. "Second, I advise that their houses also be razed and destroyed."
3. "Third, I advise that all their prayer books and Talmudic writings, in which such idolatry, lies, cursing, and blasphemy are taught, be taken from them...."
4. "Fourth, I advise that their Rabbis be forbidden to teach henceforth on pain of loss of life and limb ..."
5. "Fifth, I advise that safe conduct on the highways be abolished completely for the Jews. For they have no business in the countryside ..."
6. "Sixth, I advise that usury be prohibited to them, and that all cash and treasure of silver and gold be taken from them ...»
7. "Seventh, I recommend putting a flail, an axe, a hoe, a spade, a distaff, or a spindle into the hands of young, strong Jews and Jewesses and letting them earn their bread in the sweat of their brow ... but if we are afraid that they might harm us or our wives, children, servants, cattle, etc., ... then let us emulate the common sense of other nations such as France, Spain, Bohemia, etc., ... then eject them forever from the country ..."

Despite being fervently anti-Catholic, he allowed Catholic countries that had expelled the Jews to be useful role models.

I do not believe that we need to investigate the expressly anti-Semitic nature at the start of the Lutheran movement any further. When we read the above, we will quickly find that the Nazis followed his instructions. Should we perhaps conclude that Martin Luther, the hero of Protestant Christians, has fallen? No matter what else Luther may have accomplished, should we not look differently at him as a result of his extremely intolerant proclamations against Jews? His writings are so vile that it is almost the same as saying that the Nazis of course killed six million Jews, but Hitler did some good and built a highway system in Germany. The Nazis must at least have been pleased to have a pope who collaborated in real time and to have the father of all the Protestant movements lead the way.

We should leave Martin Luther here and move on to a short exploration of the Muslims' relationship with the Jews. Muslims believe that Jesus was born of a virgin, but not that he was God or His son and acknowledge that he was a prophet. The Islamic world has, nevertheless, found reason to be hostile to the Jews. For the sake of having reviewed all three religions stemming from Abraham, we would be remiss if we did not look into the Muslim view of the Jews.

Not all Muslims are Arabs but Arabs are Semites. It is therefore better to talk about anti-Jewish sentiment rather than anti-Semitism. In the beginning, Muhammad seemed to have a decent relationship with the Jewish tribes. The Jews also believed in one God. The Jewish fasting holiday, the day of atonement, Yom Kippur, could well have been a model for Ramadan. The story of Abraham, who was ordered by God to sacrifice his son Isaac, born to his wife Sarah at an old age, was, as we have noted already, copied but with a twist so that Abraham put at risk his son Ishmael by the woman in the Bible who is described as the slave girl Hagar.

Until 624 CE, Muslims actually prayed in the direction of Jerusalem, not Mecca. In 622 CE, Muhammad had to flee from Mecca to a place now renamed

Medina. He drew up a contract or a treaty about coexistence between Muslims, Christians and Jews. Christians and Jews were given fairly wide religious freedoms but were compelled to assist in defence of the city. In Medina, he found himself with three Jewish tribes as neighbours. He became increasingly frustrated that they did not convert to his new religion. Muhammad, the warrior, won a battle known as the Battle of Badr.

One would be forgiven for believing that Muhammad, the warrior, felt strengthened by victory and would now make an effort to be acknowledged by the Jewish tribes as the true and the last prophet. The peace between Muhammad's followers and the Jews broke down. Muhammad defeated the Jewish tribes. This victory by Muhammad became the starting point when very negative and hateful verses about the Jews began to appear in Archangel Gabriel's revelations to the Prophet. We find a similar pattern to the anti-Semitism created in the New Testament. When Muhammad found that the Jews were not ready to convert to the new religion and declare him to be the true prophet, we find verses or, in Arabic, *Surahs* in the Quran, stating that the Jews were visited with the anger of Allah.

We can find a few positive statements about Jews in the Quran, but they are substantially outweighed by the hateful ones. One should note that the Jews, according to the Islamic faith, are not seen as the killers of God being in the body of Jesus. According to Muslim belief, as noted already, the crucifixion of Jesus was an illusion set up by God himself to prevent the killing of Jesus and to bring Jesus, the prophet, to heaven.

Jews are, in Islam, said to be treacherous and hypocritical and could never be friends with a Muslim. The People of the Book, who are the Christians and the Jews, have to pay a special poll tax to be allowed to dwell in Muslim-controlled areas. But the Jews are specifically cursed by Allah, who will turn them into apes and monkeys and swine and worshippers of false gods because they are infidels.

Despite these writings, in some historical periods, Jews could live in relative peace and freedom, such as periodically under the Ottoman Empire. It is difficult to believe that the Jews felt very safe but, having come out of the Inquisition, the Ottoman Empire could be seen as a temporary haven.

Jews, as People of the Book, can be allowed to reside in a Muslim country if they pay the *Jizyah*, which is a head tax. Jews have a subordinate position in Muslim societies. It should be said that the same goes for Christians, and there is plenty of hatred against Christians, but that is not the subject of this chapter.

Apart from being turned into pigs, monkeys, and other lowlife creatures, no later than at the end of time the Jews will be wiped out. In one of the hadiths, in the sayings of Muhammad, the Jews are singled out as being the aggressors at the end of time when there will be a great battle. When interpreting this clear passage, it is impossible to conclude that this is something that can relate to any people other than the Jews. Muhammad said: "The hour will not begin until you fight the Jews, until a Jew will hide behind a rock or a tree, and the rock or tree will say: 'O Muslim. O Slave of Allah, here is a Jew behind me; come and kill him.'"

Some Muslim clerics are willing to take issue with the past and actively oppose hateful views of the Jews. Sheikh Dr. Muhammad Al-Issa is just such a cleric. He is from Saudi Arabia and is the head of the Muslim World League, an NGO funded by the Saudi government. In June 2020, he stated that the Muslim League members were proud to stand shoulder to shoulder with "our Jewish brothers and sisters to build understanding, respect, love and interreligious harmony."

Earlier in the year, the Sheikh visited the Auschwitz death camp and said, "Never again. Not for Jews, not for Muslims, not for Christians, not for Hindus, not for Sikhs. Not for any of God's children. History's greatest horror, the Holocaust, must never be repeated."

These are profoundly progressive words from a Muslim cleric in Saudi Arabia and should give us some hope. The fact that the NGO is funded by the Saudi government must be seen as positive. The Saudi strand of Islam, Wahhabism, is still teaching a very conservative form of Islam.

And there is more reason for hope. As I write, in the middle of September 2020, two Arab countries have decided to normalise relations with Israel, a Jewish-

CHAPTER 9

majority country. Israel wishes to remain Jewish as it sees itself as a place of refuge and the last resort for Jews outside of Israel who are, or may become, persecuted. First the UAE and then Bahrain started the process of normalising relations with the state of Israel. Most of the Arab countries are Sunni-majority, while Iraq is Shia majority. Iran, not considered Arab, is Shia Islam-majority. Bahrain has a Sunni royal family, although more than half of the population is Shia.

It is being speculated that the thaw in relationships between Israel and these Arab countries will be followed by more Sunni Muslim Arab countries. It is also being speculated that the reason for normalising the relationship is that Israel is a substantial military power that could help withstand the common enemy, Iran. It is, presumably, a case of the enemy of my enemy is my friend. Sunni Turkey also has regional ambitions and often ends up in conflict with even Sunni-majority Arab countries, as well as with Israel.

Only two Arab countries have previously made peace with Israel, one being Egypt, which has had peace with Israel since 1980, and the other is Jordan, which has had peace with Israel since 1994.

It will take some time for the leadership of Arab countries to change course and reverse all anti-Jewish indoctrination to which their populations have been subjected. We know this because there is plenty of anti-Jewish sentiment still around in both Egypt and Jordan.

I do not believe that we need to delve deeper into Islamic writings to understand how the anti-Jewish sentiment was stoked. Some Arab countries have, for the longest time, not allowed Jews to even visit. It seems that Saudi Arabia has relaxed its attitude towards the Jews to some extent. It may be that the animosity between Sunni Saudi Arabia and Shia Iran may also lead to a thaw in Saudi relations with Israel, in the interest of both states against the common Shia enemy.

The original writers and founders of Christianity no doubt contributed to stoking anti-Semitic sentiment as a result of the Jews (their status as the chosen people notwithstanding) being accused of being culpable in the death of Jesus, who was himself, of course, Jewish.

The original founder of the Protestant churches, Martin Luther, ensured that he bequeathed a legacy of grave anti-Semitism.

Muhammad, when he found that the Jews were not going to abandon their religion and follow him, turned against them, leaving a legacy of the hatred of Jews among Muslims.

For balance, we need to take note of the fact that in the Christian world or, rather, in the non-Muslim world, there is no lack of anti-Jewish acts: the desecration of Jewish cemeteries; the burning of synagogues; neo-Nazis marching in the US (and elsewhere) chanting, "The Jews shall not replace us." Statistically, there are rather few Jews in America, so they cannot replace the rest of the population. There are, in fact, only around six million Jews in the USA, which turns out to be substantially less than 2% of the population. In other countries, except Israel of course, where there are large Jewish populations, the Jews seldom make it up to 1% of the total population. But even leaving that aside, perhaps we should let the neo-Nazis who do not want to be replaced by the Jews keep on marching as long as they do not turn violent. The neo-Nazis might not comprehend this, but the rest of us understand that the Jews are very unlikely to want to replace them.

In Muslim-majority countries, we have already noted that Jews, and even Christians, are allowed to reside there, subject to having a subordinate position and, in accordance with holy texts, having to pay a special tax to the Muslim majority. Most Muslim-majority countries are Islamic in the sense that Islamic law governs their societies.

We find ample evidence of Muslim religious leaders who spew hatred against Jews in mosques even outside of Islamic states. We have seen how, in France, a Jewish kosher supermarket was besieged by an individual who pledged allegiance to the Islamic State, which, in turn, claims to be the true interpreter of Islam.

In Sweden's third city, Malmö, we know of demonstrations in a square where the Muslim demonstrators were shouting, "Slaughter the Jews."

If we want to go further, we could even look at schoolbooks in countries that adhere to Islamic law and find how Muhammad's hatred towards Jews has turned into childhood indoctrination.

For balance, we should remember that it was not that long ago that it was okay to preach in the churches and cathedrals that the Jews were responsible for killing Jesus. It was not that long ago that Hitler attempted to exterminate the Jews, and some Christians would tacitly let it happen. It wasn't that long ago, in parts of the Christian world, that the Jews were not allowed to enter all professions and were forced to live in secluded areas called ghettos.

Enlightenment and secular education have, at least in the rich, non-Muslim world, ensured that the power of the priestly classes has diminished over time. Not so many years ago, after two thousand years of abuse of children and church members by the Catholic Church, the secular powers at last felt strong enough to take the church on.

Not only was the church historically against allowing people to understand the Bible in their own language, but it was even against allowing such useful things as the telescope, which could make people understand that the biblical explanations of the earth as the centre of the universe were simply wrong. It was only in modern times, as late as 1992, that the church forgave Galileo for being right about the earth being a tiny speck in the universe and the sun being the centre of the solar system. Take note here! Forgive Galileo for being right.

It will be some time before the Muslim-majority countries allow science-based education to penetrate the citizenry and stop childhood indoctrination into hatred, starting at home and continuing in their schooling. The priestly classes in Muslim countries, e.g. the imams, mullahs and ayatollahs, will very likely follow the example of Christian countries and struggle to keep their power and control over the population in the self-interest of the clerical class.

It will be a political struggle for the rulers in the Islamic world to undo the tension between the ruling class and the people. Depending on your point of view, holy or perhaps unholy alliances between rulers and religious leaders will have to be broken in order to give their population a proper education. That would be a good step towards less childhood indoctrination into hatred. Reform in Muslim countries may be a necessary precondition to moving forward in the modern world. Cheap oil may not, in the long run, be an effective tool in trying to buy off the population. Change may be necessitated by the development of alternative energy sources. The economies of oil-rich Arab Muslim lands may need to integrate with the world economy, and that, in turn, may require their populations to be educated in ways that allow such integration. It may be difficult to do business with people you are indoctrinated to hate.

So, as we near the end of this chapter, we should ask ourselves: is there reason to keep hope alive, or must we borrow from Christopher Hitchens who asks whether the Jews will never be forgiven for rejecting two in a row, namely Jesus and Muhammad?

The Jews were the first of the three Abrahamic religions to believe in Yahweh. The few Jews, just under 15 million, that are left in this world just decided to stay with their original religion despite all the persecution they have suffered. One Occam's razor question would thus be: is there really anything the Jews need to be forgiven for?

Still, there are many Christians who continue to believe that the Jews are guilty of the killing of God in the form of Jesus.

Anti-Jewish sentiment also runs deep among Muslims. When the Danish lawyer and politician Rasmus Paludan organised the burning of a Quran in Malmö at the end of August 2020, despite being forbidden from doing so by both the police and the District Court of Malmö, there were no Jews nor any Jewish organisations who condoned that burning. Yet the Muslims who demonstrated against the burning of the Quran chanted a deeply anti-Jewish line in Arabic. The chanting was intended to remind the Jews about an event in Khaybar where the prophet Muhammad decapitated Jews while his very young wife, Aisha, looked on. In English, the chant would be something like the following: "Remember Khaybar, O Jews, the sword of Mohamad will return." The chant seems totally uncalled-for at any time, but especially under

CHAPTER 9

the circumstances. The chant will serve as evidence that anti-Jewish sentiment in the Muslim world is often if not always lying there, just beneath the surface.

Let us end with the following Occam's razor questions: Should we blame the purveyors of anti-Semitism or the victims? Should the burning of a Quran or a Bible be allowed as free speech, and, if not, what other form of free speech are we prepared to dispense with?

Perhaps it is as simple as this: you have the right to offend me, and I have the right to feel offended.

CHAPTER 10

Why is it ... that we are eager to believe that we have free will in relation to God but don't know what free will is?

We need to start this very simply. That means that we will not enter the discussion on modern neuroscience in terms of the extent to which we have free will.

A person is about to cross a street with many cars passing both ways in front of her. She can start with either the left or the right foot. It probably happens subconsciously, but the decision is made to start with a particular foot. Is that an expression of free will? Perhaps it is, but it is not important enough because there is no moral issue involved that would make us concerned. Nothing in the world changes, regardless of which foot she starts with when crossing the street.

Let us now assume that she suffers from Obsessive Compulsive Disorder which gives her a kind of decision tree in the following way. She always needs to start with the left foot when crossing a street. That is unless a red car passes in front of her just before crossing, in which case she needs to start with the right foot. In both cases, she needs to avoid stepping on any cracks on the street which makes her pay attention to the surface of the street rather than the traffic. Is she using her free will? Apart from perhaps delaying traffic a tiny bit, it is also not a question that we concern ourselves with too much. Okay, she suffers from the disorder, but again, there are no big moral issues at stake.

CHAPTER 10

Now let us assume that a thousand years ago, a prophetess was told the following by one of the angels of God. The prophetess is taken to a secluded place and told that all three religions that claim Abraham as their ancestor are wrong and have been corrupted. She is told that God will take on a new name and wishes from now on to be called *Xtraordinary*. She is given only one command to observe and remember, and that is that, when worshipping Xtraordinary, the worshipper must stand on only one leg for at least 15 minutes at a time and for at least one hour per day while looking up to the sky and remembering God's existence. For 20 years she keeps this to herself but then decides that she needs to tell some other people because she might soon pass to the other side. The prophetess tells nine people what the angel has told her, and they remember.

Eventually, it is decided that it is better to write it down because even these very few lines could be forgotten over time. To make sure that the prophetess' angelic revelation – now more than twenty years old – isn't corrupted, three people who have heard her instructions must agree on the wording and remember the same story for it to be approved in written form.

The story simply becomes that we should forget about all other rules and regulations in any of the Abrahamic religions and even God's old names. Those texts have been corrupted over time and this is the last true prophetess with the only true version of what God wants from you. Nothing up until that point and nothing in the future will change that. Finally, it is written down that one should pray four times a day minimum, standing on one leg for at least 15 minutes at a time, while quietly looking at the sky. Praying on both legs would be at your own risk and could be subject to the penalty of death by lightning.

A couple of generations pass, and a new self-professed holy person decides that this very simple text needs further interpretation. It is not that you have no leg to stand on, but should it be the left or the right leg? Can you be allowed to decide, on your own, whether to use one leg or the other? In certain geographical areas, the conclusion is drawn that the left foot is the right one to stand on while praying in silence because that, for most of us, is the weaker leg and standing on our weaker leg shows submission to God. It is also in that geographical area decided that even left-handed or rather left-legged people would have to use only the left leg for praying, even though that would be their dominant leg. If they were to use the wrong leg for the area, others might be tempted to follow them and pray on the wrong leg.

As it happens, in another geographical area about 300 km to the east, a different approach is prescribed. There it is decreed that people should stand only on their right leg because that is the dominant leg and that will show Xtraordinary that we submit with all our strength.

After a further few generations, the different versions have become ingrained in the two areas. The children have been taught exactly how to do this, and nobody in either area has doubts about what is the right way. When it is discovered that not too far away there is a different interpretation of the correct leg to use, squabbling breaks out between the inhabitants of the two areas.

No doubt, in both places, someone must be tempted to try the other leg than the one prescribed for them. But they are so indoctrinated since childhood and everyone in the area has prayed on the same leg for generations that any other interpretation or practice has become blasphemous. And trying to stand on the other leg could cause to you be struck by lightning, as revealed by Xtraordinary himself.

Eventually, it is decided that a chief interpreter for each of the eastern and western sects of the religion has to be appointed. It has to be a woman, with the title the Ma-Pa, and she will have the ultimate say in what is right and wrong. The Ma-Pa is elected by the separate colleges of W–Elders, consisting of 26 women.

The need for Ma-Pas is a result of detailed discussions in the communities on such important matters as what to do if a person is too sick to stand on one leg. Could they, for instance, have a close relative hold them up? Could one lean against a wall? The eastern and western Ma-Pas come to somewhat different conclusions. But the rules become more and more intricate and more and more difficult to abide by.

CHAPTER 10

Eventually and inevitably, a Protestorant movement comes about, the leader of which wants a much simpler version of all the religious rituals. She wants to go back to the original teachings of the original prophetess and decides that God, that is Xtraordinary, does not really mind and you can stand on whatever leg you want while praying.

What has this to do with free will? What we see is that our religion and how to worship and pray to God is entirely a matter of how we were educated and indoctrinated by our parents, and how they were indoctrinated by their parents, and in the end a matter of geography, of where the particular religion was interpreted in a particular fashion. The same original text has been given opposing interpretations over time, and, of course, the people on the other side must be using the wrong leg. Free will, in this context, would then mean that were you to be so naughty as to try to pray on the other leg than the one prescribed in your area, you would be risking death by lightning. We can easily imagine that the leaders of the two distinct ways of interpreting Xtraordinary's will wanted to introduce some punishment on earth. Why wait for lightning to strike you when it is possible for Ma-Pa to impose the death penalty? Free will becomes a choice between following the rules and praying on the correct leg in your specific area or risking death. In the other geographical area, praying on what is the right leg in your area would have the same dire consequences.

Let us now take a very well-known incident from real life as an example. On September 11, 2001, three planes were hijacked by Islamist Al Qaeda terrorists and flown into the Twin Towers of the World Trade Center and the Pentagon. Another hijacked plane was overtaken by passengers and crew and crashed without reaching its intended target.

The leader of Al Qaeda, Osama bin Laden, took responsibility for the attacks and claimed as motives a combination of the presence of US troops in Saudi Arabia, US support for the state of Israel, and sanctions against Iraq. Osama bin Laden, together with the hijackers and supporters of the terrorist acts, was convinced that they were using their free will in the defence of Islam.

The victims and the supporters of the victims were and are equally convinced that the terrorists used their free will in a wrongful manner to do evil. In the context of this little discourse about free will in relation to God, Xtraordinary, let us now venture into Judaism, Christianity, and Islam. We are, perhaps, getting tired of having to go over this again and again, but in all of these religions and underlying sects, God is all-seeing, all-knowing and all-powerful. The texts in the holy scriptures, however, have been written with a notable lack of clarity and many interpretations that have led to geographical differences as to how God should best be worshipped.

The religion that we receive from childhood comes from our parents and mostly from the geographical area where they live. That is where they and their parents and grandparents have for generations been indoctrinated in their belief systems and have continued to pass that on. In each geographical area, they of course believe that they are right and that all other interpretations must therefore be wrong. When parents emigrated to other geographical areas, they would bring their childhood indoctrination with them and try to keep that up for many generations. There are, of course, people who decide to convert to a religion. For some reason, a potential convert may have concluded that converting to a specific religion will be life-changing (for the better). It is no wonder that, if you convert voluntarily with such strong beliefs, you may also become a very strict follower of the religion that you are converting to. Some conversions are a result of more earthly considerations. Somebody getting married to a person from a different faith may feel inclined to convert to the faith of that partner.

Ayatollah Khomeini was a Shia Muslim cleric who founded the Islamic Republic of Iran. He took over after the Shah of Iran was deposed and went into exile. The ayatollah became the supreme leader of Iran according to a new constitution that guaranteed religious oversight over the state. After his death, a new supreme leader was appointed.

Let us now, for the sake of argument, assume that the ayatollah had happened to be born to Catholic parents, in Poland, a largely Catholic country.

CHAPTER 10

It is extremely unlikely that he would have held the beliefs that he came to hold in his capacity as ayatollah. Perhaps his writing would also have been affected by being born in Poland to Catholic parents. It is unlikely that he would have written about a man deriving sexual pleasure from a baby. Because, in his little green book, he does indeed make it clear that an adult male can enjoy a baby girl but should put his penis between her thighs instead of in her vagina. The restriction he imposes on the man is that he should not penetrate the baby's vagina, but anal penetration is a more acceptable practice. He further rules that if somehow a man does put his penis in the baby's vagina and harms her, he will have to sustain her for life. He probably felt really good about what, in his mind at least, must have been the humane thing to teach his followers in this particular ruling. He issued another ruling in the interest of divine justice in which he ordered that virgin female prisoners subject to the death penalty must be raped before they are executed. Otherwise, they could enter heaven. Another of his rulings is "If a man sodomises the son, brother, or father of his wife after their marriage, the marriage remains valid." To be abundantly clear, *sodomise* in this context means to anally penetrate. Ayatollah Khomeini also had opinions about sex with animals and wrote, "If a person has intercourse with a cow, a sheep, or a camel, the urine and dung become impure and drinking their milk will be unlawful." He does recommend sheep among the animals for sexual gratification and also recommends that the sheep be slaughtered and the meat sold to the people of a different village. One could easily assume that Ayatollah Khomeini would not have published his rulings had he not felt that he was using his free will to teach and inspire his followers to follow Allah in a good way. Whether his teachings are good or bad will, in the end, depend on the vantage point from which one looks at them. There is no doubt that from a Western liberal viewpoint, the rulings seem rather evil.

If Ayatollah Khomeini had been born in Poland, he might have become pope, instead of the Polish cardinal who eventually became Pope John Paul II. The ayatollah's outlook on life and his writings would have been different. And the opposite is equally true, that if Pope John Paul II had been educated and indoctrinated in the Muslim faith, his writing would have been entirely different and he might have become an ayatollah or a mullah.

You would think that a country like Israel would have one chief rabbi, but the truth is that there seems to be a need for two chief rabbis: one chief rabbi for the Ashkenazi Jews, and one chief rabbi for the Sephardi Jews. The chief rabbi for the Ashkenazis represents western Jews mainly from Europe, except those from Spain and Portugal. The chief rabbi for the Sephardis represents Jews from the Middle East, the Arabian Peninsula, and also those of Spanish or Portuguese descent.

Even with a few million Jews in Israel, they cannot decide on one true interpretation of holy scripture. Of course, in Judaism, as in any other religion, there are ample sects that have their own interpretation of holy scripture. We can start with the ultra-religious who do not recognise the state of Israel because the Messiah of the Jewish people has not yet arrived. We can then move on to ordinary orthodox Jews and then to more liberal-leaning ones such as conservative and reform. Even God's beloved people, of whom only around 15 million are left in the entire world, cannot agree on how best to worship their maker.

Let us choose the Sephardi chief rabbi and assume that he had been born in Saudi Arabia. He would have been educated by Muslim parents and might have ended up being the Grand Mufti of Saudi Arabia, his native country, where he would have been raised and subjected to childhood indoctrination. In that capacity, he might have taught hatred towards the Jews, in accordance with his best understanding of Islam and its traditions.

What are we to make of this? Was it really God's plan that the holy texts would be so difficult to understand? Was it really his intention to be so mysterious and refuse to make us understand? God is capable of anything, and He could write or inspire writing with such clarity that we all would have perfect understanding of His will. If God, as is stated in the *Encyclopaedia of Bible Difficulties*, instead deliberately, consciously chose to use the imperfect language of humans, He contributed to much fighting and strife between peoples with different interpretations of His holy texts.

CHAPTER 10

Either we have invented God and each geographical area just has its own invented, almost arbitrary way of worshipping him or God must be seen as sitting in heaven watching us and laughing because we do not understand how to worship Him. And He must have done so deliberately by informing us with such a peculiar lack of clarity. He must be looking down on us while we fight – even literally wage war – over the right way to worship Him.

Catholics and Protestants have been fighting for a long time, at least as far back as the 30 Years' War in the 17th century. Even the Swedish King, Gustav II Adolph, led a Lutheran army to fight the Catholics until the king died at the Battle of Lutzen in 1632. Both sides of this war were obviously living – and fighting – in the sure belief that they were exercising their free will for the good of the Lord in accordance with their particular interpretation. The problem remains, of course, that they cannot both be right at the same time. Perhaps the brutal truth is that nobody is right.

Nevertheless, at the time of the Thirty Years' War, the population on our planet was a little under 500 million people. During that religious war, around eight million people lost their lives, including about 20% of the German population. The fight was between two sides who prayed to the same God and had the same holy texts. Can we really believe that this was God's plan? To be accurate, it should be noted that although the war started as an entirely Catholic versus Protestant affair, over the thirty years, the lines became somewhat muddled. For instance, in 1635, France entered the war on the side of the Protestants. Although religion had been the original reason for the war, with Catholic France fighting on the Protestant side, it became more an issue of influence, power and land.

Northern Ireland is well known for the hostilities between Catholics and Protestants. To what extent this fighting is truly about religion is doubtful. No doubt, though, it could not have hurt recruitment efforts on both sides to know that God was on your side.

Sunni and Shia Muslims are still at odds with each other and have fought many wars. It is a matter of which side represents the truer Islam. Even here, it is certainly also a matter of gaining influence and controlling land. God is a wonderful and very practical excuse that helps the recruitment efforts on both sides.

If you are Jewish, you have the option of following the Ten Commandments or being subject to a biblical death penalty. Is that free will? The choice is to do what you are told or to die. Since the Ten Commandments were given to the Jews, it is not unlikely that non-Jews may be excluded from the death penalty for not following the commandments. We must note that Christianity has adopted the Old Testament, including the Ten Commandments. Jesus was for following these commandments except when it came to following him and leaving all else behind. To follow him, one must, among other things, hate one's parents and even oneself.

If you are Muslim and choose to leave the faith, you must die. The choice is to at least pretend to stay in the faith or be killed. The death penalty for leaving the true faith is, of course, carried out on earth. The heretic does not have to wait for the godly punishment. Is there a free choice between death and following Islam once you have been born or converted into Islam?

For all others apart from the Christians, who have found Jesus at some stage before they die, burning in hell for all eternity is what awaits you. That is what awaits every non-Christian and all the Christians who are inclined not to believe, a punishment far harsher than that for the very worst human misdeeds. You can, if punished by your fellow humans, be imprisoned for life or executed, and you may even be tortured before you die, but there is a finality to the human punishment inflicted on fellow humans. But not having the right attitude towards Jesus Christ at the end of your life will lead to your being sent to be burnt forever and ever without end. Probably somewhere between 80 and 90% of the world's population will end up burning in hell since they do not have the true faith in Jesus by the time they die. Is there a free choice here? Even if we don't know about Jesus, we are still subject to the penalty. We can, therefore, reasonably conclude that free choice is not exactly what these Abrahamic religions give us.

CHAPTER 10

And now some of us might ask: what does the Bible say? We can, for the purposes of this examination, look at one story in the Old Testament that is very well known, while remembering that even Jesus was in favour of following the laws of Moses, as was his brother James.

So, let's look at the story of the ten plagues. The story is a fairly simple one. Moses has a Jewish mother and a Jewish father and is born at a time when the pharaoh becomes afraid that a new leader will be born and come to deliver the Hebrew slaves in Egypt to freedom. The pharaoh orders the mass killing of male Israelite babies in a similar way to the New Testament story in which Herod orders babies to be killed in Bethlehem so that a Messiah could not come forth and replace him as King of the Jews. In both these instances, the question we must ask ourselves is: how in heaven's name would they know, or have any inkling of such a thing as a revolutionary leader or Messiah being born?

Moses is taken in a basket by his sister and floats in the basket on the Nile to be collected by a princess of the pharaoh's household and raised as an Egyptian prince. He eventually finds out that he has Jewish parentage and flees Egypt. In the meantime, the Israelites, God's beloved people, have been in Egypt for around 400 years and many of those years in slavery. God decides to finally hear their cries and prayers and concludes that it might be time to set them free. It is time to take them out of slavery and turn them into a free people.

God does not do the simple thing and just make sure that the pharaoh lets them leave. There has to be a convoluted way of doing this, which includes sending Moses back to Egypt to negotiate with the pharaoh about the release of the Israelites. It becomes necessary for God to inflict on the Egyptians the ten plagues, which are, in order, water becoming blood; an infestation of frogs; lice; flies; livestock becoming infested; boils; hailstorms; swarms of locusts; darkness; and finally, the killing of the firstborn.

God could very easily have skipped all of this, of course, and just forced the pharaoh to let the Israelites leave. Somehow the free will of the pharaoh seems to mean a lot in the story of the ten plagues. Let us, therefore, investigate how the pharaoh uses his free will.

After the trick when Aaron's staff is thrown to the floor and becomes a serpent, the magicians manage to copy that trick. Yet Aaron's snake manages to swallow the other snakes. The pharaoh isn't very impressed and his heart is thus hardened. God himself speaks to Moses and says, "Pharaoh's heart is hardened, he refuses to let the people go."

Could anybody else hear the Lord speaking to Moses? If pharaoh had heard a voice out of nowhere forcefully telling Moses how badly he viewed the pharaoh's behaviour, it might have helped to persuade him. But no.

God continues speaking to Moses and directing him on the actions he and his brother Aaron should take. The first plague is that all water turns into blood. The fish in the waters die and the water becomes undrinkable. For an all-knowing and all-seeing God, the next part must be beyond belief. It is even difficult for us to understand how an all-seeing, all-knowing God had no idea that the pharaoh's magicians could copy the water to blood magic trick. Since the pharaoh's magicians could indeed copy what God has done, the pharaoh's heart is hardened.

The next plague, number two on the list, and also copied by the pharaoh's magicians, is frogs aplenty. The pharaoh asks Moses to intervene to have God remove the frogs and he will let the people go. The pharaoh changes his mind once the frogs disappear, and he hardens his heart once again.

With an abundance of time, foresight and knowledge on his hands, the omniscient God is obviously aware of the fact that the pharaoh will prove to be a difficult ruler to handle. That in itself is alarming, since God knows any outcome and can direct any outcome any way he pleases. The fact is that God is waiting and playing a game with himself while his beloved people are still suffering in slavery under their Egyptian masters.

Despite his magicians' warnings about the lice plague (number three), the pharaoh hardens his heart – yet again – and still does not let the Israelites leave. This pattern continues for the plague of the flies (number four). As a negotiating tactic, Moses asks the pharaoh to allow the Israelites to leave for three days to go out into the desert to pray. The pharaoh, however, is not convinced, and

CHAPTER 10

the Israelites remain in Egypt. This causes plague number five, the death of livestock. The pharaoh's heart is once again hardened once this plague ends – as if God would not have known this in advance.

The people of Egypt are subsequently plagued with boils (plague number six) but, lo and behold, this time God himself interferes to harden the pharaoh's heart. Are we all taking note of this? God hardens the pharaoh's heart!

The next plague is hailstorms, after which the pharaoh is supposed – once more – to have hardened his heart.

Plague number eight is locust swarms, and God proudly announces that He has again hardened the pharaoh's heart.

God hardens the pharaoh's heart once again after plague number nine, darkness over the land.

Have we taken all of this in? This is a God who can read everybody's mind and understand everybody's heart. This is a God who has decided that his beloved people have had enough suffering, and he has so far used up nine plagues. It must be very surprising to a believer that the free will of the pharaoh is supposedly so important that it needs a long negotiation with many different punishments to persuade the pharaoh to let the Israelite slaves leave Egypt.

Even more surprising is that God himself intervenes and plays with the pharaoh's free will, in fact actively, deliberately robs him of his free will, his agency. He is responsible for hardening Pharaoh's heart and making him change his mind. Could he not skip all of that? What is the use of the entire exercise of respecting the free will of the pharaoh when even God himself is manipulating it? Four times God's hardening of the pharaoh's heart is what causes the pharaoh to not let the Israelites leave. Perhaps a reasonable answer is that there is no free will, especially since God knows our minds and our hearts and, according to Jesus, even knows what we are going to pray for and what He is going to give us in answer to our prayers.

We now come to the famous tenth plague, which is the killing of the firstborn. The pharaoh is warned that the tenth plague is going to be the final and truly devastating one. The pharaoh is even told that that last plague is going to be based on one of his own pronouncements. God tells the Hebrews to sacrifice lambs and eat the meat before the next morning. First, however, they should paint their doorposts with the lamb's blood. If they comply, the Angel of Death will pass over Hebrew homes and leave the firstborns in Israelite homes alone.

It is disturbing that God even needs to have a sign on the doorposts for the Angel of Death to pass over. Leaving that aside, let us assume the following scenario: some of the pharaoh's security forces are out looking to see if there is any trouble among the Israelites and discover that they are painting their doorposts with lamb's blood. They torture a few of the Israelites and find out exactly why they are painting their doorposts with lamb's blood. Imagine further that the pharaoh is persuaded, just as a precautionary measure, to paint his own doorposts with lamb's blood. There might also be some Israelites who have not received the message and therefore have not painted their doorposts with lamb's blood in time. What would have happened in this situation? Would God's Angel of death have spared the pharaoh's firstborn too since the pharaoh's palace had the doorposts painted in lamb's blood? Would the Angel of death have struck down Israelite firstborn just because they were hunkered down in dwellings where they had failed to paint their doorposts with lamb's blood?

The holiday that celebrates this event is called Passover since the Angel of Death passed over those dwellings with lamb's blood-painted doorposts. It is noteworthy that, according to three of the Gospels in the New Testament, Jesus had his Last Supper on the Jewish holiday, Passover.

Do we end this with a better understanding of the concept of free will? Are we now perhaps ready to concede that God is prepared to manipulate us to whatever end he sees fit? Are we willing to conclude that we might have very limited free will or, perhaps, none at all in relation to God? Perhaps the more appropriate conclusion is that all the biblical stories are written by humans and that there is no God or at least not a God that pretends that we have free will without understanding what that means?

It would be appropriate to end our discussion by seeing what happens next. According to the Bible, over two million people are let go from Egypt and decide to walk towards the Red Sea. After a while, the pharaoh's heart is hardened again and he follows them with his army to bring them back. God has foreseen this but lets it happen anyway. The pharaoh's army comes close to catching up to the slaves, but God, through Moses' action of stretching his hand over the sea, divides the waters in the Red Sea so that the Hebrews can march across. When the pharaoh's army approaches, many of them drown as the waters flow back again once the Hebrews have safely passed to the other side.

This is a good time to remind ourselves that, if God could harden pharaoh's heart, which in effect means changing his mind, he could have softened his heart at any earlier stage, before any plague, and just made the pharaoh let the Hebrews leave in peace.

What an incredible game God seems to have been entertaining himself with at our expense. God knows the outcome in advance since he is, among other things, a good mind-reader. Still, to amuse himself, God plays this bizarre game and interferes with the free will of the pharaoh. Do we not understand that God knows – and has known – the outcome of the interaction with the pharaoh, in every detail, all the way since creation?

Were the Hebrews slaves in Egypt? Can we find any evidence outside of the Bible that they were? We should understand that the story about Israelite slavery in Egypt lacks corroborating evidence from archaeology. According to the Bible, the Israelites who left would have been over two million in number, including women and children, and that would have been about half of the Egyptian population. There would have been archaeological finds to verify such a huge exodus. Sadly, our archaeologists find no such clues.

We can already hear people complaining about the analysis here and imagine them pointing to the Book of Job to demonstrate man's free will. According to the Bible, Job is a good man and worships God in the right way. Job does nothing wrong, according to the rule of God. Yet God himself enters into betting – and yes, that is actual gambling – with his evil opponent. The evil opponent would be the Devil, also called Satan. We must ask the question again: why is it that the all-powerful God allows an evil opponent such as Satan to even exist? One often hears the explanation that the Devil might exist to tempt us to go on the wrong path and use our free will in a wrongful manner against the Lord. I think we all know that there is enough evil in us naturally, without needing a Devil to tempt us. To those who wish to combat this idea and argue that the Devil is symbolic of the evil within us, that is not what is written in the holy texts, and for the purposes of our analysis, we are only interpreting the texts as they are written.

The bet God makes with the Devil concerns whether, by losing his assets and family, Job will end up turning against God. Satan is allowed to do anything and everything except taking Job's life. One could easily conclude that, since God knows the outcome of the bet, the cards are undeniably stacked in God's favour. Job's wealth is thus taken away from him, his family is taken away from him, and yet he remains God-fearing and God-worshipping and never utters a single bad word against God. God grants Job new wealth but funnily enough does not give him his family back. He could have done that. He doesn't but gives him a new family instead.

With God allowing a Devil to exist, there is a risk of being seen as impotent, in terms of controlling or removing the Devil. The further risk is that we do not know which of the holy texts have come about by the Devil's hands rather than being inspired by God's wishes.

Looking at this with an Occam's razor view, can one speak of free will in a situation where God knows the outcome in advance? How human is it to make bets and how ungodly is it, really?

Added to this is the fact that we do not know whether God in any way interfered with the free will of Job or, for that matter, anyone else's. We would not know, would we? But we do know from the Bible that God does interfere, and, in one of the most well-known stories of the Bible, the one about the ten plagues, it is admitted that God plays this game with himself by using the pharaoh's free will and manipulating it to whatever end He wishes.

CHAPTER 11

Why is it ... that the pope of the Catholic Church is considered infallible when so many mistakes have been made by the church?

Let us start this off by deciding what the formal titles of the current pope are. We can do that by going to the Vatican's website where the current pope has a number of titles, none of which includes *pope*. The official title or rather titles of the head of the Catholic Church are *Bishop of Rome, Vicar of Jesus Christ, Successor of the Prince of the Apostles, Supreme Pontiff of the Universal Church, Primate of Italy, Archbishop and Metropolitan of the Roman Province, Sovereign of the State of Vatican City, Servant of the Servants of God.*

When a pope is elected by the College of Cardinals, white smoke goes up from the chimney and the people are thus informed that the new pope is heading the church. Once elected, miraculously, the new pope is deemed to be a successor of St. Peter, who, in church mythology, is considered to be the first pope. There is no historical evidence that Peter was the first pope. How would Peter know that such a thing as a pope would come to be seen as the future leader of the Catholic Church?

One of the titles is biblical, and that is *Servant of the Servants of God* and is likely picked up from the Gospel of Matthew where it says, "Whosoever will be great among you, let him be your minister; And whosoever will be chief among you, let him be your servant."

At the Last Supper, Jesus goes down on his knees to wash the feet of his twelve apostles, showing them how to be servants. The supreme pope is the servant of his flock, which is made up of around 1.2 billion Catholics around the world. According to Catholic teaching, the pope is supreme. What else can we expect from a person who can miraculously trace his office back to St. Peter? It is, after all, St. Peter who was called the rock by Jesus personally. The rock on which Jesus said his church would be built.

Do we not ask ourselves here whether Jesus or Peter even knew that the church was going to be so great? Did Jesus or Peter even envisage that there would be many churches with many ways of interpreting the holy texts? Jesus seems to speak to Peter of only one church. A bit of a disconnect really, where we now have – but are not limited to – the Roman Catholic Church, the various orthodox churches and a number of Protestant churches, the Coptic church and the Anglican Church, each with their own somewhat different interpretation of what true faith is.

Northern Ireland, to take just one example, has seen quite a bit of unnecessary fighting, with deadly outcomes. The fighting has been between Protestants and Catholics in the name of God – despite both sides worshipping the same God. No doubt there were, as noted already, political, territorial and other reasons for the fighting, but it was easier to rouse the ordinary person to take a stand against the other side with the wrong faith. And, in their own particular faith, each side found both reasons and excuses for unspeakable violence against the other side.

Let us revisit the issue of whether any pope can ever be wrong. Is a pope really infallible? It would not be unreasonable to claim that all the papal titles are intended to boost the flock's belief in the supremacy of the pope, as well as his infallibility. The church believes that it is the one true religion and that the pope himself must, at any and every time of the church's history, be right. What else would all the history and all the titles imply? We can leave aside the fact that the pope is also king of the Vatican state.

The fact that pronouncements by a pope are always right has been discussed in the church since the early 500s CE. In 1870, Pope Pius IX made sure that

CHAPTER 11

nobody could misunderstand that papal pronouncements were without error by making papal infallibility part of church dogma. We find the usual play on words to shade the issue somewhat. Infallibility only applies when the pope of the Catholic Church speaks *ex cathedra*, which is from *the chair. Big difference!* is what a modern young reader might now say to herself.

Let us take the doctrine of papal infallibility as seriously as it deserves to be taken. Ever since the concept of papal infallibility was declared to be true on July 18, 1871, we can find one example of a pope speaking from the chair, and that was in 1950 when Pope Pius XII (Hitler's very own pope) announced that the Assumption of Mary was an article of faith. That must be true since the papal pronouncements from *the chair* cannot be wrong.

Ordinary followers of the church might have great difficulty believing that this is the only thing a pope could say without being wrong. Let us ask ourselves how important that pronouncement is. It serves one purpose and that is to make it difficult for people who do not believe in the Assumption of Mary to call themselves Catholic.

We would not be wrong if we came to the conclusion, with all the mysticism around the election of a pope and how he then comes to be the Vicar of Christ, that just about all his pronouncements should be without fault. Probably, for the lay member of the Catholic Church, any pronouncement by a pope ought to be seen as authoritative and true. The assertion that a papal pronouncement is only without fault if the pronouncement is made from the chair is a form of verbal gymnastics that church theologians may want to debate.

As ordinary people, we look to the pope as the leader of the many people who call themselves Roman Catholics. As the leader of the Roman Catholic Church, the pope mystically becomes the Vicar of Christ. If any pronouncement is made by a pope, even if the pronouncement is not from the chair, papal pronouncements should, at the minimum, demonstrate the wisdom of that pope to be infallible. What, otherwise, is the reason for having a head of a billion people interpreting the word of God and God's son to those who follow the Catholic faith? For the flock looking up to the pope and admiring him without question or doubt, there is likely very little difference between papal pronouncements from the chair and other papal pronouncements. Any person deemed wise enough to make infallible pronouncements should at least not make stupid pronouncements or make stupid decisions. They would indeed be incapable of doing so.

Because Pius IX made sure that papal infallibility was finally and properly acknowledged, it is reasonable that we start our investigation of papal behaviour with his papacy. The least we should be expecting from a person who has been elected to become the head of the Catholic Church is a level of decency, even if it does not go as far as infallibility. Furthermore, if you entrust somebody with infallibility in certain respects, you would expect that person to have a high level of understanding of what he is about to do or say and the consequences thereof. We know Pope Pius IX as the pope who codified papal infallibility, and we would expect him to be able to control himself and act accordingly. Prepare to be surprised.

We dealt with this briefly earlier on, and so this is a reminder of that Jewish family who lived in Bologna, Italy, and were subject to some really awful treatment at the hands of Pope Pius IX. The family had a son who had, as a baby, become very ill. The family also had a Catholic servant girl working for them and she became afraid that if the boy died, he would not be given eternal salvation. The poor ignorant girl took matters into her own hands and baptised the boy herself by sprinkling some water on him.

The story of this incident came to be known by Pope Pius IX. In his wisdom and infallibility, he decided that the servant girl's actions had made the boy a Christian. He further decided that the Christian boy had to be given a Catholic education and would have to leave his parents' home because his parents were Jewish. The pope found it unacceptable that the Jewish parents would – for obvious reasons – have given their son a Jewish education. The pope finally undertook to personally make sure that the boy was educated in the right way.

The pope had the boy removed from the parents' home and took him into his own care. The boy was at the time six years old and was taken from his family

CHAPTER 11

by the police, who delivered him to the pope in Rome. At the time, there were many protests and petitions to the pope, protests that even came from Catholic governments. The protesters wanted the boy to be given back to his parents. The faultless pope refused, and the boy eventually became a priest.

The Vatican has never apologised for the kidnapping. A papal apology for a past event or a past misdeed by the church undermines the aura of infallibility with which a pope is viewed. Despite this, Pope John Paul II did issue an apology for the persecution of Jews, and perhaps, within that, indirectly, lies some form of apology for the kidnapping in 1858.

There are conservative Catholic voices who defend Pius IX. In defending Pope Pius IX, they seem to forget that Thomas Aquinas, one of the fathers of early Christianity, argued that baptism of Jewish children against the wishes of the parents is unjust. Not only that, but the wise and infallible pope must have failed to see the other side of the coin. Let us assume that in a nice Catholic home, unbeknownst to the parents, a Devil-worshipping nanny is employed to look after their baby. She had come across as very cordial and her references were impeccable.

The little girl is about to die and the nanny, as she understands the custom of her faith, paints one of the baby's toenails black. That is the rite necessary to enter the baby into the Devil-worshipping faith. Would the defenders of Pope Pius IX be equally okay with this six-year-old girl being kidnapped by Satanists in order to be brought up as a Devil-worshipping young lady and eventually becoming a female priest in that faith? I think we can safely say that the Catholic faithful would not. We must also draw the conclusion that the pope himself would not be okay with having a young Catholic girl become a Devil-worshipping priest. The infallible pope would, in this situation, much prefer that the young girl be brought back to her parents and be raised as a good Catholic. One does not want to diminish the flock that one is set to rule over.

Let us analyse the whole chain of events so that there is no doubt that we fully understand what happened. An ignorant Catholic girl was working for a Jewish family and, in looking after the baby who was ill, sprinkled some water on his forehead. In doing so, miraculously, this Jewish boy became Catholic. A couple of drops of water on the forehead of a Jewish boy led to his being taken to the Vatican and educated to be a priest, with his education supervised by the pope himself. Shall we call this chain of events the result of infinite wisdom or an example of the stupid things people are prepared to do when it comes to defending their faith?

We can reasonably conclude that Pope Pius IX, who, after hundreds of years of debate, finally set in stone the concept of papal infallibility, was himself a very flawed interpreter of his own religion. He was a man lacking in wisdom and a man unable to see the consequences of his actions. Perhaps some will come along with the excuse that he did not make this pronouncement from the chair. However, anyone who has the ability and wisdom to make infallible decisions and pronouncements does not end up making grave mistakes.

Those who believe that the kidnapping of the Jewish boy by Pope Pius IX is the only such incident should read an article in the *Atlantic* (*The Pope, the Jews, and the Secrets in the Archives* by David I. Kertzer) that describes how French clergy were arrested in 1953 for having kidnapped two young Jewish brothers whose parents had died in a Nazi death camp. One would have expected that the boys would be handed over, after the end of the Second World War, to close relatives of the deceased parents, but that did not happen because, again, the boys had been secretly baptised, which made them Catholic. Therefore, the brothers could not be raised by Jews. Do we see this as a good example of interfaith understanding?

We should now move on to the issue of priestly celibacy. The Catholic Church's mandate for priests to be celibate might have been one of its biggest mistakes. The official reason for celibacy is that it should help the priests better perform their religious duties to their flock. We who have lived past puberty, and a few years after that, may realise that this may actually work the other way around: a celibate person may become obsessed with the fact that sex is not allowed.

Celibacy originally meant to stay unmarried, and there is a difference between sexual activity and marriage. We find exceptions to the general rule so

CHAPTER 11

that, for instance, Protestant priests who are married and who have converted to Catholicism can still serve as Catholic priests despite continuing to be married.

Early Christians, notably Paul, advised against marriage; he advised men to stay unmarried because an unmarried man can care for the things of the Lord, in contrast to a married man who cares more for things of this world. There is, from Paul, an acknowledgement that the unmarried life is not for everybody. The Vatican has recently acknowledged that the policy of celibacy has not been strictly enforced. Some priests have even been allowed to continue to serve after fathering children. And from what we know, very many continue to serve as priests in spite of engaging in homosexual activities.

The actual starting point for celibacy came through what is called the first Lateran Council, beginning in 1123 and ending in 1153. It became forbidden for priests to marry, and married priests were ordered to renounce their wives and repent.

Do we find this order for married priests to renounce their wives and repent of the marriage to be a decent and godly act? Is that an example of the wisdom and infallibility of the pope?

It should be understood that celibacy within the church can be reversed at any time if the Vatican simply chooses to do so. One has reason to suspect that there might have been financial motives for celibacy. It could have been based on the tacit understanding throughout history – wink, wink, nod, nod – *do not marry*. Quietly practise whatever sexual behaviour you may be inclined to practise. Just keep it quiet. We will, of course, not recognise your children by a woman you have had sexual relations with, and neither should you.

Lo and behold, the wealth that was originally held by the bishops did not need to be passed on to any future generations. What was likely more important to the church was that the bishops did not have *official* heirs on hand to inherit their worldly wealth. This way, the church could keep all the wealth, allowing and enabling the bishops to enjoy their opulent lifestyle during their lifetime.

A friend of mine told me about her experience in her Catholic parish in Portugal where a woman used to come to Sunday Mass with her children.

Everybody knew that the priest was the father of her children and that she would be considered his common-law spouse had it not been for the fact that he was a priest. In the interest of maintaining the double standard and the hypocrisy, everybody in the parish pretended not to know.

Remember that the priestly class was all-powerful. They were educated. They knew the biblical texts. They knew Latin, and their flock was not allowed to get a better understanding of the holy texts in their own language. The result was that the priestly class became very powerful indeed. They also were given the mandate to receive confession and the power to forgive sin, in the name of the Lord. The power of the priestly class was such that the rest of the uneducated world had no ability to take them on.

One can imagine how young girls, young boys, married women, and others throughout history may have been abused by these all-powerful priests and even by various popes. *Imagine* is sadly a wrong word to use in this context. Because there is no need for imagination when historical evidence is so horribly abundant.

In Catholicism, a religion has been created where just wishing for the things that people would naturally like, such as good sex, good food, a little more wealth than our neighbour and generally a more comfortable life, is deemed to be sinful. All of this needs to be dealt with, so you must go to your priest and confess not just your sinful acts but even your "dirty" thoughts.

The priest was, and still is – although fewer believe so – a sinner's only route to salvation, and this, of course, gives the priest immense power. The priest is a man who knows your inner thoughts because you told him. He knows what you might be most afraid of and all about your sexual activity and even your thoughts regarding sex because you told him all of it. One can imagine confessions becoming almost some kind of light – and sometimes not so light – pornography to the listening father. What we know is that some priests have acted in the foulest way having obtained knowledge through the divine power entrusted to them of being able to give a poor sinner absolution after confession.

CHAPTER 11

Do we draw these conclusions without foundation? Or is there perhaps reason to look at the history of sexual activity in the Catholic Church? We will pretend that the latter isn't a rhetorical question.

We know about the sex scandals around the world because the secular world has finally taken enough power away from the priestly class to take them on in court. We know that the priests were protected by the higher-ups and that this went all the way to the Vatican. The abusing priests were moved around and continued to serve in other parishes. We know about priests raping nuns in convents. We know of fetuses and even newborn babies buried in convents gardens.

It is amazing how far a pope is willing to go to try not to explain, but to explain away, all of this sexual abuse. The retired Pope Benedict XVI could not leave the subject alone. He came out of retirement and published a lengthy essay that included blame for the sexual abuse scandals of the Catholic Church on the sexual revolution of the 1960s and homosexual cliques among priests. Amazing stuff! Do we believe that the swinging 60s were somehow retroactively responsible for sexual scandals involving priests within the Catholic Church that go back decades, indeed centuries, into the past?

Before Pope Benedict XVI became pope, he was a cardinal who went by the name of Joseph Ratzinger. At the time, he tried to reform the church and make it easier to remove priests who had abused children. He did, in fact, as pope, actively remove hundreds of priests who had been accused of raping and molesting children. Although he tried to do some good, he also tried to explain away the inexplicable. No wonder that the pope's explanation sounded very hollow. While he served as pope, he was the Vicar of Christ. He was infallible. He should be seen to continue to be infallible. How do you lose that quality once you have been endowed with it? Yet these explanations, blaming the sexual revolution of the 1960s for priestly sex abuse, are historically, palpably, demonstrably false. Sex abuse has been going on within the Catholic Church throughout much of its history. The attempts by this pope to pretend that the sex abuse was a modern thing that started in the 1960s makes him seem less truthful than the pope should be. His explanations make him seem like a person who lacks the wisdom to be infallible.

His successor, Pope Francis, cleverly blamed the scandal on church culture, a culture that sees priests above their flock. This is a more reasonable explanation and goes back far beyond the 1960s. We all know that power tends to corrupt and that absolute power tends to corrupt absolutely. It is only in recent times that secular powers have gained sufficient strength to finally take on the Catholic Church and, within it, the priesthood where the ultimate power has been vested for far too long.

A French writer, Frédéric Martel, published a book in 2019 in which he exposes the sexual secrets of the Vatican and shows the immorality of the Catholic Church rooted in its priests' repressed homosexuality. The writer had extensive access to both priests and cardinals. He was even able to interview young male prostitutes. The conclusion he draws is that, since priests cannot take wives, the church has become a haven for gays. He further finds the hierarchy of the Vatican is full of closeted gays.

Andrew Sullivan, an American writer, wrote an interesting article in the *New York Intelligencer* called *The corruption of the Vatican's gay elite has been exposed.* Sullivan was not the only one who covered the subject of Martel's book. I quote directly from the article: "The picture Martel draws is jaw-dropping. Many of the Vatican gays — especially the most homophobic — treat their vows of celibacy with contempt. Martel argues that many of these cardinals and officials have lively sex lives, operate within a 'don't ask, don't tell' culture, constantly hit on young men, hire prostitutes, throw chem-sex parties, and even pay for sex with church money. How do we know this? Because, astonishingly, they tell us."

What is good for the goose is apparently not so good for the gander. For those who need an explanation of chem-sex, it means introducing drugs into the sex party to enhance the sexual experience. The drugs could be crystal meth or other similar substances. These parties are a form of priestly sex, drugs, and rock 'n' roll, perhaps with or without the rock 'n' roll.

CHAPTER 11

Martel is not the only one who has revealed shocking sexual behaviour by priests inside the Catholic Church. In 2010, a weekly news magazine published an article based partly on footage captured via a hidden camera which recorded, among other things, three priests as they attended gay gatherings where they engaged in casual sex.

Are we not forced to conclude that the many sex scandals that have rocked the Catholic Church, and that have been revealed to be based on documented evidence, are part of a distinct pattern of activity that has been going on for a very long time?

So, let us go back in time and see if it was only the cultural revolution of the 1960s that led to the priests no longer being able to keep their pants up. We could start this historical excursion by looking into an event called *The Banquet of Chestnuts* which took place on October 30, 1501. Celibacy had by this stage already been mandated for Catholic priests, but even if celibacy had not been introduced, it would still be surprising that such a banquet could take place and be led by a sitting pope.

Among the guests at the party were high officials of the Catholic Church and prostitutes. Really, prostitutes? Yes, exactly, prostitutes at a papal banquet! Pope Alexander VI of the famous Borgia family was the host. We know about this party because a guest wrote down precisely what occurred. There have been attempts by the church to deny the accuracy of the story, but there is little reason to believe that what we know about that infamous feast is not true.

There was, of course, no lack of excellent food and wine. The guest list included fifty of the leading prostitutes in Rome. If not the pope himself, then his son, Cesare Borgia, who was helping organise the festivities, obviously knew where to pick these prostitutes up. The prostitutes started dancing and undressing while chestnuts were thrown onto the floor. The prostitutes picked up the chestnuts from the floor with their vaginas, which enticed guests at the feast to throw other items on the floor to be picked up in the same fashion.

The guests gradually started to interact with the prostitutes and turn it into a group-sex event. All the guests, who included ordinary priests as well as cardinals, were invited to take part in a contest in which the winner would be the person with the greatest number of ejaculations. The prizes were handed out by the pope himself.

This pope very openly had several children and mistresses. One can only guess that he might well have been consumed by the power of his position. The Borgias were nothing but power-players, and becoming pope was just another step in the power-play of this family. The description of the chestnuts banquet rhymes well with the modern versions of sex abuse and sexual activity as described by Frédéric Martel and others. Many journalists have exposed the arrant hypocrisy in the hierarchy of the Vatican and its clergy around the world.

We know of stories where priests who have just finished confession in the Vatican would straight away dress up in leather outfits to go to parties at some gay sex club in Rome. We know of these stories because of good journalistic work aided by the hypocrisy of church officials in the Vatican. These Vatican officials feel that they are so infallible that even though they tell their story, and with some pride, they feel they can get away with it. And it seems they do.

The church has made sex for pleasure sinful and one must go to a priest to get forgiveness for one's sins and even for intimate thoughts. One might be forgiven for having expected better supervision and enforcement of the celibacy rules within the church itself. We would have wanted to see more stringent supervision to prevent abuse in general and, in particular, sexual abuse of children.

We see from the chestnut event that sexual scandal was absolutely not a thing exclusive to modern times. The Catholic Church has, in its history, run its own brothels, sharing in the receipts with the prostitutes. These were brothels where men could pay for sexual relief and then go into the church and ask for absolution from a priest who would extract additional funds from the sinner in return for absolution. In order not to lose sight of the importance of what we have just stated, let us be clear, the Catholic Church ran its own ***whorehouses*** for profit. If we turn to modern times, we need look no further back than 2015 when Vatileaks disclosed that Vatican properties were being "used as brothels and massage parlours where priests pay for sex".

Throughout church history, there has been an understanding of what goes on among priests. Early on, the church even decided to choose between the lesser of two evils and encouraged brothels in order to encourage heterosexual sex. After church reports in 1415 found that they needed to reduce the ongoing homosexual behaviour, they did this by setting up a municipal bordello.

In the Middle Ages, the papacy made 28,000 ducats per year from leasing property for use as brothels. In history, we find that, in regard to sex, the Catholic Church is guilty of severe double standards and hypocrisy. One standard was and is meant for activity within the church. That standard is in play because, throughout history, the leadership has not only closed its eyes to, but on many occasions actively and eagerly participated in, various sexual activities. The other standard was and is for the flock. Priests, who themselves may be sinners, will listen to "dirty" thoughts told during confession and extract some monetary punishment, as if it were a fine, and prescribe the "right amount" of prayer, as if that were the medicine.

Why are we spending so much time and effort on sex and the church? Let us think about this. Sex is a basic need. We have an institution run by the papal authority which, throughout history, has certainly been in the know and, in most instances, tolerant of the transgressions within the church. The predictable outcome of mandated celibacy would be and has been sexual abuse directed against the flock.

If a person is flawed in the sense that he has strong urges towards paedophilia, that person may want to find ways of getting close to children. Such a person might want to be a teacher in the lower grades or serve in preschool. Such a person may become a coach for junior sports or become a priest with access to choirboys – and young girls as well, for that matter. If a person found himself to be homosexual during times when it was illegal, becoming a priest might have been the best way to hide in plain sight. One might argue, and some do, that homosexual activity is preferred by some in church leadership roles because it is not as visible as priests hanging out with the opposite sex.

What has this led to? It has led to the situation where today many Catholic priests are homosexual. Joining the Catholic priesthood could, from their perspective, be seen as joining a fantastic gay club – a gay club hidden in full view. A club where a gay person may find himself safe from the condemnation of the general public.

It is only in recent years that the church has been taken on by secular courts for its misdeeds in the form of the sexual abuse of children by its clergy. The church has only reluctantly dealt with it and, in many cases, not appropriately dealt with it, by assisting priests who have been caught in the sex abuse scandals to move to other parishes without letting the new parishioners know of their background. Outside of the church world, we have sex offender registries that serve to alert ordinary citizens residing close to a sex offender who has, perhaps, recently left prison after having served his sentence.

It is not that Jewish rabbis and ministers in Protestant churches have not been abusing their flocks, both sexually and in other ways. They are, however, allowed to be married, and a Jewish rabbi in fact *should* be married. It is a known fact that the proportional numbers of sexual abuse by rabbis in Jewish congregations and by ministers in Protestant congregations, do not come close to the numbers committed by Catholic priests. One would be forgiven for concluding that, had priests been allowed to be married, the problem might not have disappeared altogether but it would perhaps have been significantly less.

St. Augustine is one of the great fathers of Christianity. He started life as a pagan and loved sex. He loved sex so much that he could not resist writing about it and making others understand how good it was. He had a long-term mistress with whom he had a child. He decided to convert to Christianity and become celibate. He is known for having written, "O Lord, give me chastity and self-control, but do not give it yet."

He was born on November 13, 354 CE and died August 28, 430 CE. He lived at a time when prostitution was tacitly allowed by the Roman Catholic

CHAPTER 11

Church. The church was then, as now, against all sex outside of marriage, but they believed that prostitution would help prevent masturbation and rape. It is true, isn't it, to borrow from Christopher Hitchens, that religion makes people do stupid things.

Let us weigh masturbation, which is a private act, against using a prostitute for sex. Is it reasonable to conclude that it might be better to allow masturbation instead of making that a sinful act? Is it possible for the church to claim that a young girl who became a prostitute in order to feed herself, consented to the sex for money? The courtesans who served the royals, the nobility, the bishops, the cardinals and the popes had a rather high status, so perhaps some of them were willing participants. The prostitutes who served the ordinary man might have been forced into their situation through hunger or some other need. Today, the church is very concerned about human trafficking, but in the old days, human trafficking for prostitution was okay with church leadership, although it meant fornicating, having sex outside of marriage.

Let us point out here that researchers have concluded that just about all of us have at some time masturbated. And believers have done so although God is watching us at all times.

St. Augustine also stated, "If you expel prostitution from society, you will unsettle everything on account of lust."

At this point, some may still want to believe that the Roman Catholic Church is a force for good. Perhaps one can look past ordinary sexual activity between consenting adults. But what about paedophilia? Can we find any pope throughout history who has actually endorsed paedophilia? Surprise, surprise, we can. That pope is Boniface VIII, who became pope on Christmas Eve 1294, and died while in office in 1303. He did not take his vows of celibacy seriously. He was discovered in a threesome with a mother and her daughter. But what he says about paedophilia is that "having intercourse with young boys is as natural as rubbing one hand against the other." When he was raping young boys, who could have stood up to him? Do his words perhaps give open approval for the paedophilia that has unquestionably gone on throughout the history of the

Roman Catholic Church? Boniface VIII was – and let us not forget that for a moment – the Vicar of Christ and God's representative on earth. At this point, it may not be terribly surprising if young seminarians or priests looking for approval of their sexual activity would be relieved and even delighted to find them in the words of this pope.

It is not that the church was ignorant about the basic need for sex. It was that they made it sinful for others and hid from the outside world as best as they could what went on inside the church.

If it is possible to make a person feel that masturbation is a sin, that sexual longing after a person who might be married to someone else is a terrible sin, not to mention that sexual activity outside of marriage and, lo and behold, gay sexual activity are sins, one would have a ready-made victim for the power of the clergy. The church has never failed to indoctrinate its flock into these convoluted sexual beliefs, nor to follow that up by giving the priests the ultimate power to be intermediaries between the sinner and God. That power must be seen as one of the causes of the sexual abuse that stretches back throughout history, and which only in recent times have we confronted in civil courts.

We know that there is a gay bubble within the church, so let's ask a supplementary question: is the gay bubble perhaps the only bubble within the Catholic Church?

We can get help from Pope Francis in finding the answer. The pope has admitted that the church was "seeing women as second-class". He also admitted that priests had sexually abused nuns and, in at least in one case, kept them as sex slaves, and that the pope who served before him had been forced to shut down an entire congregation of nuns who had been subject to priestly abuse.

Let us remember that we are talking about priests. Priests are ordained to be the intermediary between the flock and God. We are talking about priests who are educated to know what is sinful and what is not. We are talking of priests who have taken vows. It is obviously not only that women are seen as second-class within the church, but that the natural sexual urges of the priests are higher than their priestly callings.

CHAPTER 11

After Pope Francis admitted that both bishops and priests had abused nuns, he said that the church was aware of the scandal and was working on it. A number of clerics, he continued, had been suspended. Would suspension have been even close to adequate had the sexual assault been committed by employees of a private, non-religious institution or corporation?

There is obviously an ongoing bubble, and it has been admitted that, in some cases, nuns were even forced to abort the fetuses who would have become children fathered by priests. We have been taught and fully understand that if you are celibate, you should stay away from sex and that abortion is a deadly sin. Priests have been even better educated in these matters. In what kind of bubble do priests have to live to allow themselves to rape nuns, keep some in sex slavery and even force pregnant nuns to abort their fetuses? One almost needs to gasp for air. Priests who were about to become fathers – either after raping nuns or from consensual sex with nuns – were quite okay with forcing the nuns to abort the fetuses. They could simply go and confess to an understanding colleague. They would continue to take confession from their congregation and rebuke them for behaviour that was all but certain to be very much less shameful.

This priestly behaviour has, of course, been going on for almost 2000 years. We understand the conflict between vows of celibacy and the natural urges for sex. The fact that sexual urges are natural, even to priests, can be understood from the story of a former nun who, for reasons of remaining anonymous, appeared under the name Christelle. Her story was published on a French website. She had suffered, she claimed, sexual abuse at the hands of a priest of her congregation in France for two years between 2010 and 2011. She stated that the priest's gestures became more and more inappropriate, "but he kept going, until the day he raped me." He was unable to control himself, and, she further stated, "he had a split personality."

A poor, suffering, ignorant and indoctrinated person who believed she was a sinner comes to confession predisposed to believing that her sins are terrible. The priest, in his capacity as confessor, has the ultimate power to grant the sinner absolution. The priest may, if he is a good man, extract a little money and a few prayers in return for the absolution required by the sinner. He may, if he is not a good man, extract confession and ask for so much more in return for the absolution that only he can give. Shall we not allow ourselves to believe that too much of this has been going on for far too long throughout church history?

The power to relieve a self-confessing and truly believing sinner of her sins must be seen as an ultimate power over somebody troubled enough to come to confess and seek absolution. It must have been, throughout the history of the church and very likely even now, a great temptation to abuse that ultimate power. And where would it be mostly abused? We know that it is in places where people are still poor and ignorant. It would be in places where the flock has not been properly educated, and, where they are educated, this might have been done by missionaries who might have given them some basic reading and writing skills but might, at the same time, have indoctrinated them into the appropriate belief system.

We do understand that the Vicar of Christ must have wisdom enough to be infallible, and yet the Catholic Church is also guilty of many other forms of misdeeds and abuses directed towards its flock. The church did not want ordinary people to be able to read the biblical stories in their own language and burnt a translator, William Tyndale, at the stake as late as 1536 CE. The church was so against ordinary people gaining knowledge that they forbade the use of telescopes. The church understood that its own teachings might not be right and that science could, for instance, disprove the supposed age of the world or the belief that the earth was at the centre of our solar system. The church resisted by not allowing scientists to publish, banning them or executing them.

One example, Champollion, a French scientist who died in 1832 at the age of 41, was instrumental in the understanding of Egyptian hieroglyphs. He needed to be funded by the French state for his research and travels, but the church did not hesitate to impose conditions. They did not want him to publish anything that could indicate that the world was older than around 7000 years, which, according to the teachings of the Roman Catholic Church and other Christian churches, would be the time that had passed since God created the world in six days and rested on the seventh day. To be fair, this belief can be found in Judaism as well. The Jewish calendar in the year 2020 CE translates this to the years 5780/81, marking the time since creation. The fact that we find two years in the Jewish calendar is because the Jewish new year, Rosh Hashanah, happens during the autumn months in the northern hemisphere.

The treatment of Galileo can serve as another example. Galileo was punished for being right about our solar system. He was an Italian astronomer who discovered the four biggest moons circling the planet Jupiter. He was born in the mid-1500s and died in January 1642. The Catholic Church was not in favour of Galileo's scientific findings, and the Roman Inquisition in 1615, having investigated the matter, came to the conclusion that the theory that the sun was at the centre of our solar system was "foolish and absurd in philosophy, and formally heretical since it explicitly contradicts in many places the sense of holy scripture." The church knew that Galileo was right but preferred to keep us ignorant. Let us take that in. The church had a full understanding of the science but preferred to keep us ignorant.

Galileo was tried by the Inquisition and, in short, found guilty of heresy. He was to spend the rest of his life under house arrest. The church had to allow his book *Dialogue* to be read in 1822 when it had become common knowledge that the earth was not the centre of the entire universe. But, as noted earlier, it took until 1992 for the church to clear Galileo of wrongdoing. Do you, with me, have any doubt that the church would have been happier for us to continue to live in scientific ignorance? The church did not come willingly to embrace science. The church was forced, and then only belatedly, by enlightenment and scientific knowledge finally having trickled down to the ordinary person, to admit that Galileo was right.

Let us also take note of the deeper meaning when an infallible institution such as the Roman Catholic Church finally admits previous wrongs. By admitting previous wrongs, they are also opening themselves up to future papal revision regarding current teachings such as forbidding the use of condoms while complaining about humanity being at least partly responsible for climate change. Condom use would further help in preventing the spread of venereal diseases and HIV/AIDS. Right now, the rhythm method – having sex when it is perceived to be safe – is favoured in Roman Catholic theology (as well and as among orthodox Jews) because there is at least some risk of pregnancy. This being the case, the church might as well allow condom use because there is a risk that a condom may tear during sexual intercourse.

We will not go through everything that the church can be held responsible for, but let us add just a few more items to our list.

Somewhere high up on this list, we must find the Crusades when, in 1095 CE, Pope Urban II called for war with Muslims. The Crusades lasted until just before 1400 CE and ended up being unsuccessful, with the Muslims the victors. One wonders how that could be. Wasn't Jesus on the side of the Crusaders?

The list must include the burning of witches. Did the well-educated priests not know better? Did the various Vicars of Christ not know better?

We mustn't forget the Inquisition, which began in the 1100s and went on for hundreds of years, in which Muslims and Jews were continually persecuted. The church did not shy away from the worst forms of torture, and some readers may have seen historical movies that depict the kinds of torture to which people were subjected. It is fair to point out that some of these films may be guilty of exaggerating the extent and nature of the torture, but the fact remains that torture went on with papal blessing, as did the burning of "witches".

The aim of the Inquisition was for the church to get rid of heretics. In Spain, the Inquisition lasted for about 200 years, with approximately 32,000 executions and a very large number of confessions extracted through torture. In the late 1400s, King Ferdinand II and Queen Isabella of Spain blamed the corruption in the Catholic Church on Jews who had to convert to Christianity to avoid the anti-Jewish treatment of which they had been victims for centuries.

That did not help for too long because after conversion the converts were suspected of secretly practising their old religion. Jews were forced into ghettos and separated from Christians. The Inquisitor General was a man named Torquemada, who was put in charge of torturing and making converts confess to heresy. He managed, in 1481, to make around 20,000 converts confess to heresy. Hundreds were burnt at the stake while the infallible pope was watching. With minor exceptions, the Inquisition went on with papal blessing. Not only was papal blessing granted to the Inquisition outside of Rome, but there was an Inquisition in Rome directly under the pope. The Galileo incident occurred during the Roman Inquisition. Blasphemy, heresy, witchcraft and Judaism were subject to the Roman Inquisition. We again see the anti-Semitism whereby being Jewish is listed alongside blasphemy and heresy as if it were a crime. In pagan Roman times, cruel performances, with wild animals ripping people up on stage, were performed under the slogan "bread and theatre for the people". No doubt, the Inquisition served to scare the population and to create a common enemy in the heretics, as well as entertaining the people with the public executions.

We must remember that the Catholic Church sold indulgences, which can best be explained as selling for cash the absolution for sins, both sins already committed and even sins to be committed in the future. Pope Leo X lived the good life for which he needed funding, and selling absolution for future sins was a sure winner. Was Pope Leo X infallible or even wise?

Belonging to the list is also Hitler's Pope Pius XII, who could not bring himself to criticise Hitler even after he was alerted to the mass killing of Jews in 1942. There are people who apologise for his behaviour by pointing out that a few Jews were hidden by the church. It may well look to us like some kind of cheap insurance policy should Hitler lose the war.

For those who are interested, it is very easy to find many more misdeeds carried out by the church, but for the purposes of this book, we do not have to go through the entire history of papal misdeeds, misjudgments and abuse. We have seen enough – more than enough – to be able to draw the conclusion that the Catholic Church has been run in its own self-interest as seen through the actions and experiences of various popes throughout its history. We have seen more than enough to conclude that keeping the flock ignorant was the best way of maintaining power. We have seen more than enough to conclude that keeping power was paramount, almost at any cost.

We are left to conclude that neither the church nor any of its leaders are or have ever been infallible. We can also draw the reasonable conclusion that had it not been for the Enlightenment, secular education and the secularisation of society, the church would have preferred to continue to keep us in blissful ignorance.

It all comes down to the fact that the church must have known full well that the biblical stories were, at best, flawed but very likely knew that they were, in fact, just stories. Many educated priests and monks were good scientists, and they knew better. It was fine as long as this knowledge stayed within the church. As scientific knowledge spread through the population, new explanations started to appear to try to bridge the gap between biblical texts and scientific knowledge. Had the church had its way, scientists might have been burnt at the stake and scientific knowledge allowed and preserved only within the church.

Do we still want to believe that all the popes throughout history, each of them the Vicar of Christ and God's representative on earth, have been infallible? Do we still want to believe that each of the popes has, in his papal capacity, at least been imparted with the wisdom to allow him to make reasonable long-term decisions? Wise decisions are required of anybody who is supposed to be capable of making infallible decisions.

Perhaps if we take our blinders off and look at the reality of papal decision-making and actions, we would be forced to conclude that a pope is an ordinary, fallible man elected by a College of Cardinals which itself consists of ordinary, fallible men. Neither godly inspiration nor mysterious wisdom seems to have been imparted to the popes throughout the church's entire history.

With this view, the Catholic Church is an organisation with both a political and financial self-interest in retaining power and securing its survival, and the College of Cardinals votes for a pope perhaps more for political reasons than for reasons of true religion.

Let us try an Occam's razor view. Various popes have had to admit many mistakes and, in some instances, have asked for forgiveness. Is that not a simple and true indication of the fact that no pope has ever had the wisdom to be infallible and, consequently, that no pope has, in fact, ever been infallible?

CHAPTER 12

Why is it ... that Christianity decided to be anti-sex in spite of having its roots in sexy Judaism?

Whenever the topic of religion and sex comes up, we almost all have a Pavlovian reflex that brings us to believe that we need to review the *Kama Sutra*. While the *Kama Sutra* comes from India and is written in Sanskrit, it is difficult to claim that it is a religious text. It does, however, include a sex manual on sex positions as part of an exposé on how to live well. The *Kama Sutra* has no trouble with the basic notion of seeking pleasure in life. Desire, or perhaps lust, together with sexual fulfilment are reasonable goals in life. The *Kama Sutra* has passages on cheating without being too judgemental about it. The *Kama Sutra* also has passages on gay and lesbian sex, also without being judgemental.

We are all sexual beings and spend an awful lot of time thinking about sex. The great apes have alpha males that control their females for their own sexual pleasure and procreation. The status quo will continue until a particular alpha male is deposed by a stronger rival male who takes over his ladies. There is no reason not to believe that in the early times of our development we acted similarly. It is not unreasonable to believe that we still have wandering and wondering eyes and are not altogether naturally monogamous. Just look at the number of divorces and infidelities in our current societies.

CHAPTER 12

Sex is such a basic desire and need that everybody uses what they can to get more of it. People may use their looks, their influence, their power, their status or their wealth to attract partners they may desire. Almost every film made in Hollywood will have at least one overt or implied sex scene, with the female lead marketed as a goddess showing just enough skin to allow the viewer's imagination to take flight.

Showing skin, and how to do it just right, is an ancient art. Let's follow the money for a bit and see how it is being spent to enhance what we are willing and able to show. Makeup is a huge market, with at least US$500 billion spent annually. Add to this the money spent on visits to countless gyms. Add to this spending on visits to hairdressers and more or less workable diets and we can start to get a sense of the enormous amounts being expended on making ourselves more attractive to potential mates. Lingerie is a market worth about US$30 billion. Add to this the expenditure on general clothes to make us look that little bit more attractive. Let us not forget Botox injections and surgical procedures to enhance physical attraction. There is even a rise in "non-invasive" surgical procedures. At least US$1 trillion per year may be spent on just enhancing our attractiveness. I leave it to you to figure out what that money otherwise could have been used for.

We can add to this list the different ways of engaging in some form of sexual activity. Spending on pornography is estimated to be up to about US$100 billion per year. Spending on prostitution is estimated to be around US$200 billion per year. Powerful men seem to be guilty of their fair share of sexual misconduct. If we go back in history, we find that Genghis Kahn's DNA can be found in over 16 million men living at this time. Not all of the women in his life were raped. Some probably succumbed to his huge power and found that attractive. So, remember Kissinger's words, and be warned; "Power is the ultimate aphrodisiac."

Several French presidents have been known to have mistresses while being married, and at least one fathered a child while being president. President Clinton is an example of how risky someone's behaviour can get in order to get his sexual jollies fulfilled. The level of risk to which President Clinton was drawn can be demonstrated by his notoriously unorthodox employment of a cigar. Being an educated lawyer, a Rhodes scholar, and president, he must have realised that, although he might feel powerful and gratified by this act, there would be a risk, not least that his paramour might want to share, with friends or others, the details of her experiences with the president of the United States of America. Whether or not this affair with Monica Lewinsky was initiated by her, one can reasonably conclude that the president of the United States should not engage with an intern in the same way that a teacher should not engage with a pupil or a university professor with one of his students.

The recent president of the United States, Donald Trump, was so childishly proud of his fame while he was running for president that he could not contain himself and notoriously boasted that when you, just like he, are famous enough, you can "grab them by their pussy" and they will let you. Behind this may lurk an insecure man who feels he does not get to touch their genitals without his perceived fame. We do indeed get the impression of an insecure man who has found his way to a position that allows him to feel as if he were a rather greater man than he actually is. Why else would he tell the story to anyone? Are we not left with the impression that Trump's inner young boy was telling someone something, fully aware that he is getting away with something he knows he shouldn't?

Harvey Weinstein, a big-time movie producer, could not exactly be described as a lady's dream but made his way into a position where he had control and used and abused young women for his sexual pleasure. He was recently convicted for his misdeeds.

Jeffrey Epstein, a US billionaire, used his wealth to buy sex from even underage girls. He invited to his sex parties some very well-known individuals. He ended up committing suicide in jail while awaiting trial while his sometime companion, Ghislaine Maxwell, is alleged to have assisted him by recruiting or perhaps luring young girls to participate in acts ranging from nude massages on Mr. Epstein to being sexually abused by him. She is currently awaiting trial,

CHAPTER 12

and who knows what famous names may be spilled during the upcoming court proceedings? Already, Prince Andrew, a scion of the British royal family and a former associate of Mr. Epstein's, seems to have had trouble defending himself when a picture emerged of him and a young and vulnerable girl allegedly recruited into the Epstein circle to give massages to Epstein and his male friends. The girl was allegedly directed to look after the prince by Mr. Epstein and his companion, Ms. Maxwell.

The bubble in which the famous and infamous Hollywood figures live is well demonstrated by the story of how, some time ago, quite a few signed an appeal to allow the film director Roman Polanski back into the United States. Polanski has been hiding out in France for much of the last four decades, after being arrested in March 1977 in Los Angeles. He was charged with five offences against a 13-year-old girl, charges including sodomy and rape. The threat of incarceration in the US has been hanging over Polanski since then, and he has chosen not to set foot in the US since. For all his considerable artistic gifts, and with or without the involvement of the #Me-Too movement, Polanski is a toxic brand and a convicted, avowed rapist. He does not contest the accusations made against him.

We need not even look at the ultra-powerful to see examples of the gross abuse of power. Weekly, there are reports of high school teachers sexually abusing students. It is blatant coercion and abuse of power when anyone in a position of authority has sex with their subordinate – especially when the victim is a minor. It is also very common in religious and all-boys schools. Take the renowned private school, Upper Canada College, in Toronto as an example. The *Globe and Mail* described the guilty charge of a biology teacher as the "final chapter in the decades-long saga of sexual abuse at Upper Canada College".

Is there any reason to doubt that people who have certain sexual proclivities will seek opportunities to be around potential victims? Someone who has an inclination towards paedophilia may want to find employment in a kindergarten, and there is ample evidence that that has occurred and continues to occur. There have been frequent reports in Sweden regarding older women carers in asylum-seeker camps who take sexual advantage of younger men and boys seeking asylum. There are similar, and similarly shocking, stories from various refugee camps worldwide, of the exchange of food for sex.

Charitable organisations are in no way immune from predator infiltration. Two examples will suffice. Doctors Without Borders is a well-known and widely respected organisation, and yet in 2018, it was revealed that workers at the charity used local prostitutes while working in Africa. Female whistleblowers stated that the behaviour was widespread and that it was not uncommon for aid workers in the charity to use handouts of medication as payment for sex.

The United Nations peacekeeping forces are in no way exempt from sexually predatory behaviour. A Swedish diplomat, Anders Kompass, used to be employed by the UN in the field for the Office of the United Nations High Commissioner for Human Rights. He became a whistleblower and reported to French authorities about child sexual abuse in the Central African Republic committed by French peacekeepers between December 2013 and July 2014. The immediate effect of Mr. Kompass's allegations was the attempt to have him fired for not following the proper channels. There was an international uproar in which some member states criticised the UN for spending more effort on denigrating the whistleblower for having disclosed the sexual abuses than on making sure the abusers were held accountable for their crimes.

There is a lot in the above that reminds us of the cover-ups in the Roman Catholic Church's sex abuse scandal. Could we perhaps conclude that, since the church and its priests have held this position of power and influence for almost 2000 years, entrance to the clergy for less-than-pure motives could perhaps have become commonplace? Once the priesthood has, over time, become penetrated by various predators, the success of this infiltration may effectively blaze a trail for other predators seeking to gain entry into that holy cabal.

It was inevitable that sexual activity and sexual desire had to be controlled by God and regulated by various religious figures and organisations. Religious figures and organisations are keen to regulate their flock's sexual activity and behaviour while at the same time being more tolerant regarding the activities of their leadership and their clergy.

CHAPTER 12

We are all aware of the fact that in the Catholic Church, the clergy have sexually abused children. Are we also aware that Pope Francis has admitted that his predecessor, Pope Benedict, had to shut down an entire congregation of nuns who were being abused by priests who kept them as sex slaves? If we look back at the sexual history of various popes, cardinals, bishops, and ordinary priests, we find that there is good reason to believe that some of the clergy of the Catholic Church have abused their power in the same way some men outside the church have. The sexual urges are such that they are very difficult to resist, even when you enter the priesthood and give up sex as a sacrifice to the Lord. Within the Roman Catholic Church, which claims a history of almost 2000 years, there remains a brotherhood of silence and permissibility. The power of the priestly class was and, in some places, remains such that no ordinary person could question them.

And we must remember that it is not only in the Catholic Church where sex scandals have occurred.

The Church of England had its scandal through a bishop named Peter Ball who, in 2015, was sentenced to 32 months in prison after admitting that he had abused eighteen young men over a fifteen-year period. As with the Catholic Church, the archbishop and other bishops immediately came to his defence, the defence being that he had done so much good. That sounds like the Hollywood excuse for the statutory rape committed by Roman Polanski – *but he was so talented*. Even the Prince of Wales got involved and sent off a letter in support of Bishop Ball.

American televangelists are not immune and have had their fair share of sex scandals. It is reasonable to believe that what we know is only the tip of the iceberg. It is also reasonable to believe that since Roman Catholic priests have to live in celibacy, there may be a greater institutional problem within that church with so many men officially denied the fulfilment of a basic need.

Within the Swedish Lutheran church, there are some examples of priests who have pressured young, and especially vulnerable, girls in confirmation camps to engage in sex with them. Also, in Sweden, there is the story of a young woman who felt that she had to leave the Jehovah's Witnesses after some 20 years, feeling that she was a sex object. There is good reason to believe that the same behaviour occurs in similar churches and congregations all over the world.

In August 2020, Jerry Falwell Jr, one of the top evangelical leaders in the US, was caught up in his own sex scandal. It is alleged that, apart from frolicking with ladies outside of his marriage, he had also engaged a young man to have sex with his wife while he was watching. Falwell was also the head of Liberty University, a Christian university, and still wants US$10.5 million for leaving his position, insisting that he did nothing *legally* wrong. Do we not understand that he is referring to the civil laws of the United States? With Falwell's evangelical hat on, he must know that he has done something very wrong in the eyes of the Lord and has gone against his own teachings. But do not bet against his coming back and asking for forgiveness in the name of Jesus. Forgiveness for sexual transgressions is something that other evangelical leaders in the US have asked for and been given by their flocks.

We should admit that most of us will try to present ourselves in the best possible way to make us attractive to a potential sex partner. That would include showing off one's physical attractiveness, sense of humour, intelligence, income, wealth and position of power and influence. This becomes very problematic when positions of power and influence are used to coerce a potential sex partner, thus turning that individual into a victim. Using one's position of power and influence to obtain sexual advantages is never acceptable, whether that be in the hierarchy of corporations, secular organisations, the Catholic Church or other religious institutions. Let us not single out just the Roman Catholic Church but also note that there are tales of sexual abuse within some very orthodox Jewish communities, and grooming of the young and the vulnerable has occurred in certain Muslim communities in the UK. Being in a position of power over the flock in a religious congregation is apparently no different from other positions of power in other organisations, even secular ones. So, remember Kissinger's words. "Power is the ultimate aphrodisiac."

CHAPTER 12

There seems to be, among certain men of power and influence, the need to add an element, perhaps a frisson, of risky behaviour to their sexual escapades. They perhaps believe themselves to be to some extent invincible and may trust in their ability to weasel their way out of any precarious situation they might find themselves in. There is no reason or obligation to believe that the abusing priests, ministers, and rabbis are not of the thrill- and risk-seeking kind who similarly believe that they will not be found out. They may also believe that they can explain away their behaviour and, if Christian, ask forgiveness in the name of Jesus.

One can imagine that once a person engages in risky behaviour, the very riskiness becomes part of the thrill. We know, for instance, that a French journalist in 2019 published a book in which he shows that some of the most senior clerics in the Vatican are gay. Not only are they gay, but they are the same ones that give a loud voice to attacks on homosexuality, likely as a simple means to enhance their own cover. In his book, *In the Closet of the Vatican*, Frédéric Martel describes how he found a few gay priests who accepted their own homosexuality and maintained discreet relationships. But, interestingly enough, he also found others who looked for casual, high-risk sexual encounters. Martel describes the use of gay escorts, sex parties, and even drugs in the Vatican. We could add to that the fact that any sexual activity by a priest, let alone homosexual activity, must be seen as risky considering the combination of the requirement to be celibate and the biblical prohibition of homosexual acts. Power corrupts and absolute power corrupts absolutely. The priest in the Roman Catholic Church who stands between a sinner and his God and is the one who can administer forgiveness in the name of the Lord does have absolute power, in a sense, at least over the true believers in his flock.

Martel expressly does not want to confuse homosexuality with the other huge scandal in the church, namely the sexual abuse of children by the clergy. However, he does take issue with the secretive culture within the priesthood that has allowed this sex abuse to take hold and thrive. It is, he believes, the secrecy within the church that has led to a lack of confrontation of the abusers. The secrecy and permissibility have a long, long history, which we can see even from the behaviour of various popes throughout history.

There has, in short, been no lack of flagrant sexual activity of both the heterosexual and the homosexual kind throughout the history of the church. Even worse, pedophilia has been going on throughout the Church's history.

Let us now go back to the Old Testament and see what it has to say about sex. According to one of the Ten Commandments, adultery is forbidden. That sounds better than it is since we first need to know what constitutes adultery in the Old Testament. A man could have several wives and even concubines. He could buy a female sex slave from another man and keep her even beyond the six years when other slaves were to be freed. The prohibition of adultery mostly affects women and prohibits a man from engaging in sexual activity with a woman already married to another man. It is worth remembering that King David did lust after his neighbour's wife, got her pregnant while she was still married and had her husband killed. He got away with it and God forgave him, although his son eventually died. If God can forgive King David, perhaps He doesn't look that unkindly on our fulfilling the sexual desires that He has Himself, after all, instilled in us. Perhaps God does understand that when a woman looks at her neighbour's husband and feels desire, she cannot help it and it therefore cannot be a deadly sin as portrayed in one of the Ten Commandments.

With Occam's razor, one would easily conclude that even the Ten Commandments were not written by God but invented by man for a God they wanted to worship. Perhaps it was to allow the upper classes to control the lower classes in the name of God. Royals, after all, have had a long history of ruling with the grace of God or in the name of God, and also being the head of the church of their country. Why would God create us full of lust and sexual desire and then hate us for it?

In Leviticus, God tells Moses what to say to the people of Israel, and it is important to God that His people do not follow the practices of Egypt, where the Israelites once lived as slaves, or the land of Canaan, where they are going to reside. God forbids sexual intercourse with one's mother as, firstly, it would be a disgrace to one's father and, secondly, it would be a disgrace to one's mother. You should, further, not disgrace your father by having intercourse with any of his other wives. There goes monogamy out the window. Best to also leave alone your sister or your stepsister. The same goes for your granddaughter. Have no intercourse with your half-sister or an aunt on either your father's or mother's side. Also, leave alone your uncle's wife and your daughter-in-law and even your brother's wife. Do not have intercourse with the daughter's granddaughter of a woman that you have had sex with. They may be related to you and that would be incest. You should also not take your wife's sister as one of your wives as long as your wife is alive. It is forbidden to have sex with a woman while she has her monthly period and before she has ritually cleansed herself.

Apart from the above, homosexuality is also strictly forbidden. Not that clearly, however, because it seems that the sin is when a man lies with another man as he would with a woman. So, if a man lies with a man the same way as he does with a woman, they should be put to death. It is interesting to note that lesbian sexual activity does not seem to follow the same rules and must therefore be allowed, at least in the Old Testament. We do not find in the Old Testament any direct prohibition of lesbian sexual activity. We have to go to the New Testament, and specifically to Romans, where lesbian sexual relationships are put on fairly equal – which is to say *negative* – terms with male homosexual activity.

In Judaism, aside from the Bible, one finds the Talmud which is a collection – in fact two collections – of rabbinical interpretations regarding Jewish religious laws and theology. Second to the Bible, it has great importance as to how Jews should run their lives. Where the Bible is silent or not clear enough, the rabbis have constructed what is called a fence around the Torah, the five books of Moses, to ensure that there are no transgressions. Women are subject to sexual control and should be virgins when they marry. In Deuteronomy, for instance, we find that when a man has sex with his bride and comes to suspect that she was not a virgin, it is up to her family to prove that she was. If they cannot, for instance, present a bloodstained sheet from the wedding night, then she is to be stoned to death at the door of her father's house. Even rape seems to be okay in the Old Testament, as a rapist needs to give compensation to the father of the rape victim in monies, must marry her, and is never allowed to divorce her. Easier to find a wife in the olden days.

Today, it seems as if we live in a culture where many people try to define themselves as the most suffering victim of some or other injustice, and where the most suffering victim somehow wins. We now even have men who find themselves involuntarily celibate. They go by the name *incels*, and these incels are outraged that women do not want to sleep with them. They constitute, in fact, a women-hating (misogynist) extremist group, and they even believe that they are entitled to rape women. Incels have not only sexually assaulted women but have gone so far as to commit non-sexual violent acts (such as running a van into a crowd on the street) to demonstrate their immense frustration with the attractive, incel-termed *Stacys* who only wish to have sex with alpha-males, termed *Brads*.

The ancient Bible would have had a solution for them, forced marriage to a young lady of their choice. All they would have to do is rape that young woman. Luckily, biblical law does not apply, and at least in the liberal West, we live by the rule of secular laws where forced sexual activity is, as it should be, severely punished.

So, what do we learn about sex from the Talmudic writings? Firstly, we learn that sex is to be engaged in fully and lustfully. Secondly, we are made to understand that complete nakedness is preferred. Those of us who may have heard stories about ultra-Orthodox Jews who make love through a hole in the bedsheet could be either misinformed or dealing with Jews who do not understand what has been prescribed for them regarding sexual pleasure. Thirdly, we are made to understand that a man can use his wife for sex in any way he wishes, which would include oral and anal sex, but he *must* also bring pleasure to his wife. A little note here is that Muslim men are also allowed to enjoy their wives in any way they desire, but they are also to bring sexual pleasure to their female partners.

If we move forward to the 1500s, it seems that some leading rabbis turned against oral sex and even looking at the vagina. Amazing how far you can go and how much you can interpret if you really want to control people's lives. So, when engaging in sex, touch, be naked, enjoy the pleasure of sex but be sure not to look and preferably do it in the dark.

While the sex act is fine with the rabbis, it seems that the desire for sex affects the male body in a similar way to a demon and makes the man sin. The rabbis are not quite in agreement about whether a man can pay a woman for sex or not. One influential rabbi was of the opinion that, in ancient times, a man could pay a woman to have sex with him and leave after completion of the sex act. That made her a whore. But once the Torah was handed to the people, it was written, "There shall be no whore of the daughters of Israel." Another influential rabbi was of the opinion that a whore can be defined as one who is available to any man. A woman who is available only to one man is a concubine and acknowledged in the five books of Moses. Eventually, the more stringent interpretation won the day, and the famous Rabbi Maimonides' interpretation is now the rule of law. It is not permitted to be either a whore or a concubine, even to kings.

In the Old Testament, we find the Song of Songs, the authorship of which is attributed to King Solomon. The impression one gets from reading that psalm is that it is highly erotic, perhaps even slightly pornographic, and that there is no mention of God in the entire piece. The way rabbis and many Christian theologians try to explain the Song of Songs is that it is a description of the relationship between God and his people, a relationship that is similar to the longing, love, and sexual tension between a man and a woman. It seems far-fetched to try to put God somewhere in these verses, but it is done only because these verses have found their way into the Bible. Perhaps the Song of Songs is just there to entice the man who spends his time studying holy scriptures to find somewhere to get sexually aroused before going home and having to produce sexual pleasure for his wife. It is because of our God that these verses find their way into the Bible? Is it perhaps either bad editing or a deliberate entry intended for sexual arousal?

The Song of Songs is a celebration of sexual tension between two lovers who are longing for each other and giving each other invitations to pleasure. If one wanted to show how God loves his people, it could have been done in ways that were much easier to understand. Without mentioning God at all in the text, without mentioning anything about the biblical laws in the text, rabbis, priests and ministers have had to find ways to explain away the meaning of the Song of Songs. It was helpful, of course, to have King Solomon's authorship ascribed to the Song of Songs to have it admitted into biblical texts. God could have just written something with fire in the sky in a way that would find no scientific explanation, and the Song of Songs would not have been needed as a way of explaining the great love our God has for us.

How much of God's love for his people do we find in the following lines from the Song of Songs? "You ravish my heart, my sister, my promised bride, you ravish my heart with a single one of your glances, with one single pearl of your necklace."

Or how much God in the following? "Your lips, my promised one, distil honey. Honey and milk are under your tongue; and the scent of your garments is like the scent of Lebanon."

Perhaps there is more of God in the chorus of the song of songs: "What makes your beloved better than other lovers, O loveliest of women? What makes your beloved better than other lovers, to give us charge like this?"

Does it start to become obvious to us that the Song of Songs has no Godly reason for being in the Bible, no matter how much one would like to explain away its inclusion? Perhaps God would be pleased when the bridegroom states, "Your two breasts are two fawns, twins of a gazelle."

For clarity, it needs to be pointed out, again, that the Old Testament, with very few exceptions, is identical with the Jewish Bible. King Solomon, who is the biblical author of these highly erotic verses, lived around a thousand years before Jesus. Yet, Christian attempts are being made to reinterpret these erotic verses as being about Christ. How credible is that? Let us step back in time and ask ourselves, how credible is it that King Solomon authored the erotic Song of Songs?

The Sabbath is holy and no work should be done on that day. Nothing new should be created, such as light by turning on electricity. Nor should one press an elevator button to go to a specific floor in a building. Yet sexual activity between husband and wife is encouraged on the Sabbath. On Friday evening, which is the eve of the Sabbath, a song *Lecha Dodi* is sung by the congregation. The translated meaning of the song's title is *Come my Beloved*, and in welcoming the Sabbath, one is joined with the beloved. In this song, God is definitely mentioned. But the Sabbath is described as a bride, in words such as, "Dress in your garments of splendour, my people," or "Rouse yourselves! Rouse yourselves! Your light is coming, rise up and shine. Awaken, awaken, utter a song." And, although God is mentioned immediately after this, it does leave a bit of the Song of Songs feeling, with what may well be interpreted as somewhat erotic text, to remind the men before going home to their wives that they have duties to perform.

It is said that the author of *Lecha Dodi* drew from the interpretation that rabbis have given to the Song of Songs, where the young lady symbolises the Jews and the lover symbolises God. It is, frankly, a bit of a stretch to get to that interpretation. Could God not have expressed himself more clearly to us?

There is no doubt that Judaism embraces sexual activity with the understanding that sexual activity does not always have to be engaged in with the intent of procreating. In Judaism, man and woman were created as whole beings, including all their physical features and all the elements of their personalities. It is also a fact that Judaism does not find celibacy to be recommended. A rabbi should be married when he starts to lead a congregation to diminish the temptation to use his power over the congregation to make some of the congregants engage in sexual activity with him. That, of course, doesn't mean that sexual abuse by rabbis never happens. It does. Some rabbis entice some members of their congregation to engage in somewhat *holier* sexual activity. In a conservative Jewish congregation in Toronto, a rabbi who was counselling a woman with marital problems made her engage in sex acts with him. That turned out to be a costly event for the congregation once the rabbinical misdeeds were discovered and a settlement reached with the abused woman.

Judaism does incorporate the belief that a human being has a soul and agrees with Christianity that life was breathed into God's first creation which, according to the Old Testament, was done in the following way: God formed man of the dust of the ground and breathed the breath of life through his nostrils, and *man became a living soul.*

After acknowledging the breath of life blown into man, the Jewish religion doesn't make that strong a distinction between body, soul or the third element, the spirit in a human being. There is a life to come in Judaism. It is hard to pin it down in the same way as in Christianity, and it seems to be that, in Judaism, the life to come will be in a future messianic time. In Judaism, it becomes less fruitful to try to distinguish between the sinful body and the soul that will survive an individual's death.

It may be fruitful here to look at Roman Catholicism and its relationship to sex. The Catholic Church can easily be a stand-in for other Christian denominations. After all, the Roman Catholic Church has a leader who is the Vicar of Christ and can speak for the church and interpret holy texts without fault. In Judaism, a rabbi is no more than an individual educated and trained in biblical and ancient rabbinical texts, the same as a carpenter has been trained to do woodwork. Each Jewish individual is responsible for her or his own relationship with God. Some rabbis have been given by their followers an almost prophetic status, but that is a matter of choice and not a matter of dogma.

Once theology distinguishes between a sinful body and the other two components of life, namely soul and spirit, it becomes easier to explain to a sinner that it is her body playing tricks on her and she should do her utmost to keep her soul and spirit clean. We must by now be wondering what the differences are between the soul and the spirit. The way Catholics explain this is that the soul is what makes us human and feel emotions and it is subject to human limitations. The spirit, however, is that through which we make a deeper connection with God, especially when we believe in the Lord and receive Jesus Christ as our Lord and saviour. As we notice, there are quite a few people out in the world who do not receive Jesus Christ as Lord and saviour, and thus they may not have a spirit. Or do they perhaps have a spirit that is sinful? That spirit, in not giving itself up to Jesus Christ, does not have the right connections with a or the higher authority.

In Thessalonians in the New Testament, one sees the beginning of the human entity being divided into three parts: "And the God of peace himself sanctify you wholly; and may your spirit and soul and body be preserved entire, without blame at the coming of our Lord Jesus Christ." We can easily count the three parts, namely **body**, **soul** and **spirit.** There are other New Testament passages of a similar nature but, for our purposes, it is enough to conclude that in Christianity a human being consists of the three parts.

Origen, one of the early church fathers, in the late-100s to mid-200s, comes to the view that only souls existed in Paradise and the body came later once Adam and Eve had been cast out of Paradise. There is no evidence for that in biblical texts. On the contrary, Adam and Eve were ashamed of their nakedness after having eaten of the forbidden fruit. Let's give this one to Origen and perhaps agree that the soul can be naked and embarrassed. However, if Adam and Eve had no bodies, from where did Adam's rib come for the creation of Eve? Very few Christians were able to read at the time of Origen, and he had no reason to believe that, eventually, we would all be schooled and learn to read. Origen likely felt that followers who could not read for themselves were just going to have to trust him in regard to the division of a human into a sinful body and holier soul. Is it perhaps that with theology you can invent anything and, with a bit of hope and luck, make people believe it? Origen concludes that the body is geared to lust and sin. There we have it. The beginnings of almost 2000 years of sexual guilt.

St. Augustine is a wonderful fellow. He started off as a pagan and, as noted already, enjoyed sex so much that he could not stop telling everybody else about it. For instance, he wrote that when he was sixteen years old, "the frenzy gripped me and I surrendered myself entirely to lust." Eventually, he became a Christian and started to go against contraception. He also stated that sexual intercourse should be engaged in only with the aim of procreating and performed exclusively within marriage. In many ways, St. Augustine shaped how the Roman Catholic Church views sexuality. He was instrumental in making Catholics understand that marriage is for procreation and in ensuring that divorce and birth control should not be allowed. He also introduced the best element in the drive to surround sex with guilt and that is that sex should be subject to the greatest self-restraint. Finally, he felt that celibacy was the greatest gift or perhaps the greatest sacrifice you can give to God.

All of this is, of course, a rather easy position to come to once you have enjoyed a sex life to the fullest and are maybe at a somewhat older age when you no longer have the same physical needs. But his influence was such that he imposed the views developed in his later life, after his Christian conversion, on younger people who still have the urges but should thenceforth feel guilty about them. He was, supposedly, 31 years old when he converted to Catholicism. He had quite a few years in his pagan days that were notably lustful and filled with what was later to be seen, even by himself, as sinful sex. Only God knows how long St. Augustine continued to have lustful sex, while no longer telling us, after becoming a Christian, but he is known, as we have already seen, for having stated, "O Lord, give me chastity and self-control – but do not give it yet." That tells us all we need to know about that hypocritical father of sexual guilt in Christianity, not just in Catholicism.

This leads us to confession. Masturbation is terrible and you must feel guilty. Masturbation is seen as residing somewhere between a mortal sin and something that is just terribly wrong. Let's quote Pope John Paul II who, in his encyclical, writes, "Masturbation not always incurs grave sin, or mortal sin, but it cannot be said that masturbation is not "gravely wrong" nor constitutes a "grave matter". Masturbation needs to be confessed so that you can be cleansed from that dirty and gravely wrong act. Confession is to a priest in the Catholic Church. The priest has been given the power to absolve you of your sin. We know of course that just about everybody masturbates or at least has masturbated from time to time. In whose interest is masturbation something that needs to be confessed? Is it in the interest of the individual who has done something fairly natural and very likely could not help himself? Is it perhaps in the interest of the entire Church to have people need to go for confession and contribute to this vast and expensive organisation for its upkeep? The head of the Catholic Church is the Vicar of Christ and God's representative on earth and yet they live on earth where they need funding. They do not exactly get it from God, who could have supplied them with whatever He wanted them to have. They get it from their followers and more likely than not more from sinners who go to confess than from others.

How do you confess impure thoughts? A lot of Catholic thinking has gone into this one. If the impure thoughts lead to impure actions, the impure thoughts need not be confessed separately. They would be part of the bigger sin. If, however, you stopped with just impure thoughts, of course, they need to be confessed and absolution sought from the priest receiving your confession.

We can see that in the Catholic Church, we have an organisation that is indispensable to its sinners because very many human impulses could be seen as sinful and require interaction with your priest. Did God know that you had impure thoughts or that you were masturbating? Of course he did. And if we believe Jesus, God knows what you are going to pray for and what he is going to give you as a result of your prayers before you even start praying. It is reasonable to assume that the same thing applies to going to confession.

A Jew can also sin, but he has to make up with his God on his own without any intermediary. The Catholic Church has become powerful by making almost everybody in their flock a sinner in need of redemption. If it were not a religion, it could be seen as a very good business proposition.

The soul can have eternal life, but the life of the soul after the body is dead depends on how we have lived our lives. If we are not the right kind of Christian or don't have the right kind of faith or haven't followed Christ in the right way, we, that is our souls, are doomed to eternal damnation. There is a desire in us to believe that bodily death is not final. That makes the ever-living soul a beautiful proposition to believe in. So, in the realm of belief, there is the body, the soul and the spirit. In science, there is the body and the brain inside the body where our personal traits and personalities reside. Perhaps we can posit this comforting thought: if we follow science and understand that there are no ghosts, there is no soul, there is no spirit outside our brain, then there is no eternal life. Would not that in some way be comforting to know, that when life is over it doesn't matter how we have lived it? Dead is dead and nobody will be there to punish us for having followed our human instincts in the way God created us. For many of us, it is a comforting thought that death is final. Do we need confession or religious institutions if death is final?

When we look at Catholicism, we must delve into celibacy, which is compulsory for its clergy. It is not at all the case that celibacy started at the beginning with St. Peter (who was married). On the contrary, it took until the 12th century for the Roman Catholic Church to go from sexual self-restraint to mandatory celibacy in the priesthood. Let's follow the money. Originally the bishops were very wealthy and in a princely class of their own. If clergy were not allowed to get married, they would not have their own families or a need for inheritance and therefore would have no need for personal wealth. The wealth would stay within the church.

What remains to be asked is: how seriously did the church leadership and the priests take their celibacy? Let's go back to Martel's book, *In the Closet of the Vatican: Power, Homosexuality, Hypocrisy*. Martel's conclusions are that a substantial number of the Vatican gays do not take their celibacy vows seriously but treat them with contempt. More interesting is how we know that even the ones in the Vatican who are constantly railing against homosexuality hire prostitutes and pay for sex with church money and engage in sex parties with

CHAPTER 12

drugs. Well… the answer is jaw-dropping. We know this because they tell us. They know they get away with it and that the true believers are unlikely to challenge their behaviour. Do we not find this to be Donald Trump-like behaviour? They engage in risky behaviour and, like the little boy getting away with something he knows he shouldn't, they simply cannot resist telling.

How seriously did the Catholic Church take celibacy? We know about quite a few popes who have misbehaved. Pope Boniface VIII, who served between Christmas Eve 1294 and died in office in 1303, was caught having sex with a mother and daughter at the same time and is recorded as having said, *having intercourse with young boys is as natural as rubbing one hand against the other.*

Is this a pattern? Let's continue to the infamous Chestnut Banquet that occurred on October 30, 1501, and was recorded by an attendee. The banquet was arranged by Cesare Borgia, the son of Pope Alexander VI. This is the account we find in Burchard's diary: *On the evening of the last day of October 1501, Cesare Borgia arranged a banquet in his chambers in the Vatican with "fifty honest prostitutes", called courtesans, who danced after dinner with the attendants and others who were present, at first in their garments, then naked. After dinner the candelabra with the burning candles were taken from the tables and placed on the floor, and chestnuts were strewn around, which the naked courtesans picked up, creeping on hands and knees between the chandeliers, while the Pope, Cesare, and his sister Lucretia looked on. Finally, prizes were announced for those who could perform the act most often with the courtesans, such as tunics of silk, shoes, barrettes, and other things.* (source Wikipedia.)

It is hard to believe that somebody would have made this up, although we should understand that the church, and even people at the time, contested the accuracy of this writing.

We know the following about the church, that they did not want anybody to read the Bible in their own language. They did not want us to be able to use instruments to see out in the sky and understand that the earth was not the centre of our solar system. They did not want to fund Champollion, who came to understand how to read Egyptian hieroglyphs. The church was afraid that

Champollion would come back with evidence that the Earth was older than what church teaching allowed.

Why was the church so eager to prevent us from knowing the truth? A reasonable explanation is that they knew the truth themselves. The clergy were the most educated and they had enormous power. They were afraid that once the masses knew the truth, the church would lose its power. That prediction is slowly coming true since in the liberal West we now have scientific education that explains the ways of the universe to us better than the Bible does.

We must conclude that the priestly class knew the truth. Doesn't this tell – or remind – us that the church is an organisation that is run in its own self-interest and not exactly in the interest of its flock. What about sex, then? The Catholic Church and its priestly class have led with absolute power. One can be certain that nobody investigated the sexual activity of the priestly class, especially since several popes were themselves heavily involved in outré sexual activities. However, some popes did not mind flaunting their mistresses and their illegitimate children.

Did many priests perhaps join the priesthood because it was such a fabulous profession? Did perhaps not all but still a substantial number join the priesthood because it gave them the power to use and abuse their flock for sexual pleasure? Who would challenge them? This question demands to be repeated. Especially among ordinary people, who would challenge them?

Celibacy could be abolished by any ruling pope. Nobody has yet dared abolish the mandatory celibacy despite the abuse of the flock and the sexual abuse of children that, we can be certain, must have been going on for a very long time, if not throughout church history.

Once we understand and acknowledge the fact that the Catholic Church did not even want us to know the truth about science, why would they not also, to secure and hang on to power, allow – indeed actively encourage – us to feel guilty about our sexuality? Why did they make us feel guilty about our sexual desires? The church has let us understand that *lust* is when we desire sex without the intent of procreating. It would be interesting if the Catholic

Church released statistics on how many of the priests, bishops and cardinals have been excommunicated after being caught with their pants down. As far as we know, many have been moved to other parishes. As far as we know, many still roam around, unsupervised.

Shall we perhaps also draw the conclusion that, whereas a Jew is responsible to God personally without any intervention from an organisation, a rabbi or a Jewish priest, a Kohen, a Catholic believer can get help from an organisation that thrives on the believer's lack of knowledge. Does not the believer's fear of the unknown make a huge difference? This, especially, as the Catholic Church sets itself up as the organisation that can alleviate the unknown and bring eternal life, help with salvation and ensure that the soul will not burn in hell. There was even a pope who, in 1517, took advantage of the ignorance and sold indulgences for money. Nowadays, it is, thankfully, impossible to buy indulgences because the sale was prohibited back in 1567, but you can, with good deeds and charitable contributions, perhaps still earn indulgences.

We need to understand that indulgence is part of the Catechism of the Catholic Church. It is "a remission before God of the temporal punishment due to sins whose guilt has already been forgiven, which the faithful Christian who is duly disposed gains under certain prescribed conditions through the action of the church which, as the minister of redemption, dispenses and applies with authority the treasury of the satisfactions of Christ and all of the saints."

Isn't it amazing that the church has the power, through its actions, to arrange for lesser or no punishment for sins? Can we think of any greater power?

Pope Francis is really trying to move with the times. An article in the *New York Post* on September 10, 2020, tells us that the pope has been interviewed for a new book by Carlo Petrini. The pope now says that sex and eating, among other delights, are gifts from God. Even more interesting is the fact that the pope now claims that the Catholic Church's condemnation of life's enjoyment of food and sexual pleasures are "overzealous morality … A wrong interpretation of the Christian message." Popes before him have either not agreed with Pope

Francis's new message or disagreed publicly while indulging in these pleasures themselves.

Let us hope that this is the beginning of Christianity taking the guilt out of sex and food. It is also another example of how the leadership of the Catholic Church has, over time, not been wise enough to be infallible. Let us also hope that a future pope does not come to a different conclusion and puts the guilt back on the table. This is likely not Pope Francis' best pronouncement. For a man who has the ability to put on the infallibility cloak, he inadvertently makes us understand that the church may have been wrong for millennia. The church may even now be wrong in many other respects.

Future popes may conclude that the current pope has been wrong. Let us agree with the pope on food. In the rich part of the world, we can allow ourselves to indulge in the flavours of food and how it is presented for our visual delight. We therefore gladly allow the pope to give credit to God for our enjoyment of food on the understanding that it follows that, if God gave us the pleasure of food, he must also be responsible for the ones who don't get enough of it. For now, though, let's take these papal pronouncements as good news. Petrini's book is named *Terra Futura: Conversations with Pope Francis on Integral Ecology*.

Is it perhaps reasonable to conclude that the church has been interested in making and keeping sex sinful for its own organisational and financial reasons? One is left to assume that there are many within the hierarchy of the Catholic Church who disagree with the pope on his new take on food and sex, as it may diminish the need for coming to a priest for confession. Throughout history, the church has not been terribly interested in letting us understand the truth. The church has been more interested in encouraging – or even forcing – us to believe in its teaching. To be fair, we find in Corinthians in the New Testament a passage regarding the fact that God has deliberately made sexual activity to be enjoyable. The passage, however, ends with the warning that a lack of self-control will lead to Satan tempting us. It is not that we do not learn from Christianity, and even in common parlance, the term for desiring sex is *horny*, which clearly indicates the Devil's influence in a feeling of sexual desire given to us by God.

CHAPTER 12

Body and soul and spirit stand in contrast to our natural being. If we just exchange *soul* and *spirit* for personality, we end up in the brain. We have no evidence for either a soul or spirit as part of our human being, but we do have evidence of the fact that we are endowed with a brain. Following the evidence leads us to conclude that the human being's entire persona, including personality, is entirely natural. We can now locate which parts of the brain react to emotions and which to rationality. Why don't we draw the reasonable conclusion that our entire being is entirely natural?

The Occam's razor question is: is it likely that there would be some unnatural, *outer-worldly* part of us that makes us live on after death? Is it more likely that our soul and spirit are part of our personality and reside within our brain? Will we cease to exist when we die and our brain stops functioning?

Many people would like there to be a soul and spirit so that they may feel comforted in the belief that they will have a life after death. Think about this, because you are likely then to believe that you have done your worshipping of Jesus absolutely right. If your particular way of worshipping Jesus is not what Jesus expects, you may end up in the wrong place where there are eternal fires after death. Might it not, with Occam's razor, be more advantageous to know that when we are dead, we are dead and there is nothing of us left to be either lauded or punished in eternity after death? The knowledge of finality, to both human physical life and the personality that comes with it, may relieve a lot of sexual guilt and allow for what is supposed to be sexual pleasure. You have first to believe that there is a punishment after death to be afraid of any punishment after death.

We shall end our discussion here.

Afterword

There are still many who wish to believe that the holy scriptures in Judaism, Christianity and Islam contain high morality and absolute truth and that the texts are to be interpreted precisely the way they are written.

The problem in any book with many pages is that it is easy to find contradictory commands or prescriptions.

The Verse of the Sword in the Quran, when read alone, stands in contrast to other verses that call for tolerance, patience and forgiveness. It reads, translated into English, "*When the Inviolable Months have passed away, kill the polytheists wherever you find them. Seize them, besiege them, and wait for them at every place of observation. If they repent, observe prayer, and pay the obligatory alms then let them go their way. Allah is forgiving, merciful.*"

Many Islamist terrorists and suicide bombers recite this verse when they commit terrorist acts. The text seems fairly clear to them: after the holy months you can kill nonbelievers unless they repent and observe prayer. The general impression to a non-Muslim reader would be that if the polytheist converts to Islam, he should be allowed to live. The conversion needs to be genuine, whatever that means, and the alternative is death. The polytheist could also be kept alive to learn to see the light. This comes with adhering to the only "true" religion.

It is very difficult to make out which command supersedes any other in the Quran regarding the prescribed violence against polytheists, but, for our purposes, it is enough to understand that many followers of Islam believe that the text gives them somewhere between a command and the permission to kill the polytheist nonbelievers. If Allah wanted to have a specific order in which the texts would be interpreted, he could have let us know.

The Quran is supposed to be a miracle and the perfect and final word of God. Allah should not have left us to have to come to different interpretations, even within Islam, of His holy texts as dictated by the Archangel Gabriel to the last prophet, Muhammad. If this Verse of the Sword is not to be read as it is written, we can conclude that Allah could have dictated it more clearly to the Archangel Gabriel, who, in turn, dictated it in a cave to Muhammad, a perfect man with perfect memory but no ability to write. Muhammad, in turn, dictated it to some of his followers who *could* write. Before it entered the Quran, it was rechecked and several sources had to agree. There cannot be any transmission problem between Allah and the Quran since in Islam the Quran is perfect. What Muslims and non-Muslims should agree on is that the Verse of the Sword did not have to be transmitted to Muhammad. It could have been made clear in the texts of the Quran that Islam is a religion of peace. It could have been made clear that Islam requires its followers to be merciful when they defeat an enemy. It could also have been made very clear that forced conversion to Islam is not permissible.

We find in the Quran, as we find in the Old and New Testament, conflicting commands and prescriptions which we humans seem not to be able to interpret clearly for our full understanding. In all three religions, and the many denominations thereof, not only ordinary people but also theologians cannot agree on the true meaning of the holy texts. Could we not expect better from God or Allah? Allah could have made clear, beyond any doubt, to the followers of Islam that forced conversions to Islam are wrong for several reasons. For instance, the Quran could have stated that Islam is so attractive that only fools will not voluntarily join the religion. Further, it could have been stated in the Quran that the unbeliever should be left alone since they are also children of Allah, although for the time being misguided in their faith. Would it not have also been good if these fictional statements had been followed up with something along the following lines: *these eternal truths are everlasting and must be followed even where a believer finds, in this Holy Book, other commands that may seem contradictory or confusing?*

If similar writings had been found at the beginning of the Old Testament, the genocide of the people in the lands to be conquered by the Israelites would have been avoided. The Israelites would just have had to co-inhabit these lands.

If similar writings had been found at the beginning of the New Testament, there would have been no reason for the crusades, no reason for the Inquisition and no reason for the forced conversion to Catholicism when South America was conquered.

Followers of Catholicism may perhaps rightly feel that Roman Catholicism has been singled out in the preceding chapters. There is no intention on my part to claim that Roman Catholicism as a religion has more or less truth than any other religion. As far as I'm concerned, there is no truth in any of the religions. Religions promote a lack of knowledge and a lack of understanding. Furthermore, religious organisations try to have their followers blindly believe in their need for these organisations. Roman Catholicism has a pope who stands as a dictatorial leader, and the Catholic Church has the largest following among all Christian denominations.

Much can be said about televangelists. They line their own pockets at the expense of the poor and ignorant. Some have even come up with a prosperity gospel wherein they enrich themselves by proclaiming to the poor and ignorant that the more they give to their evangelical preacher, and his church, the greater chance they will have to achieve riches themselves. We will only hear of the very few who perhaps win the lottery after giving away their last hundred dollars, and they will serve as an inducement for other followers to continue to give and line the pockets of the leaders of their flocks. Do we believe that these preachers of the prosperity gospel perform their duties in the interest of themselves or in the interest of their flock? Is it not a bit odd that they pray to Jesus to induce their followers to give the leaders money but do not ask Jesus to supply them with the wealth they so blatantly believe that they deserve? Better still would be to pray to Jesus that their followers' financial circumstances improve without their having to give away their last penny.

Let us move to the Old Testament and from there pick a well-known story regarding the erection of the Tower of Babel. The story tells us that men got together to build the tower that was intended to reach Heaven. God got nervous about this and was concerned that, if man could reach Heaven with the tower, what else could man come up with? God, who is Almighty, had no reason to be nervous. It seems that the writer of this story must have forgotten how Almighty the Lord actually is, and he could have just let them get on with it and build the tower up to the five or six floors they could conceivably have managed at that time. But he did not. Instead, and to prevent humankind from reaching that high, God decided to scatter the builders around the earth and give them different languages so that they could never cooperate to infringe on God's heavenly abode or in other ways interfere with God's domain.

Let us think about this. We live at a time now when all of us seem to learn English, when it is possible to build skyscrapers with a height of more than 500 m and when we can even fly more than 10 km above the surface of the earth. Why is God not nervous about it now? Besides, God, being all-seeing and all-knowing, knew already, at the time that the Tower of Babel was being constructed, that we were, in the future, going to learn English, build much taller towers, fly aeroplanes high above the ground, and even land on the moon. Doesn't that make, from God's perspective, the mere scattering of the people who tried to construct the Tower of Babel, and giving them different languages, a nonsensical exercise? Would this not tell us that this is a man-made story and has nothing to do with God? Very likely, it is a story intended to try to make sense of the fact that we have different languages.

Let us now move to the New Testament and the story of the three wise men who came from the East to worship the baby Jesus. The story tells us that they followed a star from the east all the way to Bethlehem and brought with them gifts for the new king. How would these three wise men even begin to imagine that looking at a star or even a comet was a sign that a king of the Jews was being born? And why would these wise men from the east care in the first place? Let us note that they arrived when Jesus was about two years old. The way the Nativity is celebrated at Christmas is definitely wrong in pure scriptural terms. The wise men did not come to the manger and see a mother and father with a newborn baby. How do we know that it was two years later? We know because, according to the New Testament, the evil King Herod wanted all the male children two years old and younger killed in Bethlehem to prevent the new King of the Jews from growing up among the toddlers in Bethlehem. This can be described as another story without any historical accuracy. After two years, how could anybody know where Jesus and his family would have moved from Bethlehem? And then we find out that, luckily, Jesus and his family had escaped to Egypt. The killing of the toddlers in Bethlehem is given the name "the Massacre of the Innocents", which must be intended to give us the feeling that it was a very substantial event. There is no historical evidence that this occurred. That leaves us with two possible explanations: the first one is that it never happened, and the second is that it was such a small event because very few toddlers of that age group lived in that small place called Bethlehem. Occam's razor would be a good filter when trying to find the truth in this wonderful tale.

When the three wise men looked at a star, how would they even have come up with the idea that it indicated that a king would be born somewhere far away and they needed to go there with gifts? Of course, there is no way of explaining that.

Here is a challenge. Go out on a clear night and pick a star and try to follow it anywhere specific. Perhaps it is not a star but a comet. Make the same thought experiment: how would you follow a comet to a specific place? In the New Testament, that specific place was not the manger. The three wise men ended up in front of King Herod and while asking him about the new King of the Jews spilled the beans about the fact that such a child had been born. That, in turn, led to the biblical story of the killing of the innocent babies and toddlers in Bethlehem. These three wise men must have been pretty unwise to give it all up to King Herod.

CHAPTER 12

Is it now perhaps time to conclude that all the holy texts are man-made to try to explain a world that was inexplicable to the writers, especially as the texts were written before any reasonable scientific knowledge.? We should be guided by Occam's razor and find the simplest answer to any question, including questions about God or religion.

A Swedish comedian and thinker, Tage Danielsson, wrote in 1963, "If God had existed, he would not have been stupid enough to create pagans."

Do not be afraid to ask the difficult questions about your own belief in the same way that you are prepared to ask difficult questions about other people's beliefs. And remember Occam's razor when you answer the questions: the simplest answer is almost always right.

Postscript

I finished my fact-gathering at the end of October 2020 and my writing soon after. Late November my manuscript went to my brilliant editor Karl French, who has been able to make the text much more understandable. He has improved my language in a way that makes it so much more readable. Karl, an accomplished author in his own right, has also clearly demonstrated his knowledge regarding the various topics included in this writing. I must add that I am envious of his command of the English language. I am greatly in his debt.

It is now February 2021, and a few comments on occurrences since October 2020 are warranted.

Our scientists have come through for us and we have, at record speed, been supplied with several vaccines against the Covid-19 pandemic. It is still unclear how effective the vaccines and the rollout of vaccinations will be in order to save our way of life and our economies and allow us to get back to normal.

In mid-January 2021, a 20-year-old Muslim Afghani, residing in Sweden as a migrant, visited a supermarket armed with a knife and tried to rape a female employee who was working in a small, secluded area of the shop. She managed to get help, and, when the young man was arrested, he claimed that it did not matter whether or not the girl was interested in having sex since everybody needs sex. We can view this in at least two ways. One would be that it is just an anecdotal incident. Another view is, perhaps, that violent occurrences among young Muslim immigrants are so frequent that it is systemic and the result of culture or religion. Perhaps better put, culture *and* religion, since it is very

CHAPTER 12

difficult to distinguish between the two regarding people who have been subject to indoctrination in childhood and beyond and believe that they own the only true religion and follow the last prophet who was the bearer of God's true word. We will all have to make up our own minds as to where we stand on this, in particular, our views when it comes to respect for women. But we do know that, among Muslims, one too often finds a negative, derogatory view of women. Let us also remind ourselves of the relationship that ultra-Orthodox Jewish men have with women and also remember that fundamentalist Christian men require obedience from their women.

In early February 2021, Ayaan Hirsi Ali's new book *Prey* came out, and in it, she draws a link between the immigration of Muslims to the West, Islam, and the erosion of women's rights. As we know, she has a Muslim background and was subjected to female genital mutilation. Her view is that Muslim migrants to Europe brought with them systemic violence against women. She has given several interviews in connection with the publication, in the course of which she praises the Danish approach with emphasis on values and norms while depicting Sweden as a country that sees itself as a moral superpower. In reality, though, she feels, that Sweden betrays not only its citizenry but the immigrants as well. It is particularly the women in Sweden who should feel betrayed. The Swedish political power structure is not interested in seeing the situation for what it is. Neither is the political power structure willing to acknowledge that immigration has changed Sweden.

Regarding violence committed in the name of Islam, we may wonder what happened to the body of the young man who beheaded the French teacher Samuel Paty for having shown pupils in his class cartoons of the prophet Mohammad. The young man was given a hero's funeral in Chechnya. The Chechen leader agreed with the Chechen mufti (the title *mufti* is granted to an expert in Muslim legal matters who has the power to issue rulings in matters of Islam) in claiming that the French president is the number one terrorist in the world. Interestingly, the Chechen leader accused President Macron of being a terrorist one hundred times worse than the actual murderer. No blame, in their view, falls on the killer of the French teacher but rather on the French president and the French people. This, again, leads us to wonder how peaceful the religion of Islam really is when its religious and political leaders interpret it the way they do.

Cultural and religious hatred continues to be spewed from even a United Nations refugee organisation as it has done since Israel became a state over 70 years ago. UNRWA (The United Nations Relief and Works Agency for Palestine Refugees) is the organisation in question, and it is now looking after the third and fourth generation from the original refugees.

I am a refugee myself, and in 1955, ten years after the Second World War, quite a few of us were still languishing in a refugee camp outside Salzburg in Austria. My family was taken in by Sweden, a country with which we had no connection and of whose language we knew not a word. I do not believe there are any camps and settlements where refugees have been kept from generation to generation without being placed in other countries, aside from those under the care of UNRWA. In late January 2021, Canada started to probe UNRWA's funding of textbooks promoting hatred against Jews. This is not merely a clear example of the Palestinian political and religious hatred of Jews but of a policy of indoctrination being aided and abetted by a United Nations organisation. Instead of this, surely UNWRA should have done all that it could to find a place for these refugees generations ago and stopped all the hatred that is promoted even in school textbooks. UNWRA may have started with the best of intentions, but it has since found a life for itself that is difficult for the people who make a living from it – and gain influence through it – to give up.

The fact that religious beliefs can make people do stupid things can be evidenced in many ways. While the pandemic is raging, many religious people, from all three Abrahamic religions, find it unacceptable that they cannot congregate in their houses of worship the way they want to. They also believe that they are so special that they can congregate anywhere and do not have to abide by rules set up by a mere political government in the interest of

POSTSCRIPT

everybody's health. Perhaps they believe that God will look after them, although the evidence seems to suggest that he just doesn't do this, either inside or outside of the houses of worship.

In Israel, for example, there are some areas where ultra-Orthodox Jews live, and they totally disregard the physical distancing rules (generally called *social distancing*) to the detriment of their own societies and Covid–19 contagion outside of their areas. It may seem to be a matter of the leaders controlling their flock so as not to lose them. On January 22, 2021, the *Jerusalem Post* (an Israeli newspaper in English) published an opinion piece stating that the prime minister of Israel may almost have an easier time launching an attack against Iran's nuclear facilities than he would trying to stop these religious people's insurrection. What these religious people spend so much time and effort on is ensuring that they and their flock studiously avoid the Internet lest they get what, from a Godly perspective, is fake news. This is the same as when the Soviet Union claimed that the West was so corrupt that Soviet citizens were forbidden to even listen to radio broadcasts from the West in order not to get corrupted. The obvious conclusion to be drawn from this is that if you are so afraid of other opinions, your own position must be very weak.

The pope of the Roman Catholic Church has again, in late December 2020, come out with a statement that is somewhat baffling. He rightly claims that the coronavirus vaccines are morally acceptable and that one should take them. What the pope is alluding to is the fact that Covid-19 vaccines have been developed using lines of cells that come from aborted fetuses. In the absence of any alternatives, the vaccines can be used in good conscience according to what the pope has stated. Similarly, condom use would prevent not only unwanted pregnancies but also limit the spread of sexually transmitted diseases, as well as HIV/Aids. But, to state the obvious, Pope Francis has not, thus far, come out in favour of condom use.

Pope Francis *has* come out in favour of a more important role for women within the hierarchy of the church so that they could, for instance, read mass. The New Testament clearly says, "do not permit a woman to teach or to exercise authority over a man; rather, she is to remain quiet." We ask ourselves again if the pope does not, inadvertently, demonstrate more and more that the Roman Catholic Church is a gigantic social organisation that only invokes God and the Bible when it suits the sitting pope?

Another example from Sweden, and this one comes from the government agency *The Living History Forum*. The case made by the forum is that media and other organisations that should be working against anti-Semitism are focusing on a small clique of Swedish neo-Nazis but hardly at all on the approximately one million immigrants from Muslim countries where the hatred of Jews is cultural. It is, the forum believes, a matter of trying not to offend the immigrants from these Muslim countries. Again, the victim is to blame, and the perpetrators of hate are left alone in order not to upset them.

Finally, a point on media and how carefully they treat religion. On January 20, 2021, just before 9 AM Eastern time, before the new president, Joe Biden, was inaugurated and before President Trump had left office, CNN had a panel that commented very positively – even admiringly – on President-elect Biden's true faith. He was going to church, and it was interesting, they noted, that he was a frequent churchgoer, not like some other politicians who did not have his genuine faith. Do the commentators really know how genuine President Biden's faith is? More disturbing, though, is that the panel's admiration was directed towards a man, one about to become president, who potentially has a completely irrational belief system. There is no reason to believe that all religious presidents would be treated equally. President Biden is Roman Catholic, which, nowadays must be considered mainstream in the US. That leaves the question still hanging there: would the panel have been equally full of admiration if the president-elect had been a devout Muslim or Jew?

In difficult times, when tough, vital, urgent decisions have to be made, should we admire a president who goes down on his knees and asks God for guidance? The issue isn't that we believe that President Biden would not be able to make the right decision. But this is to serve as an example of the deference with which

CHAPTER 12

religion and religious people are handled in the media. What if we had a truly religious president who, rather than reacting decisively as deadly missiles were heading for the US, chose instead to pray for God to intervene. Would God answer? Would God give guidance? Would God intervene?

Acknowledgements

I have been helped and supported by so many that I have to choose the ones I acknowledge here. If you do not find yourself here, rest assured you are not forgotten.

The assistance and input I have received have been on a personal level, and I feel uncomfortable identifying the people I owe thanks to. I will therefore do so in a way that they will recognize themselves and, for the rest of you, it doesn't really matter who they are.

Jan Sterner is a journalist I got to know as a young man while I was still living in Sweden. We started off in a professional relationship and he interviewed me in my capacity as a tax advisor a number of times for newspapers he worked for. He would later, from time to time, call me to discuss tax and economic issues. We have, over the years, developed a friendship, allowing us to discuss my views on religious matters. It is Jan who is responsible for urging me to finally get my thoughts down on paper and write this book. If you enjoy the read, I will be happy to take credit. If you do not enjoy the read, I would prefer that you blame Jan. Over the years, he has been able to follow the development of my thinking in these matters, which is why he has been invited to write the foreword for this book.

Thanks go to TR who read a very early version of my economics chapter and helped me understand how it could be presented more succinctly. His son SRM who is currently in high school read a few chapters and provided me with effective feedback based on his religious studies at school.

CHAPTER 12

MK read quite a few of the chapters and gave me input based on his Jewish background.

Similarly, Gus gave me input based on his Muslim background.

AMDFA went over the manuscript with me page by page and gave me valuable feedback based on her Roman Catholic background. AMDFA owns every comma in this book.

ÅF has a Swedish background with a father who was a clergyman in the church of Sweden. He read several of my chapters and gave me valuable criticism of sections where improvements were needed.

Peter, with his background in the Church of England, read the entire book and engaged in several conversations with me. His input led to several important changes in the manuscript.

GE read several of the chapters. His background is both Swedish and international. He was able to give me feedback on both improvements of the text and how to clarify issues he felt were left unclear.

JB, a Swedish self-proclaimed atheist residing in the UK, has read several of the chapters and helped me modify some passages in my writing.

PEJ, a churchgoing Christian residing in Canada, has given me his perspective on how the book reads.

BU, who is both an atheist and a wordsmith par excellence, read the entire manuscript and noted that it was a substantial body of work but that it needed a hard edit, which it did, and which it has had thanks to my editor, Karl French.

My good friend S, with a secular upbringing and background in the Swedish church, read several chapters. He made a number of points that worked their way into this book. He further pointed out that the early version of the manuscript he read was interesting but needed attention in terms of syntax. After several revisions, but especially with the help of my editor, Karl, I feel that I have been able to deliver a much more readable text.

I also owe thanks to MS who is an Orthodox priest. In his very busy schedule, he took time to read the entire manuscript and deliver a thoughtful and extremely well-worded analysis of my writing, chapter by chapter. It is not that any of us have changed our minds, but I find it very useful to receive the opinions of people I do not agree with since I learn more from people who do not share my views.

I must acknowledge and give great thanks to RAM who has, over a very long time, helped me improve my thinking and made me understand the requirements of a modern younger reader. I hope RAM finds that her efforts over many long hours were not wasted.

Anna Eriksson and Janice Poon have across the Atlantic collaborated on the book cover. I believe that the result matches the writing. I would be remiss if I didn't acknowledge Wikipedia. Wikipedia has made it so much easier to find information that I knew I had read somewhere. It was also a great resource; in fact, it was invaluable to have a second reference on things I knew. Even better, it was a great place to check what I thought I knew but really didn't.

My editor Karl French has already been thanked in the postscript. I want to add that when he suggested passages to be deleted, it took me a while to come around to his thinking. He was right. I also want to acknowledge that when my writing was over-the-top and perhaps too playful, he very gently pushed me in the right direction. I have not always taken his advice and, should a reader still find passages that could be seen as somewhat insincere, the blame must fall on me. Since I lack adequate words of praise for my editor, I need to borrow from the former president, Donald Trump, and say that Karl is tremendous.

INDEX

Abel, 8, 74
abortion, 37, 86, 90, 148, 232
Abraham, 6, 9, 18, 78, 81-3, 104, 124, 176-7, 190, 194-5
abrahamic religion, 2, 6, 78, 81-82, 87, 94, 126-8, 139, 154, 177, 200, 203, 210, 218
Adam and Eve, 8, 11, 74-6, 107, 111-2, 140, 169, 181, 255
Adams, John, 84
Afghanistan, 88, 99
Africa, 53, 84-5, 169, 244
Al Jazeera, 93
Alexander VI, Pope, 227, 259
Ali, Ayaan Hirsi, 92, 271
Al-Issa, Sheikh Dr. Muhammad, 196
Allah, 93, 78, 83-6, 93, 98, 195-6, 264-5
Allen, Dave, 138
Alpha Centauri System, 163
Al-Qaeda, 87, 90, 145
Amanpour, Christiane, 146-8
Amish, 138
Ammonites, 18
Andrew, Prince, 243
Antipas, Herod, 182
Aquinas, St. Thomas, 158
Archer, Dr. Gleason L., 25, 38-40, 106

AstraZeneca, 52
atheism, 2, 7, 76, 25, 178, 192
Atlantic, 222
atonement, 132, 194
Atonement, Day of, 131-2, 194
Augustine, St., 143, 230-1, 256
Avinu Malkeinu, 181
Ayaan Hirsi Ali Ayatollahs, 199
Badr, battle of, 195
Baha'I, 84, 126
Ball, Peter, 245
Bangladesh, 99
baptism, 140-2, 220-2
Barbary Pirates, 84-5
Barker, Dan, 76
Behe, Michael, 170-1
Benedict XVI, Pope, 188, 225
Benedict, Pope, 147, 245
Biden, Joe, 274
Big Bang Theory, 159-60, 176
Boko Haram, 88
Boniface VIII, Pope, 231-2, 259
Book of Revelation, 185
Borgias,
    family, 63, 227-8
    Cesare Borgia, 226, 259
Breivik, Anders Behring, 91
Brussels, 88
Buddhism, 94, 126

burqa, 95
Cain, 8, 74-6
capitalism, 57-8
Carlin, George, 5
celibacy, 221-2, 226-8, 233, 245, 256, 258-60
Champollion, Jean-François, 234, 259-60
Chava (Eve), 107
Chechnya, 99, 271
Chestnut Banquet, 227, 259
China, 57
Christus, 184
Chukchi, 169
circumcision, 144, 176
Climate Change and Inequality (Pope Francis), 32, 44, 138
Clinton, Bill, 241-2
Collins, Dr. Francis, 24-32, 42, 109, 122
communism, 55, 57
confession, 37-8, 134, 137, 140-1, 224, 228-9, 233-4, 256-7
Constantine, King, 187
conversion 144, 206, 236, 256
forced conversion, 86, 94, 98, 264-6
Covid-19, 58, 60, 63, 154, 165, 270, 273
Council of Nicaea, 187
creation story, 12, 23, 37, 74-6, 107-112, 156
Crossan, John Dominic, 191
Cuba, 55
Darwin's Black Box (Behe), 170
David, King, 19-21, 104-5, 145, 184-5, 190-2, 248, and Goliath, 19
Dawkins, Richard, 5, 7, 71-2
death penalty, 86, 93, 128, 205, 207, 210
Deuteronomy, 107, 121-2, 177, 249

Dimon, Jamie, 33, 45-8, 53
divine intervention, 26-7, 35, 170, 261
divorce, 34, 80, 128, 139
DNA, *See* Genetics
Doctors Without Borders, 243
Ebola, 166
economy, 45-61, 169
Encyclopedia of Bible Difficulties (Archer), 25, 38-40, 107, 208
Enlightenment, 104, 199, 235, 238
Epstein, Jeffrey, 242-3
Erdogan, Recep Tayyip, 100
Esau, 13-6
Eucharist, 123
Evangelical, 40, 76, 106, 150, 246, 266
evolution,
    theory of, 67-76, 111, 167-70, 176, reeding hen, 73, elephant, 71-2, eye, 171-4, guppy, 72, 168, human, 68-71, 168-9
exorcism, 35-6, 65, 139
Falwell Jr, Jerry, 246
Fascism, 91-2
fasting, 194
Feletti, Father Pier, 142
Ferdinand II, King, 236
Finding Darwin's God (Miller), 30
Forbes, 52
fossil fuels, 46, 55
Francis, Pope, 150, 261-2, 273-4, on economics, 44, 54-6, 60, 64, on same-sex unions, 148, on science, 25, 32-7, 138-9, on papal abuse, 226, 232-3, 245
free will, 4, 13, 26-28, 127, 202-6, in Christianity, 143, 209-16, in Islam, 95, 100, 205-7, 210, in Judaism, 210-16
Frum, John, 152

INDEX

Fry, Stephen, 21-2
fundamentalism, 86, 90
Gabriel, Archangel, 77, 79, 81-3, 98, 195, 265
Galilee, 181, 184
Galileo, 199, 235, 237
Garden of Eden, 8, 11, 74-6, 111-2, 140
Gaza, 99
genetics, 24, 67-72, 168-9
genetic mutation, 168
Gervais, Ricky, 5
God Who Hates, A (Sultan), 92-3
Gospels, 104, 145, 179, 185-6, 189-91, 214, 266,
    Matthew, 20, 103-4, 179, 217, Mark, 137, Luke, 20, 103-4, 135-6
Grand Design, The, (Hawking and Mlodinow), 158
gravity, law of, 42, 157
Great Fire of Rome, 184
Greatest Show on Earth, The, (Dawkins), 71-2
Gustav II Adolph, King, 209
Hadiths, 3, 196
Hagia Sophia, 150
Harris, Sam, 90
Hawking, Stephen, 158
heaven, 64, 107-10, 121, 140, 142-3, 149, 151, 179-80, 187, 195, 207, 267
Herod the Great, 131, 182, 211, 268
Hitchens, Christopher, 5, 35, 200, 231
Holocaust, 93, 196
Holy Spirit, 38, 122, 124
homosexuality, 10, 140, 144, 147, 249,
    in Catholic Church, 146-8, 225-6, 229-30, 247-9, 258, in Islam, 92, in Judaism, 128, lesbianism, 147, 249
Human Genome Project, 24
Ice Age, The, 163-5
In the Closet of the Vatican (Martel), 247, 258
Incel, 250
incest, 11, 75-6, 80, 249
India, 53, 57, 105, 126, 240
indoctrination, childhood, 1-2, 6, 23-4, 206, 272,
    in Abrahamic faith, 18, 21, 41, in Islam, 92, 94-5, 99, 197, 199-10, 208, 270-1
Infidel (Ali), 92
infidel, 93-4, 98-9, 196,
intelligent design, 167, 171, 174
International Council on Biblical Inerrancy, 40
interpretation of religious texts, 3, 5-6, 39, 204-6,
    Abrahamic, 78, 113-5, 118, 120, 203, Judaism, 208, 249, 251-3, Christianity, 179, 189-92, 209, 218, 261, Islam, 81-4, 85, 98-9, 149, 265
Inuit (Eskimo), 169
Iran, 92, 94, 99, 197, 206, 273
Ireland, Republic of, 22
irreducible complexity, theory of, 167, 170, 174
Isabella, Queen, 90, 236
Iscariot, Judas, 182, 188
Ishmael, 81-2, 195
ISIL (ISIS), 88, 90
Islam, 34, 42, 95, 96, 100-1, 126, 128,
    anti-Semitism, 194-5, extremism, 90-3, 97-9, 145, 205-6, 264-5, 271, indoctrination, 86-7, 94, 206-8, interpretation, 81-4, 98-9,

102, 105, 123, 149, 265
Islamophobia, 101-2
Israel, 19, 36, 91, 94, 117, 128, 150-1, 197-8, 208, 272-3
Israelites, 121, 129-30, 211-5, 248, 266
Jacob, 14-7, 190
Jefferson, Thomas, 84
Jephthah, 18
Jerusalem Post, 273
Jerusalem, 195,
    temple of, 131, 134-7
Jeshu, 178, 189
Jewish Sanhedrin, 182, 189
Jizyah, 84, 196
John Paul II, Pope, 207, 221, 256
Josephus, Titus Flavius, 133-4, 184
Judah, 19
Julian, Emperor, 131, 134
Kahn, Genghis, 241
Kalin, Ibrahim, 100
Kama Sutra, 240
Kantzer, Kenneth S., 38-9, 41
Kardashians, The, 47, 56, 62
Keating, Charles, 59
Kertzer, David I., 222
Khomeini, Ayatollah, 205-6
Kissinger, Henry, 241, 246
Kistner, Sally, 52-3
Kohanim, 129
Kompass, Anders, 244
Korea, 168-9
Lane Fox, Robin, 5
Language of God, The, (Collins), 24-32, 122
Lateran Council, 223
Lebanon, 99
Leo X, Pope, 54, 237
Levites, 129-30, 132
Leviticus, 106, 132, 134, 248
Lewis, C.S., 25-6

LGBTQ+, *See* Homosexuality
Liberty University, 246
light-year, 163-4
limbo, 143
Living History Forum, The, 274
Lot, 9-10, 18
Lutheran church, 120, 138, 194, 209, 245
Macron, Emmanuel, 99-100, 271
Malmö, 97, 199-200
Martel, Frédéric, 225-5, 246, 257
Martin Luther, 138, 192-4, 198
Martin, Father James, 146-8
Marx, Karl, 101
masturbation, 231-2, 256-7
Maxwell, Ghislaine, 242-3
McDonald, John H., 171, 174
Mecca, 80, 195
Medina, *See* Mecca
Mennonites, 138
Messiah, 20-1, 144-5, 150, 185-6, 191
Me-Too movement, 243
Michener, James, 5
Miles, Jack, 130
Miller, Kenneth, 30
miracles, 41, 145, 265
missionaries, 86, 144, 234
Mlodinow, Leonard, 158
Moab, 11
Mohamad, Dr. Mahathir, 101
morality, 10, 12-3, 17-19, 21-2, 92, 113, 226,
    'moral law', 25-6
Mormonism, 138
Moses, 105-6, 215, 248
    plagues, 211-2, books of, 249, 251, commandments, 114-5, 122, 124, law of, 8, 179, 211, death of, 107, 175
Mount Ararat, 13

INDEX

Mullahs 199, 208
Musk, Elon, 46
mythology, 127, 129, 217
National Academy of Sciences, 157
National Institutes of Health, 24
natural disaster, 26, 165
natural selection, theory of, 72, 159, 168, 170, 172-3
Nazism, 92, 178, 188, 194, 222, neoNazi, 91, 198, 274
neanderthal, 68
Nero, Emperor, 184
New York Intelligencer, 226
Nice (France), 101
Nigeria, 88
Noah, 11-3
Northern Ireland, 5, 209, 218
Norway, 89, 91, 100
Numbers, 106
Obama, Barack, 97
obesity, 169
Occam's Razor, 4, 22, 32, 43, 66, 76, 124, 153, 156, 166, 173, 176, 186-8, 200-1, 216, 238-9, 248, 26, 268-9
On the Origin of Species (Darwin), 170
Origen, 256
Orion, belt of, 164
orthodoxy,
    Judaism, 86, 90, 128-9, 208, 250, 273, other, 138, 218
Oslo, 91
Ottoman Empire, 196
Paedophilia, 229, 231, 243
Pakistan 87-8, 99, 105
Paludan, Rasmus, 200
Paradise, 85, 255
Passover, 182, 214
Paty, Samuel, 99-100, 271

Peter, St., 217-8, 258
Petrini, Carlo, 262
Piketty, Thomas, 33, 45-6, 48, 50, 52-3, 62
Pilate, Pontius, 181-4, 186-9
Pius IX, Pope, 142, 218-22
Pius XII, Pope, 219, 237
plague,
    biblical plague, 211-6, black plague, 37,
Polanski, Roman, 243, 245
poverty, 47, 58, 64
Prey (Ali), 271
priests, 32, 37-8, 63, 132, 137, 139, 224, 257,
    female, 144, 221, celibacy, 222-3, 258, Jewish, 129, 230, 261
Prince of Wales, 245
Problem of Pain, The, (Lewis), 25-6
Psalms, 105, 121, 251
pseudo-science, 156
Quran, 42, 77-81, 86, 149, 153, 264-5,
    desecration of, 97-98, 100, 200-1, interpretation of, 83-5, 96-8
rabbis, 36, 117-8, 128-9, 254
chief rabbi, 208, female rabbis, 128, 144, marriage of, 230
Ramadan, Tariq, 98, 102
rape, 10, 17, 26-7, 148, 207, 233, 250
Ratzinger, Joseph, *See* Benedict XVI
real estate, 50
Resurrection, 137
Romans, 135, 178, 181, 184
Rosling, Prof. Hans, 58
Sabbath, 74, 86, 90, 117-8, 154, 180, 253
sacrifice, 18, 81, 129, 131-7, 214, 245

Satan, 141, 186, 215-6, 262
Satanism, 127, 221
Saul, King, 19
science,
    compatibility of science and religion, 24-31, 33-38, 42, science and evidence, 68-9, 73, 76, scientific approach, 25, 32, 34, scientific theory, 157, 167-8
Scientology, 73
selective breeding, 168
sexual selection, 72, 167-8
Sharia law, 92
Shia, 5, 34, 92, 197, 209
Silverman, Sarah, 63
sin, 9, 20, 37-8, 137, 139-41, 188-9, 224, 228, 232-4,
    bodily sin, 254-62, original sin, 140, sin offering, 132-4
slavery, 18, 21, 30, 64-5, 85, Israelite slaves, 210-14, sex slavery, 232-3, 245, 248, slave trade, 60
social media, 51, 56, 60-2, 97, 99
Sodom and Gomorrah 8-11
sodomy, 207, 243
Solomon, King, 131, 251-3
Song of Songs, 251-3
soul, 254-5, 258, 263
South Pacific, 152
Soviet Union, 273
St. Peter's Basilica, 54
stillbirth, 140-3
Stockholm, 88
suicide bombers, 88, 97, 264
Sullivan, Andrew, 226
Sultan, Wafa, 92-3
Sunni Muslims, 5, 197, 209
Supplemental Nutrition Assistant Program, 62

Sweden,
    economics, 52-3, 58, Islam, 97, 100, 199, 270-1, 274
Syria, 88, 92-3
Tage Danielsson, 269
Talmud, The, 134, 193, 249-50
technological innovation, 33, 44, 138
Ten Commandments, The, 113-24, 170-80, 193, 210, 248
Teresa, Mother, 59
terrorism, 87-8, 90-100,
    counterterrorism, 9, 88,
theism, 28-9, 121,
    monotheism, 123
Thor, 29, 31, 161
Tiberius, Emperor, 181
Torah, 106, 122, 249, 251
Toronto, 146, 243, 254
Torquemada, Tomás de, 236-7
Transubstantiation, *See* Eucharist
Trump, Donald, 242, 278
tsunami, 145, 165
Turkey, 100, 150, 197
Uganda Game Department, 71
Unauthorised Version: Truth and Fiction in the Bible, The, (Fox), 5
United Nations Relief and Works Agency for Palestine Refugees, The, 272
United Nations, 52, 152, 244, 272
University of Delaware, 171
University of Lund, 58
Upper Canada College, 243
Urban II, Pope, 236
Uriah, 19-20
Vatican,
    pope, 217-8, scandals, 220-9, 247, 258, wealth, 54, 58
Vatileaks, 229
Virgin Mary, 20, 35, 139, 190-1

INDEX

virginity, 10, 249
Wahhabism, 197
Walmart, 61-2
watchmaker argument, 174-5
Weinstein, Harvey, 242
witches, 92, 236-7
World Redistribution Agency, 52
Yahweh, 119, 121-2, 133, 200

Yom Kippur, 133, 194
YouTube 5, 21, 58, 63-4, 76, 93, 138-9
Zayd, 79
Zaynab, 79-80
Zeus, 43, 152
Zion, daughters of, 17

www.ingramcontent.com/pod-product-compliance
Lightning Source LLC
Chambersburg PA
CBHW020902080526
44589CB00011B/397